# Documentary Screens

# Documentary Screens

*Non-Fiction Film
and Television*

**Keith Beattie**

First published 2004 by
PALGRAVE MACMILLAN
Houndmills, Basingstoke, Hampshire RG21 6XS and
175 Fifth Avenue, New York, N.Y. 10010
Companies and representatives throughout the world

PALGRAVE MACMILLAN is the global academic imprint of the Palgrave Macmillan division of St. Martin's Press, LLC and of Palgrave Macmillan Ltd. Macmillan® is a registered trademark in the United States, United Kingdom and other countries. Palgrave is a registered trademark in the European Union and other countries.

ISBN 0–333–74116–1 hardback
ISBN 0–333–74117–X paperback

This book is printed on paper suitable for recycling and made from fully managed and sustained forest sources.

A catalogue record for this book is available from the British Library.

A catalog record for this book is available from the Library of Congress.

10  9  8  7  6  5  4  3  2  1
13  12  11  10  09  08  07  06  05  04

Printed in China

*For my mother, and to the memory of my father,*
*Reginald Joseph Beattie (1922–1998)*

# Contents

# Acknowledgements

This book began as a series of questions raised in the course 'Documentary Film and History', coordinated by Professor Roger Bell at the University of New South Wales, Sydney. Multiple thanks are due to Roger for involving me in the course during its inception and to the students in the course whose insights and enthusiasm provided a stimulus for the writing of this book. For their generous and long-standing support of my endeavours in the areas of film and media I'd like to thank Dr Geoff Mayer, Head, Cinema Studies Department, La Trobe University, Melbourne; Dr Richard Pascal, School of Humanities, at the Australian National University, Canberra; and Associate Professor Roy Shuker, Head, Media Studies Programme, Victoria University of Wellington, New Zealand.

The Australian Centre for the Moving Image, Melbourne, allowed me to screen many of the works examined here. I would like to thank Fiona Villella of ACMI for her assistance. Aysen Mustafa of the Australian Film Institute also helped locate film titles. My thanks to Dennis O'Rourke for agreeing to speak with me.

At Palgrave Press I am particularly grateful to Catherine Gray for her patience and support. Also at Palgrave, Sheree Keep, Beverley Tarquini and Kate Wallis provided timely and efficient assistance. Comments by Palgrave's two anonymous reviewers of the manuscript were productive and welcome.

Louise and Michael Thake were, as ever, supportive and encouraging in the best possible way. Dr Julie Ann Smith offered an inestimable degree of support and extremely helpful comments on the manuscript. The English language cannot do justice to such a contribution, and so: Grazie, molte grazie, brava dottoressa … adesso è ora di passare ad altro.

Any errors in this book remain, of course, my own.

# Introduction

A 72-year-old director takes up a digital video camera and travels the highways and back roads of France to shoot a series of startling real life vignettes which turn an unlikely topic, scavenging, into a story of loneliness, loss, ageing, and human fortitude at the beginning of the twenty-first century (Agnès Varda's *Les Glâneurs et la Glâneuse*, 2002). Subjects appearing in their homes and other locations testify in verse and song to the part alcohol plays in their lives (in the British Broadcasting Corporation's [BBC] *Drinking for England*, 1998). A self-described explorer and adventurer with little experience of filmmaking journeys to the far north of Québec and directs a group of Inuit people in a reconstruction of their past way of life (Robert Flaherty's *Nanook of the North*, 1922, the first 'documentary' film). Documentary productions encompass remarkable representations of surprising realities. How do documentaries achieve their ends? What types of documentary are there? What factors are implicated in their production? Such questions – which constantly return us to the representations themselves – animate this study.

*Documentary Screens* critically examines formal features, evidentiary capacities, patterns of argumentation, and histories of selected central documentary films and television programmes. This study situates these features, and the documentaries themselves, within varying contexts which inform and impact on the documentary texts in multiple direct and indirect ways. The contexts identified and examined here are, first, subgeneric formations and, second, broader and more significant material settings. By gathering together selected works into nominated subgenres I am not suggesting that documentaries have necessarily fallen into discrete categories. Constructed as a genre within the field of non-fictional representation, documentary has, since its inception, been composed of multiple, frequently linked representational strands. In a related way, the various subgenres of documentary referred to here are not textual codifications, but general categories composed of works sharing orientations and conventions

1

recognized by both the producer and the viewer (Neale, 1980: 11). The existence of these categories is manifest in everyday references to documentary such as those found in television programming guides, which routinely classify non-fictional work as historical documentaries, science documentaries, autobiographical work, works 'based on a true story' and so on. Similarly, academic studies commonly construct or allude to subgenres of documentary, among them, direct cinema, ethnographic film or compilation film. The particular subgenres confronted in this study are by no means exhaustive of the possible range of documentary categories, though they do include works prominent within the documentary tradition.

The subgenres returned to and reassessed here are: ethnographic film, direct cinema and cinéma vérité, autobiographical documentary, drama-documentary and documentary drama, indigenous documentary productions, compilation films and television documentary journalism. This book also examines recent so-called popular factual entertainment, a category which, in its multiple forms and revisions of documentary representation, overflows and refuses subgeneric positioning. The reassessment of documentary subgenres undertaken here is timely – perhaps even overdue. It is virtually impossible to pick up any of the growing number of books on documentary without reading of the 'blurring' of documentary forms and generic hybridity. Focused almost exclusively on contemporary works, such analyses usefully outline emergent processes of overlap and intersection between various forms of documentary representation. However, recognition of what is being blurred, an identification of the formal boundaries that are being crossed, is assisted by an understanding of pre-existing forms and subgenres of documentary film and television. We need to know where we have come from to know where we are going. This study assists such an endeavour.

Just as documentary is predicated on a series of refusals (it is not fiction; it is not the item-based presentation of the evening news[1]) so, too, this book is not concerned with practical aspects of documentary production, or detailed study of viewing patterns or audience reception of documentary on film or television (though viewing habits are implicated here in the theory of documentary and in the 'readings' or interpretations of documentary television programmes and films). This book is a critical examination of forms and histories of documentary selected from cinema, television and new media contexts. Different formal characteristics are suggested by the various media, and attention is paid to the features of work within each medium, from the Griersonian documentary film, through camcorder television, to convergent forms of new media. In addition to an emphasis on various media, the analysis includes works exhibited and broadcast internationally – specifically, the United Kingdom, the United States and Australia – and recognizes the differing productive bases and broadcast ecologies which influence work from various countries. An understanding of national specificities allows comparisons to be drawn between productions from different countries without falling into either a national parochialism that refuses to acknowledge international trends or a media transnational essentialism that denies national differences.

This attention to national productive practices and international comparisons is informed by reference to the specific material contexts which affect works of each subgenre, be they, for example, the disciplinary concerns of a field of study (ethnography's focus on the Other, the context of Chapter 3), the historical and political determinants referred to as colonialism (the context of Chapter 4), or the economics of production (the context of Chapters 2, 10 and 11). In this way the analysis undertaken in *Documentary Screens* situates selected documentary films and television programmes and subgenres in relation to the larger disciplinary, ideological, historical and economic forces which impact on documentary form and content. This method constitutes the basis of what is called here a 'documentary studies' approach, one that can be distinguished from existing theoretical and practical orientations to documentary.[2] The media theorist John Corner has usefully outlined three different frameworks for academic interest in documentary, each of which is paraphrased here as a way of positioning the approach undertaken in this study.

The oldest strand of interest in documentary analysis is that conducted within vocational and practical film schools worldwide. Here the emphasis is on learning the practical techniques and skills required to make effective films and programmes. While the focus on the acquisition of practical productive skills has tended to marginalize theories of documentary, Corner (2001b: 124) has noted that 'a great deal of clear and focused thinking about the nature, form and function of documentary work has developed from such teaching. The wish to make good documentaries has been a great motivator of analysis and criticism' (Corner cites Rabinger, 1998, in this regard, to which can be added Kriwaczek, 1997).

A second strand of interest in documentary developed from within film studies and its close connection with literary and textual analysis. 'In film studies, the chief if not exclusive concern is with questions of aesthetics and textual form. A highly developed and often dense analytic agenda surrounding the organisation of the image, narrative structure, *mise-en-scène* and the symbolic and imaginary conditions of spectatorship provides the focus of study', observes Corner (2001b: 124). The approach derives some of its analytical and interpretive method from the study of fictional texts, and some of it from the demands of documentary practice. Corner notes the contributions by Nichols (1976 and 1991) and Renov (1993c) to this approach. 'Film studies has tended to regard documentary film as constituting a special case of "realism"…one in which complex questions of ontology and epistemology (the status of the film image and its use as a means of knowledge) are linked to particular political and social intentions' (Corner, 2001b: 124).

An interdisciplinary media studies, with its links to cultural studies, constitutes a third strand of study. This approach emphasizes documentary texts as media products which can be considered in relation to other such products, among them television news and soap operas. Whereas the film studies approach has tended to ignore documentary on television (within its focus on independently produced documentary cinema), media studies has moved toward greater attention to the televisual forms of documentary expression. Separate aspects of media studies examine the institutional features of television, the professionalization of its practices, and its demand to engage an audience. The research of Kilborn and Izod (1997) and Corner (1996) extends the media studies orientation to non-fictional texts (Corner, 2001b: 124–5).

The approach undertaken in *Documentary Screens* is separate from, though informed by, the three strands of study outlined here. Questions of form prominent within film studies approaches to fictional texts are rephrased in relation to the non-fictional texts examined in this book. Following the perspectives of media studies, this study includes on forms of documentary representation on television, with reference to institutional features such as public and commercial broadcast environments, and aspects of television scheduling. These approaches are extended within attention to the contextual factors which impact on documentary form and content. The connections between form, content and context which are implicated in documentary studies are outlined in the following descriptions of each chapter.

Chapter 2, 'Men With Movie Cameras', examines the work of the founders of English language documentary, Robert Flaherty and John Grierson. Specifically, the chapter draws upon Grierson's important essay 'First Principles of Documentary' as the basis of an examination of the formal features of Flaherty's *Nanook of the North* (1922) and Grierson's *Drifters* (1929), films which in differing ways marry informational content to narrative as the basis of a work referred to as documentary. The differing formal approaches adopted by the filmmakers are contextualized through reference to the filmmakers' divergent approaches to production finances: Flaherty's alignment of documentary with commercial distribution and exhibition, and Grierson's focus on sponsored documentary as a tool of citizenship. Grierson's reliance on both corporate and government sponsorship is emphasized within the chapter as a prime factor in the development of documentary film. This chapter presents historical background to the development of documentary as a genre which, since the days of Flaherty and Grierson, has come to contain a number of subgeneric categories.

Chapter 3 confronts one of the earliest identifiable subgenres, that of ethnographic film. Often excluded from analyses of documentary film, ethnographic film is a key focus for questions of cross-cultural representation. The chapter examines the formal regime of ethnographic representation within an account of the rise and expansion of ethnographic film. The plotting of the historical dimension begins with 'salvage ethnography', a practice exemplified by Flaherty's *Nanook of the North*, a film which seeks to save or rescue a culture believed to be 'disappearing'. The so-called reflexive turn in ethnographic filmmaking is analysed through reference to the film *The Ax Fight* (1974), and Dennis O'Rourke's film '*Cannibal Tours*' (1987) serves as the basis of an analysis of self-reflexive modes of ethnographic film. The most recent phase of ethnographic depiction, the rise of a 'new ethnography', and its impact on ethnographic filmmaking, is also examined. The broad context for this analysis is the notion of Otherness as it operates in ethnography and ethnographic film. Throughout most of its history, ethnographic film has, like ethnography itself, functioned as a representational practice in which the culture of the non-Westernized 'Other' has been treated as scientific datum subject to the gaze of Western ethnographic science. Within this recognition, the chapter explores ways in which ethnographic film constructs or contests categories of 'us' and 'them', self and Other.

Opposing what are frequently the objectifying practices of ethnographic film, indigenous peoples worldwide have used sound and image technologies in various forms of self-documentation. Chapter 4 focuses on the use by indigenous Australians of media technologies to produce, disseminate and consume their own images as a practice capable of revising documentary representation as part of a wider process of contesting the effects of colonialism, the context for this chapter. The revision of colonial representation, a process referred to here as 'decolonizing the image', is examined through reference to selected works produced by indigenous Australian documentary producers.

Chapter 5 studies the developments in documentary filmmaking referred to as cinéma vérité and direct cinema, and the theoretical positions adopted by these practitioners in relation to the representation of truth. In terms of direct cinema and cinéma vérité, truth refers to the camera's capacity to depict or reveal authentic moments of human experience. Such a conception of truth revolves around the question of behaviour modification – the degree to which behaviour is altered by the presence of the camera. Questions of behaviour modified by the presence of the camera fed demands from within television journalism and the social sciences in the late 1950s for portable camera technologies that could be used to capture truth. These demands, and the new camera technology – the contexts for the development of direct cinema and cinéma vérité – are examined in relation to the claims, methods and forms of *Chronicle of a Summer* (*Chronique d'un été*), a foundational work of cinéma vérité filmed in Paris in 1960 by Jean Rouch and Edgar Morin and released the following year, and *Don't Look Back*, a prominent example of direct cinema made by D.A. Pennebaker in 1966.

Behaviour modification and performance are also central concerns within autobiographical film practices in which the filmmaker/author adopts a persona and performs an identity, as in the case of Ross McElwee's comedic display in his film *Sherman's March* (1985). Within the informing context of the construction of personal identity, Chapter 6 examines self-authored film and video through reference to selected autobiographical works produced over the past 20 years. The works studied include *Sherman's March*, a film in which McElwee's performance complicates conceptions of autobiography as a simple reflection of an authoring self, and Rea Tajiri's *History and Memory* (1991), an innovative record of the experience and memory of internment suffered by her Japanese American family during the Second World War. The chapter also considers the visual grammar of camcorder-based autobiographical work, particularly works from the video diary form, including Robert Gibson's *Video Fool for Love* (1995), a feature-length diary of romances lost and found that significantly extends the visual language of camcorder autobiography.

Chapter 7, 'Finding and Keeping', considers features of compilation or so-called found footage film, those films edited from pre-existing footage. Compilation films are produced within a context that raises fundamental issues to do with the availability of, and access to, footage. The context informs compilation filmmaking in direct ways, notably in determining which topics will be addressed and how they are treated. Within this context, this chapter studies formal features of selected compilation films as they are deployed in the construction of historical arguments. The selected works analysed in this chapter are Emile de Antonio's *In the Year of the Pig* (1969), a work which mixes archival footage and interviews to build a politicized rhetorical history of the Vietnam War, and *The Atomic Café* (1982), a 'pure' compilation film which eschews interviews within an exclusive reliance on the recoding of source footage to construct a history of Cold War tensions and nuclear proliferation. The chapter also discusses recent avant-garde compilation works produced through the practices of 'image piracy'. In their open confrontation with copyright laws and their challenge to the commercialization of image archives such works foreground the contextual factors of availability and accessibility of source footage.

'The Fact/Fiction Divide', Chapter 8, addresses the intersection of documentary and dramatic elements in works produced for television. This intersection, in works of documentary drama and drama-documentary, has at times been the subject of critical, even political, controversy. Unease has been felt in certain viewing quarters over a form that joins elements of fact and fiction or drama and documentary within works that may contain contentious or politically sensitive content. In a number of cases controversy has impacted on broadcast practices and policies leading to regulatory provisions and, in one notable case, to the ultimate restrictive practice: banning of such work. Within the contexts of controversy and broadcast regulatory policies, this chapter examines Peter Watkins' *The War Game*, a devastating documentary drama depiction of nuclear war, produced in 1965 for the BBC, though banned for 20 years. *The War Game* raises issues concerning the effectiveness of a form capable of representing events, such as a 'ground zero' view of nuclear holocaust, which would otherwise be beyond the capacity of a camera to document.

The capacity of dramatized documentary/documentary-drama to narrate events when there is 'no other way to tell it'[3] has been deployed in journalistic investigations of particular incidents (*Why Lockerbie?*, Granada, 1990, a report of events surrounding the bombing of a Pan Am passenger jet over Lockerbie, Scotland, is an example here). Investigative journalism and television reportage of contemporary events combine in other ways in the long-form news documentary, the subject of Chapter 9. The chapter focuses on the television news documentaries produced by renowned journalist John Pilger, in particular his report *Cambodia: The Betrayal* (1990), one of a series of investigative reports undertaken by Pilger into the devastating legacies of the Khmer Rouge regime. The contexts for Pilger's work, and the long-form documentary news report generally, are the practices of journalistic investigation and impartiality in broadcasting.

Chapter 10 traces phases in the development of 'popular factual entertainment' through reference to the central factor impacting on this history, namely, production economics, specifically, the cost of production and revenue returns from advertisers. Within this context, the chapter addresses formal features of works which draw on and transcend, or hybridize, forms and modes of a number of subgenres and televisual formats. Particular attention is paid in the chapter to the characteristics of crime-based 'reality television (TV)' (specifically, the influential US example *Cops*, 1989), so-called docusoaps (with reference to Music Television's (MTV) *The Real World*, 1992, and other examples) and the newer forms referred to as 'gamedocs', principal among them the worldwide television phenomenon *Big Brother*.

The final chapter, 'The Burning Question', steps out of the subgeneric classificatory frame of earlier chapters and looks to the future of documentary. This chapter previews current and emerging media technologies and speculates on the forms of documentary that will appear within the near future in film and cinema, television and new media. The determining contexts here are media technologies and their convergence, and the economic factors which have an impact on the production of new documentary work.

As this outline of chapters suggests, *Documentary Screens* traverses a wide range of documentary works and subgenres, and in doing so, it explores a number of formal strategies and historical changes to the depictive patterns adopted in documentary representation. Chapter 1 provides a basis for the analysis and constitutes a tool kit of formal features that can be applied to the nuts and bolts of documentary forms studied in the subsequent chapters. Descriptions and explanations of the 'mechanics' of documentary may be somewhat 'dry' and, at times, intricate. The insights to be derived from the tool kit are, however, useful for interpreting documentary representation as it operates in the various subgeneric forms of documentary.

This book is intended to be read 'interactively' with the films and programmes it examines. To this end, a final section provides details of where copies of the central films or programmes studied in each chapter can be purchased or hired in the United States, the United Kingdom and Australia. The final section also includes lists of further resources available to support the analysis of each topic. This book, as its title suggests, tunes in to cinema, television and computer screens and focuses on the documentary representations found there. It is hoped that reading this book, and watching the screens, will contribute to a deeper understanding and appreciation of what are often fascinating, sometimes challenging, always interesting documentary representations of the world.

## CHAPTER 1

# 'Believe Me, I'm of the World': Documentary Representation

Documentary concerns itself with representing the observable world, and to this end works with what Grierson called the raw material of actuality. The documentarian draws on past and present actuality – the world of social and historical experience – to construct an account of lives and events. Embedded within the account of physical reality is a claim or assertion at the centre of all non-fictional representation, namely, that a documentary depiction of the socio-historical world is factual and truthful.

Of course, saying that a documentary representation makes a truth claim is not the same as saying that it presents truth. Distinctions of this kind inform the growing and increasingly sophisticated positions offered within documentary theory, pointing to the complex relationship of representation, reality and truth. The generalized truth claim of documentary representation may encompass a number of individual truth claims.[1] Furthermore, not all truth claims are beyond dispute; indeed certain claims made in a documentary may be the subject of what is at times intense debate and critique (Corner, 1996: 3). Operating within such parameters, the so-called truth claim is based on a particular orientation or stance toward subject matter which is summarizable in the position, 'Believe me, I'm of the world' (Renov, 1993a: 30). In these terms documentary can be defined, generally, as a work or text which implicitly claims to truthfully represent the world, whether it is to accurately represent events or issues or to assert that the subjects of the work are 'real people'.

This chapter begins with an analysis of one aspect of the truth claim, that which rests on a 'contract' or a bond of trust between producer and viewer. The other component of the truth claim – the documentary interpretation of reality – is examined through reference to the styles, conventions, rhetorical and narrative strategies, modes and genres of documentary representation.

## 'Believe me': the documentary contract

Truth claims reflect a tacit contractual agreement or bond of trust between documentary producers (whether an individual filmmaker or broadcasting institution) and an audience that the representation is based on the actual socio-historical world, not a fictional world imaginatively conceived. Documentary producers and filmmakers adhere to this long-standing mandate through detailed research of a topic and the verification of the identity of witnesses relied on in a documentary report. In certain contexts, this commitment is reinforced through guidelines and codes issued to producers by broadcasting or commissioning authorities, and in some instances contraventions of such guidelines can result in punitive censures. *The Connection* (1996), a programme produced by Carlton Television for Britain's commercial Channel 3, is a case in point. Carlton was fined £2 million for fabricating scenes using professional actors and for failing to label the scenes as reconstructions, as demanded by the Independent Television Commission code of practice (see Chapter 9).

*The Connection* raises various ethical issues, not the least the betrayal of good faith inherent in the documentary contract (see Winston, 2000). In most cases the 'contract' between producer and audience is undertaken informally by producers concerned with maintaining evidentiary standards (Tunstall, 1993: 32), and reinforced in handbooks and manuals written to provide instruction in the production of film and television documentaries. Exemplifying such routinized directives, one handbook states that, 'It is the implicit duty of every documentary maker to stand by the accuracy of the film's claim to truth' (Kriwaczek, 1997: 42). This commitment is extended in what have been called 'situational cues' or 'indexes' (Carroll, 1983 and 1987; Eitzen, 1995; Plantinga, 1996 and 1997). Such cues include advertisements for a film or programme, distribution releases, reviews, notes in a television programme guide, explicit labels or written descriptions in the title sequences of a film or television programme which alert potential viewers to a work's non-fictional content. In specific situations these cues include statements such as 'the untold story' or 'a television history' which underline a producer's commitment to veracity and providing a full and accurate account of a subject.

In turn, the 'constituency of viewers' (Nichols, 1991) comes to a documentary with a set of expectations regarding the work's authenticity and veracity. This is not to suggest that viewers fail to question information contained in a documentary. Studies of reception point to the fact that viewers interpret or decode the documentary text in complex and sophisticated ways and frequently balance and validate the information and interpretations provided in a documentary against their own experiences and other sources of information (see, e.g. Corner and Richardson, 1986). Such a process of negotiation is, however, undertaken in relation to a text which is generally expected to have been produced in good faith with standards of evidentiality.

The pervasiveness and strength of viewer expectations have been demonstrated in the case of a work which purposively subverts the documentary contract. *Forgotten Silver* (TVNZ: 1997), a 'mockumentary' produced by Costa Botes and Peter Jackson (director of the *Lord of the Rings* trilogy) for New Zealand television, highlights the issues raised here. Unlike most mock documentaries, in which the viewer is alerted in advance through situational cues to the fact that the work is a fabrication, the Jackson and Botes programme was intentionally screened without such warnings. The programme recounts the story of Colin McKenzie, a figure responsible for various ground-breaking inventions, including, most notably, the invention of powered flight and cinema. The programme's outlandish assertions are rendered plausible through interviews with a series of known experts and through a reliance on carefully staged footage which supports the experts' testimony. Viewer response to the faked documentary was mixed. According to letters to newspaper editors, many viewers accepted the programme as a truthful account of historical events. When the hoax was publicly exposed many viewers were, again according to a flurry of letters to editors, incensed by what they took to be the bad faith of the broadcaster and the producers in breaking the documentary contract (Roscoe and Hight, 2001). As the hoax demonstrated, viewers expect a documentary to engage the world in ways which present real people and events, not invented ones. The process which supports this expectation involves not only situational or extratextual cues but also cues *within* the documentary text itself (Nichols, 1991: 18–23). A film or television programme deemed to be documentary is structured by intratextual conventions which mediate viewers' reception and interpretation of the work as an accurate and verifiable depiction of the world.

## 'Of the world': interpreting reality

The status of a representation as a legitimate depiction of the socio-historical world is informed by certain properties commonly understood to be inherent in the photographic image. The photochemical process of photography and traditions of photographic practice function to rally viewers' belief in the photographic image as an authentic and accurate representation of the object before the camera.[2] This position is reflected in the popular summation of the photograph's truth claim: 'the camera cannot lie'. The philosopher Charles Peirce argued that the photograph is made under circumstances in which it is 'physically forced to correspond point by point to nature' (quoted in Nichols, 1991: 149). Peirce termed this connection between image and object an indexical bond. The bond between representation and referent, that is, between the image and the real world, produces an impression of authenticity which documentary draws on as a warrant or guarantee of the accuracy and authority of its representation.[3]

The notion of an indexical bond – a point-by-point, unmediated relationship between image and object – suggests a definition of representation as an act of recording. However, documentary representation exceeds a recording function; a documentary representation is an interpretation of physical reality, not a mere reflection of pre-existent reality. The interpretation and manipulation of reality occurs at all stages of the documentary process. The presence of a documentary camera and sound and light equipment is likely to affect the world being filmed in multiple direct and indirect ways such as a simple rearrangement of furniture to accommodate a film crew in a cramped space, to alterations of behaviour in which subjects 'act' naturally for the camera. The raw footage shot on location is filmed according to certain codes and conventions, and the footage is further manipulated in the editing process. The final edited film or programme is also 'reworked' in descriptions of the text used to promote the film or programme. The multiple transformations point to the various 'realities' which documentary encompasses: putative reality (the world as it is understood to exist without the intrusion of the camera), the world in front of the camera (so-called profilmic reality), and the reality screened in the film or programme (Corner, 1996: 21).[4] Traversing these levels, the documentary manipulation and interpretation of reality is expressed through representational styles and conventions and forms of argument and narrative which together work to produce a realistic and authoritative representation of the socio-historical world.

## Documentary realism and its conventions

Style refers to patterns of use, conventions or techniques in which particular meanings and effects are produced. Style in documentary is rarely used for its own sake as technical virtuosity or ornamentation; dominantly, it is deployed to develop a work's perspective and to convey information (Plantinga, 1997: 147). Stylistic features are not universal; individual filmmakers will bring their own style of filmmaking to a work, and different documentary forms are marked by different styles. These variations typically function, however, within a realistic impulse which functions to produce the effect of the filmmaker 'having been there' and, by extension, of us – the viewers – 'being there' (Nichols, 1991: 181). Realism operates in both fiction and documentary, with differing effects. Fictional realism, particularly the classic realism of Hollywood film, functions to make an invented world seem real. A 'realistic' fictional film or programme thus seeks to render its characters, actions and settings believable and plausible. This stance differs from the operation of realism in documentary, where it functions to render persuasive the arguments and claims made in a film or programme about the socio-historical world. As Corner (2001a: 126–7) points out, such claims and arguments about the world operate in documentary in two, linked, ways: first, at the indexical level of the image – 'this *is* the ship that brought survivors back, this *is* the captain of the ship' – and, second, at the level of exposition, that is, through spoken propositions and directives provided in voice-over commentary or the on-camera testimony of witnesses: 'these *are* the known facts relating to the shipwreck, this *is* the judgment it is most sensible to make as to what happened'.

Corner informs the distinction between realism in fiction and documentary realism by noting that the former essentially provides a kind of '*imaginative* relationship' between the viewer and the events on the screen. 'What this means is that the narrative of the realistic fiction is designed to engage imaginatively (and selectively) with viewers' perceptions of the real world and what can happen in it. There is often a pleasing play-off here between fantasy and reality.' Documentary, in contrast, provides an *inferential* relationship between the represented events and the viewer. 'In the documentary, we are offered bits of evidence and argument and have to construct truths from them, truths of fact and perhaps truths of judgment. However, we should remember that imagination plays a part here too' (2001a: 127). Within its capacity to continually engage viewers' perceptions of reality, styles of realism have changed over the decades. The realism of one era can look hackneyed or appear unconvincing in another era. The realism of *The Bill* (ITV, 1984–present) or *Hill Street Blues* (NBC, 1981–87), for example, is a different variety of realism to that of earlier programmes such as *Dixon of Dock Green* (BBC, 1955–76) or *Kojak* (CBS, 1973–78) (Kilborn and Izod, 1997: 34). If the basis of a realistic work is a perceived 'truth to life' (O'Sullivan *et al.*, in Kilborn and Izod, 1997: 44), then changes in style constitute and reflect varying perceptions of truth. Different viewers will, however, depending on their varying expectations and experiences, carry and form different understandings of the same object (Branigan, 1992: 203). In this way, realism, 'both as a practice and a critical concept – is the subject of never-ending contestation' (O'Sullivan *et al.*, quoted in Kilborn and Izod, 1997: 44).

Within this pattern of contestation and change, Kilborn and Izod have usefully set out various aspects of realism (1997:43–52), and Corner identifies two principal stylistic approaches. In both of the forms outlined by Corner, any effect of reality is not solely achieved through the style itself; rather, the styles operate within the broader context of the documentary truth claim to produce a 'reality effect' (Corner, 2001a: 127). The first form that Corner identifies, what he calls *observational realism*, produces the effect that what we are seeing is a record of reality as it unfolds. The style strongly suggests that the events we are witnessing are beyond the intervention or control of a film crew (Corner, 2001a: 127). The impression is that the events we see on screen '*would have happened, as they happened, even if the filmmaker had not been present*'

(Roscoe and Hight, 2001: 21. Italics in original). The emphasis here is on seeing, watching and observing and the camera style is unadorned ('raw'), an effect that contributes to the idea that the events are captured as they occurred and not filtered through an authoring consciousness. This type of realism is a central component of the observational mode (discussed below).

The second kind of realism can be called *expositional realism*, a style closely aligned with commentary and the expository mode (see below). Expositional realism exceeds mere observation, and involves the organization of sound and image in support of an argument or rhetorical position. The style operates through a close fit between word and image, between what is seen and what is heard, and presents evidence in such a way that one outcome from the array of evidence appears inevitable and ineluctable. Within the style, scenes may function metonymically, serving as a typical account of more general circumstances. The combination of word and image functions here to ' "win the viewer" for the particular case that the documentary is making' (Corner, 2001a: 127).

The effects of both observational and expository realism are enhanced by the conventions which are routinely deployed in documentary. Conventions include profilmic practices, those relating to events which occur before the camera, and filmic techniques, stylistic features adopted within the text itself, though not all of the possible range of conventions and techniques need be apparent in a work for it to be understood as realistic. Profilmic conventions evoke immediacy and direct access to the real and include location shooting (as opposed to filming in a studio) and interviews at-the-scene with witnesses to 'real-life' events. Filmic conventions vary widely from form to form and include, for example, the eschewing of a presenter and voice-over commentary in the observational documentary, and the expositional techniques of long-form television news documentary, which typically utilize an on-screen presenter and voice-over narration. Other filmic conventions include the hand-held or shoulder-mounted shaky camera shot, a practice that has been replicated to the point of cliché as a sign of documentary authenticity. Documentary filmmaking manuals and critical assessments of documentary practice identify (and in certain cases, prescribe) various filmic conventions. For example, one manual advises the documentary filmmaker to avoid using artificial lighting and light reflectors in outdoor scenes and instead to rely on natural light which has a 'realistic feeling to it that is desirable in documentary'. The same manual suggests that the camera should be unobtrusive in crowd scenes in order to prevent subjects looking into the lens, and insists that the camera should not be used to record incidentals, and only moved to follow action (quoted in Branigan, 1992: 206).

Despite such prescriptive regulation, conventions are not aesthetic straitjackets. The documentary tradition contains a number of examples of aesthetic innovation and experimentation. New technologies such as the invention of sound and lightweight portable cameras produced new approaches and styles. In other ways, experiments involving voice-over narration have produced remarkable results, among them the verse narration written and read by W. H. Auden for *Night Mail* (1936), the Whitmanesque lyrical narration of Pare Lorentz's *The River* (1937), Richard Wright's blues-inspired narration for *12 Million Black Voices* (1941), and the narration for the innovative *Drinking for England* (BBC2, 1998), in which subjects recount their experiences in verse. In another way, the films of Errol Morris rely on various visual and aural techniques, including, for example, the *film noir* visual components and sonic elements (supplemented by a haunting music soundtrack by Philip Glass) of his film *The Thin Blue Line* (1989). Documentaries may employ visually spectacular and aesthetically composed shots, as in the films *Kooyanisqatsi* (1983) and *Baraka* (1992), while nonfiction surf films typically rely on heightened and intensified visual spectacle for their aesthetic effect (Beattie, 2001a).

Generally, however, the conventions of documentary realism tend to impose a degree of aesthetic restraint on the text. The documentary film theorist Bill Nichols (1991) points to this effect in his description of documentary as a 'discourse of sobriety' which represents the world within formally 'sober' ways. Documentary shares this aesthetic restraint with other fields such as science, politics, economics and journalism, which like documentary, adopt a rhetorical stance designed to persuade audiences that the information presented is legitimate and important (Nichols, 1991). In these terms, aesthetic innovation is generally subservient to documentary conventions, and their contributions to the maintenance of an argument about the socio-historical world.

## Argument and narrative

Documentaries are frequently organized around an argument. Documentary works construct an argument from sounds and images which are presented as evidence of the real world. It is useful to contrast this understanding with the ways in which sounds and images are deployed in most fictional texts, where they are circulated as elements of a plot which occurs in an imaginary world. While a fictional text will focus on motivation, characterization, the plausibility of actions and events and an internal consistency of story, a documentary concentrates on a strategy that persuades viewers that the evidence it presents is a fair representation of issues (Kilborn and Izod, 1997: 119).

Arguments can be presented in a variety of forms, including essays, diaries, reports, eulogies, manifestos and exhortations (Nichols, 1991: 125). The forms appear in a variety of media, including documentary, where certain forms, particularly the journalistic report, have commonly adopted an argumentative or rhetorical stance. Within its various forms, argument produces two representational outcomes: a perspective on the world, and a commentary about the world (Nichols, 1991: 125). Perspective refers to the point of view adopted in the text to the material that is presented; it is an implicit and continuous form of argumentation, as in the case of a 'fly-on-the-wall' documentary that structures its interpretation of the observed world through indirect, though continually controlled, ways. Commentary, in contrast, is an overt form of argumentation that is routinely provided by voice-over narration or direct testimony provided by subjects in the form of 'talking heads'. Commentary is an explicit way of presenting evidence and it differs from perspective in the manner it constructs and directly presents conceptually richer aspects of an argument.

The case about the world constructed in argument is extended in other ways. The rhetorical thrust of a voice-over can be reinforced by particular vocal inflections. At one point in the documentary series *Vietnam: A Television History* (PBS, 1983), for example, the male narrator's voice announces in a deep, measured tone full of foreboding and imminent crisis, 'And then came Tet' (in 1969, Tet, the lunar new year, marked a North Vietnamese military offensive launched during the Vietnam War). The form of delivery informs the argumentative thrust of the series in which the Vietnam War is interpreted as a debilitating and, for the United States, disastrous political event. Music can also be used to advance an argument. At the end of Emile de Antonio's *In the Year of the Pig* (1969) the stirring, patriotic strains of *The Battle Hymn of the Republic* ironically underlines the film's thesis concerning the criminal folly of US intervention in the Vietnamese civil war (see Chapter 5).

Central to the documentary presentation of an argument or arguments about the world is the role of narrative. Narrative in documentary tends to differ from that in fictional texts, where it principally functions to emphasize the motivation of characters operating within a plausible world. Fictional narrative rests on a relationship of cause and effect: an event or action (cause) sets in train a series of actions (effect). The novelist E. M. Forster specified this particular feature of fictional narrative by contrasting two simple statements. According to Forster, the statement 'The king died' does not construct a narrative, whereas 'The king died and as a result the queen died of grief' establishes a narrative of cause and effect (in Maltby, 2003: 455). Fictional narratives inform the unfolding of a causal chain by situating the action within the boundaries of a specified time and place ('far away and long ago' would be sufficient for the fairy tale-like example of the king and queen).

Narrative in documentary operates in ways different to its function in fiction, though certain documentary forms maintain elements of fictional narrative. The simple narratives of documentary 'city symphonies', for example, order events in a 'day in the life' of the city in a sequential chain of events unfolding in time (24 hours) and place (a nominated city). In particular, narrative in documentary adopts the principles of sequencing in order to advance an argument about the socio-historical world. Documentaries often replace cause and effect with a simple problem-solution structure: a problem is posed, the historical background to the problem is examined and current dimensions of the problem are explained. A solution or solutions to the problem (or ways to find a solution) are then outlined or suggested (Kilborn and Izod, 1997: 119). This structure is popular in varieties of television current affairs journalism. In another example, Pare Lorentz's *The River* (1937) adopts this structure to analyse flooding and soil erosion along the Mississippi River. In Lorentz's film, the problems of erosion and flooding are established within a description of long-standing exploitative land use practices along the Mississippi. The solution, government intervention in the form of dam building projects, appears within the terms of the argument as the only viable ameliorative response to the situation. Though constructed primarily on a problem-solution structure, *The River* also follows a simple narrative based on a journey from the headwaters of the Mississippi downstream to the Gulf of Mexico.

Underlining the importance of narrative to documentary strategies of argumentation, the film historian Brian Winston (1995: 113) insists that narrative is a feature of all documentary work, and objects to descriptions of documentary as a non-narrative system.[5] In a similar way, the film theorist Bill Nichols (1991) acknowledges the place of narrative in documentary, though he argues that narrative structure is pronounced in certain documentaries and only partial in others. Following this observation, it can be noted that narrative is especially prominent in the drama-documentary, which exceeds routine narrative conventions in documentary through re-enactments of events reminiscent of fiction film (see Chapter 8). Much less prominent, but nevertheless present, are the narrative elements of 'fly-on-the-wall' documentaries, which situate subtle cause and effect relationships in a specific time and place (discussed in Chapter 6). Other forms, such as so-called docusoaps, routinely narrativize events in obvious ways, while in 'reality TV' narrative vies with a rigorous stylization that moves representation from the referential to the realms of pure aestheticization (these issues are discussed in Chapter 10).

## Documentary modes

The conventions of documentary, together with forms of narrative, are extended in the codes and representational strategies of modes of documentary. Among the various topologies of documentary modes (Renov, 1993a; Corner, 1996: 28–30), the schema formulated by Nichols (1985 and 1991: 31–75) is a particularly useful interpretation of the communicative functions of the diverse modes of documentary depiction. Nichols has identified five modes of documentary representation: expository, observational, interactive, reflexive and performative. There is a certain historical progression of the modes, from the expository mode prominent in early documentaries, to the performative mode of a number of contemporary works. However, modes are not mutually exclusive, and the formal innovations of newly emergent modes coexist with established practices. At the same time, modes may overlap within a work and in this way a documentary may exhibit features of more than one mode.

The first of Nichols' modes, the expository, relies heavily on commentary in the form of intertitles or voice-over narration to anchor meaning and construct authority. The expository mode was prominent in documentaries of the 1930s produced in the United Kingdom by John Grierson and his co-workers, in which the spoken commentary was often presented in the form of a deep, authoritarian male voice-over narration by an unseen speaker (the so-called voice of God commentary).[6] Variations of this method exist today in many television documentaries in which the voice of a commentator encodes expertise and authority translating the subject matter to a lay audience. The spoken word in the expository mode reverses the traditional emphasis in film on the image. Images function in the expository mode to complement, reinforce, or elaborate the impressions, opinions, reactions and written research articulated in the spoken commentary. Argument in this mode emphasizes broad and general features of the subject and tends to eschew particularities or incidental detail. Argument is advanced by styles of editing focused on the maintenance of rhetorical continuity and perspective, with less emphasis being placed on indications of the passage of time or the organization of space. The expository mode creates the impression of an objective and balanced approach to its material. The voice of God commentary seems to exist above and beyond the arguments being presented – an all-knowing and all-seeing viewpoint. This impression of objectivity aligns the expository mode with journalism, from which it borrows an emphasis on research, evidence and a value-free style of representation.

The observational mode, Nichols' second mode, is closely linked to developments in camera and sound recording technologies during the late 1950s. These developments culminated in portable 16 mm cameras and portable sound recording equipment synchronized to the camera. Liberated from the restraints of the studio, the camera was free to simultaneously record image and sound in almost any location. The impression of unmediated observation achieved within the mode is informed in the editing phase in which footage is assembled with respect to temporal and spatial continuities, eschewing voice-over commentary, intertitles, non-diegetic sound effects and a complementary musical track. The result of these practices is an attempt to replicate an immediate 'slice of life' which is presented in lived or real time. The feigned denial of the presence of the camera in the observational mode is summarized in the assessment that the camera becomes a 'fly on the wall', an unobtrusive and all-seeing eye on the world. A sense of direct and unmediated access to the world characterizes the film and programme making practices of direct cinema, analysed in Chapter 6.

In contrast to direct cinema's observational claims, other practitioners accept the disruptive presence of the camera, using it as a catalyst to inspire and reveal what they insist is true and authentic behaviour. Working with this approach in the early 1960s, Jean Rouch and Edgar Morin modified observational techniques to an openly interventionist practice. The resultant film, *Chronicle of a Summer* (1961), a work which the filmmakers labelled cinéma vérité (see Chapter 6), popularized a mode structured around the interactions between filmmaker and subject. The interactive mode stresses dialog and the verbal testimony of subjects. While in the observational mode of direct cinema there is an attempt to deny the filmmaker's presence, in the interactive mode the filmmaker may appear on camera in the role of interviewer, or be heard off camera asking questions of the subjects.[7]

Interviews include medium shot or close-up shot of the interview subject talking to the interviewer on camera, or to camera responses by an interviewee to an unseen interviewer's questions. This practice, the so-called talking head, offers a personalized basis to knowledge, and it is useful to distinguish between the use of talking heads to represent an official or authoritative point of view, and the use of talking heads as a form of testimony by people who are telling their own stories (Martineau, 1984: 259). Authoritative knowledges are represented by a person deemed to be an expert in a field, who is often interviewed framed against a backdrop that reinforces a sense of authority (standing against shelves of books, or seated at a desk with a computer, for example), or who appears on a specially constructed set, as in studio-based segments of current affairs television journalism. In contrast, people narrating their own experiences are often framed at the location of the events being described. In this way, the subjects of *The Life and Times of Rosie the Riveter* (1980), a film by Connie Field dealing with US women in the workforce during the Second World War, are depicted at the sites of their wartime employment. By relying on the recollections and testimony of participants elicited through interview, Field's interactive documentary functions in the manner of an oral history, providing first-hand interpretations of historical events often overlooked by more traditional forms of historical analysis. Argument in Field's film arises from comments provided by witnesses, as opposed to the rhetorical strategies of the expository mode in which a voice-over commentary is relied upon to present and advance an argument. Ross McElwee's *Sherman's March* (1985), a film marked by a series of interactions between the director and the women he encounters on a journey through the South, deploys the interactive mode within an autobiographical frame. In *Sherman's March* (examined in Chapter 7) the autobiographical merges with the interactive to the point that McElwee's life is revealed within and through interactive moments of conversation and interrogation.

Nichols' fourth mode, the reflexive, self-consciously draws attention to the processes of representation. While the expository mode centres on commentary, the reflexive mode engages in metacommentary, reflecting on its own constitutive practices. Reflexive documentaries are concerned with exposing objectivity by revealing the filmmaker as a subjective authorial presence willing to provoke action and to reflect on the results of that provocation, as in *Chronicle of a Summer*, or someone who actively dismantles and interprets (or reinterprets) filmed footage, as in Timothy Asch's *The Ax Fight* (1974), a film discussed in Chapter 3.

An emphasis on experimentation is extended in the performative mode in which stylistic, expressive and poetic features push documentary away from a referential basis and patterns of argumentation toward the formal aesthetic realm of avant-garde cinema (Nichols, 1994: 94–5). However, the performative work remains dominantly within the realm of documentary through the fact that it retains a referential claim on the socio-historical world. The word 'performative' does not here necessarily refer to dramatic performances by subjects (though many of the actions of subjects within the performative text are excessively stylized). A performative documentary is one in which the text 'performs' – 'draws attention to itself' and its visual and expressive virtuosity (Nichols, 1994: 97). Nichols includes in this category the works *A Song of Ceylon* (Jayamanne, 1985), *Tongues Untied* (Riggs, 1989) and *Looking for Langston* (Julien, 1991), among others. Generally, the mode is characteristic of films produced for art house exhibition and is rarely utilized in television documentary. Indeed, the works from which Nichols constructs the five modes of documentary representation are largely drawn from documentary cinema with little or no attention to documentary screened on contemporary

television. It can be noted, however, that recent developments in
television documentary practice constitute a substantial revision
of, and departure from, pre-existent modes. Such developments
function as the basis of two newly emergent modes, one of which
can be termed the 'reconstructive', the other as 'observational-
entertainment', a hybrid term which reflects the hybrid status of
the mode's melding of aspects of observation and 'entertainment'.

The reconstructive mode encompasses the increasingly prominent practice of dramatic reconstruction of historical and
contemporary events and experiences, such as those used in
drama-documentary and documentary drama. Reconstruction,
the dramatic restaging of events, operates through many of the
conventions of fictional realist drama, including multiple camera
set-ups on film sets. The 'second order' experience of the world
(Paget, 1998: 81) located in dramatic restaging operates through
conventions of acting and performance, including rehearsals,
scripted dialogue and pre-planned shots which are rallied within
the reconstructive mode to maintain belief in the authenticity of
the depicted world. Though borrowing heavily from fictional
techniques, the reconstructive mode works to locate the text
within the sphere of the documentary truth claim, and to this end
employs a variety of extratextual and formal features to indicate
that the content is derived from the socio-historical world. The
presence of these features in drama-documentary, and distinctions
between their deployment in drama-documentary and documentary drama, are examined in Chapter 8. Reconstruction has
become a standard feature of television tabloid news documentaries where it has commonly, though controversially, been used in
reports of crimes. In another way, reconstruction is innovatively
melded to the conventions of tabloid news formats and *film noir* in
*The Thin Blue Line*'s incisive and subtle investigation of a murder
case which mixes reconstructions with features of the interactive
and reflexive modes. Reconstruction of a different kind has prolif-
erated through an increasing reliance on the manipulations made
possible by digital media. The intersection of digital media representation and natural science topics has produced programmes such
as *Walking with Dinosaurs* (BBC/Discovery, 1999), *The Ballad of Big
Al* (BBC, 2000) and *Walking with Beasts* (BBC, 2001) which use
putatively realistic dramatizations to re-create the look and behaviours of extinct animals.

The other newly identifiable mode, referred to here as 'observation-entertainment', comprises various features exhibited in recent factual forms such as 'reality television', the docusoap, and reality game shows (see Chapter 10, where the term 'popular factual entertainment' is used to describe these forms). The new mode relies on observation, though the sense of closeness, or intimacy, with the subject achieved within the mode outstrips that of 'traditional' observationalism and leads in one way to a 'snoopy sociability' in which the spectator is situated as a bystander to the routines of people's working lives (Corner, 2001a). In another way it verges on a form of surveillance, replete with camera angles reminiscent of closed-circuit surveillance camera footage, that pries into otherwise proscribed spaces. In both cases, the looking and hearing of classic observationalism are replaced with the voyeuristic and gossipy pleasures of peeping and overhearing. The subject's denial of the camera's presence in classic observationalism is also replaced in the newer mode with a degree of self-conscious performance by subjects. Performance, and a sense of playing to the (hidden) camera, is a prominent feature of the reality game show *Big Brother*, a programme which revises and replaces the traditional purpose of documentary as argument about the world with the viewing pleasures derivable from looking or spying and over-hearing. The voyeuristic pleasures of the mode are heightened through techniques which include musical enhancement of mood and a visual style which in certain cases is reminiscent of rock music video. Corner (2000a) uses the phrase 'documentary as diversion' to describe the pronounced move to entertainment in the observation-entertainment mode.

The array of theoretical tools confronted here – realism, style, conventions and modes – form part of the 'communicative package', the 'particular visual and aural "shape" of a work', as Corner calls it (1998: 97). Importantly, the formal features outlined here operate within documentary texts which circulate within, and are informed by, disciplinary, historical and discursive settings. The following chapter examines the foundational documentary films of Flaherty and Grierson, paying attention to sponsorship as a context within which documentary film developed. Subsequent chapters extend this approach by examining the content and representational forms of work from a range of documentary subgenres through reference to the varying settings or contexts in which they occur.

## CHAPTER 2

# Men with Movie Cameras: Flaherty and Grierson

The list of foundational figures in the history of documentary – those documentary filmmakers whose work has been identified as integral to the development of documentary practices – is a varied one. Dziga Vertov, Walther Ruttmann, Joris Ivens, Pare Lorentz and Leni Riefenstahl are prominent in accounts of world documentary cinema, while two figures, Robert Flaherty (1884–1951) and John Grierson (1898–1972), are generally considered to be the founders of English language documentary. The pioneering status of both Flaherty and Grierson rests on the fact that both filmmakers developed practices, methods, techniques, and most notably in Grierson's case, institutional arrangements and a body of theoretical writing that in varying ways, formed the bases of documentary as it continues to be practiced in numerous countries worldwide.

Flaherty was born in Michigan and grew up in Canada where he spent much of his youth exploring remote areas with his father, a miner. As a young man Flaherty led surveying expeditions into sub-Arctic Canada and in the early 1920s, after a brief training in film-making, he travelled to northern Québec where he made his first and best-known film, *Nanook of the North* (1922). A strong narrative drive mixed with dramatic reconstruction informs this film and Flaherty's other work including *Moana: A Romance of the Golden Age* (1926), *Man of Aran* (1934), *The Land* (1941) and *Louisiana Story* (1949).

Grierson was born in Stirling, Scotland, and enlisted in the naval minesweeping service during the First World War. In 1919 he enrolled at Glasgow University and eventually graduated with a

Master's degree in philosophy and literature. Grierson spent from October 1924 to January 1927 studying in America, where he was influenced by the ideas of Walter Lippmann, a writer on issues related to public relations, democratic theory and propaganda. On his return to Britain, inspired by Lippmann's ideas, Grierson contacted the Empire Marketing Board (EMB), the British government's largest publicity organization, where he was appointed as an assistant film officer. From this position, and in his other government appointments, he established a basis of support and professional contacts which he relied on to extend the production of documentary film. Grierson directed only one film, the influential silent era work *Drifters* (1929), though he produced hundreds of others, including a number of outstanding documentaries within what became known as the British documentary film movement, among them *Song of Ceylon* (1934) directed by Basil Wright, and *Night Mail* (1936) by Wright and Harry Watt. On one level the documentary 'movement' under Grierson's stewardship can be characterized as a group of directors, editors and researchers who collaborated with Grierson during the 1930s and the 1940s in the making of documentary films. On an institutional level, the movement coalesced around government and corporate sponsoring bodies such as the EMB and later the General Post Office which were concerned with film as a medium of public education.

Grierson consolidated his thoughts on documentary film in a series of essays he published during 1932–34 in the journal *Cinema Quarterly* under the title 'First Principles of Documentary'. Notoriously contradictory and inconsistent in his writings, Grierson presents here a unified and systematic statement of his early position on the aesthetic and social approaches of documentary. Importantly, he referred to the essays as his 'manifesto', a word which evokes modernist declarations of creative (and political) intent and one which reinforces the systematic and purposive elaboration of ideas contained in 'First Principles' (Grierson, [1932–34] 1998: 83). Though Grierson was later to revise a number of the statements he made in the essays, the work nevertheless stands as an effective and significant summation of his early ideas on forms of documentary, including Flaherty's *Nanook of the North* and his own film *Drifters*.

This chapter draws on Grierson's 'First Principles of Documentary' as the basis of an examination of the form and stylistic strategies of Flaherty's *Nanook of the North* and Grierson's

*Drifters.* The divergent formal approaches to the documentary representation of reality – the dramatized narrative of *Nanook* and the imagistic method of *Drifters* – are contextualized through reference to Flaherty's alignment of documentary film with commercial distribution and exhibition and Grierson's focus on sponsored documentary as a tool of citizenship. The latter, Grierson's reliance on sponsorship, by both corporate and government funding bodies, is emphasized here as a central factor in the development of documentary modes of filmmaking.

## Grierson and the 'speedy snip-snap', 'shim-sham mechanics' and 'documentary proper'

Grierson opens his essay 'First Principles of Documentary' by critically outlining the formal features and practices of documentary filmmaking. To date, he comments, 'all films made from natural material have been regarded as coming within [the documentary] category'. He notes that films made from what he calls natural or raw material, by which he means footage shot on location, include educational films, scientific films, illustrated lectures and newsreels. He refers to such works as the 'lower categories' of filmmaking, which, he argues, are distinct from documentary. According to Grierson, films in the lower categories merely record or describe events. The newsreel, for example, 'is just the speedy snip-snap of some utterly unimportant ceremony', that is, uninspired footage of a public event which has been rapidly edited for quick release. For Grierson, newsreels represent a 'purely journalistic skill' which is unlikely to 'make any considerable contribution to the fuller art of documentary'. The 'documentary proper', in contrast to the lower categories of factual filmmaking, does not merely describe natural material; it arranges and creatively shapes the 'raw material' that is reality. In this way Grierson situates documentary as a unique category of non-fiction film, one in which the filmmaker 'dramatizes' an episode to extract or highlight certain features which will expose essential characteristics of the filmed event (Grierson, [1932–34] 1998: 81–5).

What Grierson calls the documentary film's 'creative shapings' of the profilmic world (a description that resembles his earlier and best-known description of documentary representation as the 'creative treatment of actuality'[1]), also distinguishes documentary from the studio produced fictional film (Grierson, [1932–34] 1988: 83). A documentary film is derived from selected profilmic observations depicting people in their unscripted daily lives, as opposed to the fictional film which depicts professional actors in scripted stories in studio settings.[2] Documentaries capture the 'spontaneous gesture' and the unrehearsed actions of non-professional 'actors'. For Grierson, documentary is capable of achieving 'an intimacy of knowledge and effect impossible to the shim-sham mechanics of the [commercial film] studio' (Grierson, [1932–34] 1988: 83).

From these observations and declarations Grierson assembles three points which serve as the bases of his early theory of documentary. Speaking on behalf of documentary filmmakers he wrote ([1932–34] 1988: 83):

> (1) We believe that the cinema's capacity for getting around, for observing and selecting from life itself, can be exploited in a new and vital art form. The studio films largely ignore this possibility of opening up the screen on the real world. They photograph acted stories against artificial backgrounds. Documentary would photograph the living scene and the living story. (2) We believe that the original (or native) actor, and the original (or native) scene, are better guides to a screen interpretation of the modern world ... They give it power of interpretation over more complex and astonishing happenings than the studio mind can conjure up or the studio mechanician recreate. (3) We believe that the materials and stories thus taken from the raw can be finer (more real in the philosophic sense) than the acted article.

Grierson's reference to representation which is 'more real in the philosophic sense' has caused some critical confusion. He here makes a distinction between empirical reality (what he elsewhere calls the 'actual'[3]) and 'the real'. For Grierson, observable, empirical content was selected and edited by the documentary filmmaker to reveal truths (which are 'more real in the philosophic sense') about the world.[4] He argues that documentary is not a mere reflection or mimesis of reality. A documentary representation is one in which the carefully selected raw material, or edited footage, is creatively or 'artfully' edited or 'interpreted' to reveal truths which would otherwise evade the camera. In this way, the evidentiary and informational role of documentary is incorporated into a form which transforms empirical evidence into revelatory and insightful – 'truthful' – perceptions of its subject.

In his explication of the basic principles of documentary, Grierson refers to the formal techniques and approaches Flaherty employed in *Nanook of the North* as exemplary of the newly emerging documentary practices. Grierson locates the specific features of Flaherty's work within two points: first, notes Grierson, 'Flaherty does not simply describe an action, he employs a method which interprets the action. Interpretation involves a style of editing which juxtaposes details and relies on staging or re-enactment. Second, Flaherty digs himself in for a year, or two maybe. He lives with his people so the story is told "out of himself" ' (Grierson, [1932–34] 1988: 85). Flaherty's practice of what has since become known as participant observation is used to create a story from narrative elements found on location. Grierson takes it for granted that the story form – narrative – is the basis of documentary. Re-enactment or staging is not used for its own sake, nor is editing used for purely aesthetic ends. Such methods are deployed to structure a story in order to reveal the reality and truths of the events it narrates. Grierson notes that fictional cinema, or 'Hollywood', also deals with stories. Hollywood, however, begins with a script and actors and a purpose-built studio, imposing a 'ready made dramatic shape on the raw material'. In contrast, Flaherty creates a story 'on the spot' from what is at hand. 'With Flaherty', wrote Grierson, 'it became an absolute principle that the story must be taken from the location, and that it should be (what he considers) the essential story of the location' ([1932– 34] 1988: 84).

Grierson's implicit criticism of Hollywood, evident in his contrast of Hollywood's artificial studio methods and effective documentary practices, was not, however, a position shared by Flaherty early in his career.[5] Flaherty, unlike Grierson, looked to Hollywood for commercial distribution and exhibition of his films and in doing so he screened *Nanook of the North* in New York for a number of distributors, including an unsuccessful presentation for staff at Paramount.[6] Flaherty eventually found a commercial distributor, the French film company Pathé Frères, and secured a premiere for his film at New York's largest and most important theatre at the time, the Capitol. The two linked achievements – a distributor for a feature-length non-fiction film, and a successful premier for such a film at a prestigious New York venue – are significant in the development of documentary film. The backing of Pathé Frères provided the financial support necessary for Flaherty to establish the 'documentary proper' in the form of *Nanook of the North*. The New York premiere created a large audience for the finished work and in the process opened a path for the production of documentary films for commercial cinema release. Ultimately, however, the financial success of *Nanook of the North* stemmed from a reliance on a form in which, as Grierson observed, factual 'raw material' was structured into a dramatized narrative. The formal structure of *Nanook of the North* was, in commercial and aesthetic terms, an impressive achievement.

## *Nanook of the North*: dramatized narrative

*Nanook of the North* deals with a family of Itivimuit, a group of Inuit living on the shore of Hopewell Sound in Québec. The narrative of this silent film involves a series of simple experiences and daily routines: Nanook repairs a kayak, he and his family travel to a trading post to trade their furs, Nanook fishes in the frozen sea and hunts a walrus, the family builds an igloo and retires for the night. The next day the family members depart in dogsleds for a day of hunting seal. The day ends with a blizzard and the family is forced to take shelter for the night in a disused igloo.

The first footage of Inuit life shot by Flaherty was burnt in a fire, forcing Flaherty to re-shoot his footage. Flaherty was dissatisfied with his original footage, which reminded him of a travelogue, unstructured scenes of life in exotic places, one of Grierson's 'lower categories' of filmmaking. An alternative model to the travelogue for the representation of native peoples existed in the form of Edward Curtis' *In the Land of the Head Hunters* (1914), a film built around the lives of the Kwakiutl natives of the northwest coast of North America. Curtis' film is a fanciful melodramatic tale of headhunting, warfare, a despicable villain and a woman pressed against her will into marriage. The basis of Curtis' film is the fictional melodrama, which he lays over any evidence of Kwakiutl life as it was lived at the time.

Flaherty, however, invented a form which was distinct from both the travelogue and the fictional structures of Curtis' film. Flaherty's groundbreaking achievement in *Nanook of the North* was the construction of a narrative which transcended a mere series of travelogue scenes in a way which did not impose a predetermined structure upon its content. Specifically, Flaherty's significant contribution to documentary cinema was the recognition that scenes from reality could be edited into a narrative that relied on the dramatic effects of fictional cinema. Pointing to the centrality of narrative to his understanding of what became known as a documentary representation, Flaherty stated that 'a story must come out of the life of a people'. The film theorist Siegfried Kracauer saw in this statement a basis of what he called Flaherty's filmmaking 'formula' (in Williams, 1980: 101–2). In drawing out the implications of Flaherty's use of the verb 'come out', Kracauer implicitly distinguishes Flaherty's filmmaking practice from Curtis' method. According to Kracauer, Flaherty's statement reflects his insistence on constructing a story from the 'raw material of life', as opposed to subjecting this material to pre-established filmic frameworks. Kracauer highlights this demand by pointing to Flaherty's idea of 'discovering the *essential human story from within*' the observable world (in Williams, 1980: 102. Italics in original).

Grierson (1932–34) argued that what he called the 'story form' is the basis of *Nanook*'s essential documentary quality. As Grierson recognized, this form relies on Flaherty's creative, or artful, or dramatic, manipulation of factual information. Grierson's use of the word dramatic carries two meanings: a narrative which builds a certain emotive and ideational intensity, and actions which are enacted for the camera (Corner, 1996: 14). In *Nanook of the North* the two meanings of the word dramatic coalesce in numerous examples of enactment and reconstruction, including the film's notable and emotionally intense seal hunting scene.[7] Having apparently hooked a seal, Nanook pulls hard on the harpoon line, as if struggling to land the seal. In fact, the scene was enacted, with the harpoon line leading off camera to a group of men who tugged on the line. The family in the film is also 'enacted' or dramatized in the sense that Flaherty brought together a number of individuals to represent a typical Inuit family group. Nanook the Bear was played by Allakariallak, his wife Nyla was played by Alice Nuvalinga, who cares for the baby Rainbow and son Allegoo (played by Phillipoosie). (The place in the family of another woman, Cunayoo, Nanook's second wife, is discreetly left undefined.)

These 'characters' are set in a drama that is a nostalgic reconstruction composed of anachronisms. Nanook hunts with a spear when at the time the Inuit were well acquainted with rifles, just as they knew of gramophones, contrary to the scene in which Nanook encounters a record player. At the time of Flaherty's film, the Inuit no longer wore fur clothes though Flaherty redressed them for his film in traditional clothing. Through these and other manipulations Flaherty consciously set out to evoke a former 'primitive' way of life which accorded with his conception of the 'real' Inuit condition. While the use of such methods were increasingly looked upon in subsequent documentary film practice with suspicion, they were acceptable to Flaherty as a way of retrieving or locating central truths concerning the subject. Flaherty famously summarized his awareness of the irony of his situation – approaching truth through dramatizations, reconstructions, or what he called manipulations – by saying, 'Sometimes you have to lie. One often has to distort a thing to catch its true spirit' (quoted in Calder-Marshall, 1966: 97).

The various manipulations and historical re-enactments are structured into a narrative that draws together various random acts and scenes. As the film historian Brian Winston has noted, prior to the intertitle 'Winter comes', which appears 23 minutes into screen time, the film is a series of vignettes and unconnected incidents: building a fire, going to the river, meeting a trader at the trading post. The incidents serve to establish the location for the film, though there is no sense of causal relationships between the incidents. After the 'Winter Comes' intertitle, however, the film adopts a simple though effective narrative based on a journey in which Nanook catches a fox, builds an igloo, hunts a seal, struggles to control his dogs, is trapped with his family in a blizzard, and eventually finds shelter with his family in an abandoned igloo (Winston, 1995: 100). The journey is integrated temporally across two days and two nights, and events are causally related: the hunt for food motivates the journey, which involves capturing a seal, which leads to the sled dogs fighting over the seal meat, which dangerously delays the family's search for shelter as a blizzard approaches, and the eventual refuge from the storm in a disused igloo. The narrative builds dramatic tension – 'will Nanook and his family escape the blizzard?' – that is satisfactorily resolved when the family finds shelter (Winston, 1995: 101).

Intertitles play an integral expository role in the narrativization of these events. The intertitles provide contextual information, assisting in locating the events in place and time, and underline crucial developments in the narrative, as when they draw attention to the effect of the dogfight in delaying and hence endangering the family's search for shelter as the blizzard closes in. Elsewhere the intertitles add moments of dramatic tension to specific sequences within the broader narrative. This process is exemplified in footage of Nanook constructing an igloo, against which an intertitle reads, 'Now only one thing more is needed.' The suspense created in this title is maintained as Nanook is seen cutting a block of transparent ice. The mystery of the 'one more thing' is unravelled when Nanook adds the ice to the igloo as a window. Other techniques are used to build and maintain drama and suspense. Many of the scenes, such as the seal hunt, for example, are shot in long takes with the action unfolding in real-time, uninterrupted by editorial cuts which would hasten a conclusion and dispel the suspense.

The scenes referred to here, as with the majority of scenes in the film, were not shot in any particular sequence. Flaherty did not work from a script; instead he structured his footage completely in the editing stage, allowing, as he insisted, for the story to emerge from the filmed material. What Winston (1995: 103) calls Flaherty's 'genius' was his ability to construct a story from incidents that were not shot in sequence or necessarily filmed for the purposes of being included in a narrative. Drawing on Flaherty's film, Grierson had noted in 'First Principles of Documentary' that a documentary was a story with a dramatic form. The dramatization of narrative distinguished documentary from the 'lower categories' of factual film such as newsreels and travelogues which do not dramatize material. In turn, while fiction cinema dramatizes stories, it does not a share a direct claim on the real in the way of documentary or the 'lower categories'. The result of Flaherty's innovations was a unique positioning of documentary as a form which dramatized, through enactment and narrativization, the 'raw material' of reality.

## Citizenship and documentary film

Having praised Flaherty in 'First Principles of Documentary' for establishing the story form based on drama, Grierson then qualifies his assessment of Flaherty's achievement. (Throughout his early writings he adopted this tactic in relation to Flaherty's work: praise followed by criticism. In later writings he denied that he was influenced by Flaherty.) Grierson argues that while Flaherty's dramatic story form is adequate as a way of interpreting the place of the individual in a harsh natural environment it is incapable of revealing 'the essentially co-operative or mass nature of society'. According to Grierson, the 'world of complex and impersonal forces' that is modern society requires the abandonment of the story form for a different order of documentary representation. For Grierson, the purpose of documentary was not to represent the novelty or romance of the 'noble savage on [an] exotic landscape', but to inform or instruct citizens in the operations of modern society (Grierson, [1932–34] 1988: 85–7).

Grierson understood industrial society to be a unified object characterized by an interdependence and harmony of social and political institutions, and he conceived documentary film as an agent of civic education capable of explaining and promoting the essentially harmonious and consensual nature of society to its citizens. Grierson rejected the idea that society was inherently divided between irreconcilable interests. While he acknowledged the existence of different social classes, indeed his conception of documentary rests on the existence of an educated elite which will instruct and inform the general public, he did not see class as a divisive condition within society. The emphasis in the Griersonian documentary on consensus and integration denied social division and differences and any need for social transformation. Grierson's ideas on the functions of documentary were, then, inherently conservative in their reinforcement of the status quo. Grierson did, however, hold that the state could play a reformist role in addressing issues such as ill health and poverty, and under Grierson's stewardship the British documentary film movement of the 1930s moved toward a form of journalistic reportage that sought to highlight and ameliorate social problems. Such documentary reports were extensions of what Grierson understood to be a basic principle of documentary, namely, the education of citizens in matters concerning the social interconnections and operative forces of industrial society.

In 'First Principles of Documentary' Grierson introduces a form that he considers adequate to this educative task through a discussion of Walther Ruttmann's *Berlin, Symphony of the City* (1927). Ruttmann's film was one of a number of so-called city symphonies produced in the late 1920s and throughout the 1930s, among them Dziga Vertov's *Man With a Movie Camera* (1929). These technically innovative works are structured around the diurnal activities of a city (Berlin in Ruttmann's case; Vertov constructs a generic Russian city from footage shot in Moscow, Kiev and Odessa).

Grierson admired the ways in which the 'smooth and finely tempo'd visuals' of Ruttmann's film 'floated along in procession'.
According to Grierson, '[i]n so far as the film was principally concerned with movements and the building of separate images into
movements, Ruttmann was justified in calling it a symphony'.
Significantly, Grierson argues that the film represents a 'break
away from the [dramatic] story' form of Flaherty: 'In *Berlin* cinema
swung along according to its own more natural powers: creating
dramatic effect from the tempo'd accumulation of its single observation' (Grierson, [1932–34] 1988: 86).

While he accepts the film's technical innovations Grierson
insists, however, that the poetic imagery of *Berlin* lacks a social purpose. Grierson criticizes Ruttmann's film, and the city symphony
genre in general, for an 'aesthetic decadence' that fails to comment on social issues such as the place of labour and working conditions. In contrast, Grierson seeks a form of realist documentary
which 'fulfils the best ends of citizenship' and which adopts a
'sense of social responsibility' by revealing the working conditions
of modern industry and the ways in which labour and industry
interrelate, thereby persuading viewers of the effectiveness of the
modern industrial system (Grierson, [1932–34] 1988: 86–8). Such
a persuasive, rhetorical, approach is, he argues, exemplified by his
own film *Drifters*.

## *Drifters*: 'deep-seeing, deep-sympathizing' and deep-sea fishing

Critical assessments of the history of British cinema have described
Grierson's silent film *Drifters* as an important and influential film
within the British documentary film movement of the 1930s
(Aitken, 1998: 11; Le MeMahieu, 1988: 214). *Drifters*, a film produced as a promotional tool for the British fishing industry,
focuses on the work of deep-sea herring fishermen. The film's
uncomplicated narrative depicts fishermen walking to their
trawlers, the ships putting out to sea, a night of fishing, the return
to harbour and the sale of the catch. Grierson ([1932–34] 1988:
78) described the film in terms of a series of vignettes: 'the gathering of the ships for the herring season, the going out, the shooting
at evening, the long drift in the night, the drive hard against the
head sea, and (for finale) the frenzy of a market in which said
agonies are sold'.

As with Flaherty's *Nanook of the North*, Grierson's film relies heavily on reconstruction and manipulative directorial intervention. For example, the fishing village from which the trawlers depart is a composite of a number of villages in the Shetland Islands. The interior of the trawler featured in the film was shot on a set especially constructed for the purpose, and the exterior shots of the men on deck were composed of shots of two different ships. The catch of fish and eels, seen swimming in a net as it is hauled to the trawler, was filmed at the Plymouth Marine Biological Research Station. Indeed, reconstruction played a central role in Grierson's conception of documentary. Within Grierson's well-known definition of documentary as 'the creative treatment of actuality', 'treatment' was synonymous with reconstruction which, in turn, was often replaced by its synonym 'dramatisation' (Winston, 1995: 99).[8] Treatment, or dramatization or reconstruction – the practice referred to in 'First Principles of Documentary' ([1932–34] 1988: 83) as 'the creative shapings ... of natural material' – was for Grierson, as his comments on Flaherty's deployment of the practice reveal, a way of approaching 'documentary proper'. Such 'shapings' were complemented and extended through the film's formal characteristics, in particular a pattern of associative montage indebted to Eisenstien and, more particularly, Pudovkin.

Associative or relational montage, a form of narrative montage whereby shots create meaning through their relationship to one another, was developed from the editing practices and experiments of Soviet filmmakers of the early twentieth century. An experiment conducted in the early 1920s by filmmaker Lev Kulushov provided the basis for claims of the efficacy of Soviet montage techniques. Kulushov juxtaposed a close-up shot of the face of a well-known Russian actor, Ivan Mosjoukine, with three shots – one of a bowl of soup, another of a woman in a coffin and another of a child with a toy bear. Mosjoukine's expression did not change from shot to shot though, according to a contemporary report of the experiment by Kulushov's pupil Pudovkin, viewers perceived changes in the actor's expression as he responded pensively to the soup, sorrowfully to death and happily to a child at play (Pudovkin, 1949: 140). Working with the suggestive power of relational montage, the Soviet director Sergei Eisenstein extended the dramatic possibilities of the technique. In his films *October* (1927), which depicts the events surrounding the October Revolution of 1917, and *Battleship Potemkin* (1925), based on the true story of a mutiny on board a Russian battleship in 1905, Eisenstein edited shots to produce startling contrasts. His 'montage of collision' (see Taylor and Glenny, 1994) constructed meaning dialectically through a thesis or argument (as established in a shot or series of shots), antithesis (a contrasting shot or series of shots), leading to synthesis (a new meaning created from the radical opposition of shots).

Having prepared the intertitles for the US version of *Battleship Potemkin* Grierson was familiar with, and greatly impressed by, Eisenstein's film. Grierson's emphasis in *Drifters* on quick cutting and unusual camera angles are reminiscent of Eisenstein's techniques, and the focus in *Drifters* on a group of workers, not an individual, corresponds to Eisenstein's refusal to celebrate the individual and his attention to the experiences of various social groups. However, the similarities between Eisenstein and Grierson end there. As numerous critics have pointed out, Grierson had no sympathy for the revolutionary politics of Soviet cinema and, generally, his indebtedness to Eisenstein's style has been overstated (see Winston, 1995: 48). Though traces of Eisenstein's formalist influence can be found in *Drifters*, equally if not more evident are elements of the approaches of Eisenstein's Soviet contemporaries Victor Turin (whose film *Turksib* [1929] Grierson admired) and Pudovkin (Aitken, 1990: 86–7). Unlike the radical disruptive oppositions constructed by Eisenstein in his style of editing, Pudovkin sought to establish and maintain narrative meaning through an editing style that linked shots in a sequence. Similarly, most of the formal structure of *Drifters* is composed of linked sequences of shots which gradually build an impression of the subject.

In 'First Principles of Documentary' Grierson refers to the technique of *Drifters* as 'imagist', an impressionistic style of realist filmmaking that constructs sequences from varied and often seemingly unrelated shots. In a statement typical of his self-promotional attitude, he claims that the 'rhythmic effects' in *Drifters* 'outdid the technical example of [Eisenstein's] *Potemkin*'. According to Grierson, shots in *Drifters* are 'massed together, not only for description and tempo but for commentary' on the subject ([1932–34] 1988: 89). Grierson's emphasis on the communicative ability of shots and sequences emphasizes the place of editing in his narrative method of filmmaking. In a written commentary on *Drifters*, Grierson ([1929] 1988: 79) explained how he structured

a montage of provocative images into a narrative sequence of the
passing of day into night, into day:

> For the setting of darkness, not darkness itself, [but] flocks of birds sil-
> houetted against the sky flying hard into the camera repeated and
> repeated. For the long drift in the night, not the ship, not the sea itself,
> but the dark mystery of the underwater ... For the dawn, not a bleary
> fuss against the sky ..., but the winding slow-rolling movement into the
> light. Then a bell-buoy. Then a Dutch lugger rolling heavily into the
> light. Three images in a row.

Grierson ([1932–34] 1988: 88) referred to his style in the film as
one which is 'deep-sympathising', an approach which romantically
depicts what he calls the 'high bravery of upstanding labour'.
Further, he considered his representation to be one which is 'deep-
seeing', by which he meant a creative and insightful reworking of
textual elements to produce not merely a mimetic record but an
interpretation of, and argument about, industrial forms of modernity and its relationship to nature. Throughout the film, images of
human labour, nature (birds, sea, sky, fish) and machine (the
ship's engine and winches) are juxtaposed. The editing style suggests the connection and interaction of various elements: (male)
worker and machine, worker and nature and machine and nature.
Over-lapping dissolves are used to draw attention to the relationships of elements. Grierson's patterning and layering of images
demonstrates the ways in which aspects of the process of herring
fishing are interconnected and, in turn, the visual practice constructs an argument concerning the interaction of social relations
generally (Aitken, 1990: 191).

An extension of the film's evocation of social relations is inti-
mated in the final scene in which the catch is sold at the market.
The presence of the market suggests an industrial and economic
context for the relations presented in the film. The intertitles at
the end of the film read: 'And the sound of the sea and the people
of the sea are lost in the chatter and clatter of the market for the
world', followed by 'So to the ends of the earth goes the harvest of
the city.' Having linked the fishing industry to global markets, the
poetic and non-specific language of the intertitles, however,
retreats from any direct reference to the role of economic forces in
the lives of 'upstanding labour' or any reference to the fact that the
labour-intensive and dangerous deep-sea fishing industry may be
exploitative.

Grierson acknowledged his lack of commentary on the relation-ship of labour and economic context when he stated that, 'As the catch was being boxed and barrelled I thought I would like to say that what was really being boxed and barrelled was the labour of men' (quoted in Winston, 1995: 37). Winston argues that Grierson could not say what he wanted to say about work and the domi-nance of the market because of the censorious presence of the sponsor (Winston, 1995: 57). Indeed, it would have been diffi-cult for Grierson to raise the issue of the exploitative power of market economics given that *Drifters* was produced for a government agency, the Empire Marketing Board, which existed to promote and publicize an impression of the benefits and advantages of free-trade markets. For Winston (1995), Grierson's failure to confront the political implications of the scenario constructed in *Drifters* is symptomatic of the entire tradition of the British documentary film movement and its implication with the demands of govern-ment and private sector sponsorship. Harry Watt, who made a number of films for the General Post Office Film Unit after Grierson had moved there from the Empire Marketing Board in 1933, admitted that 'The truth is that if we had indulged in real social criticism to any extent, we would have immediately been without sponsorship and a whole experiment [in documentary film production], would have finished. So we compromised' (quoted in Armes, 1978: 133). As Watt highlights, in a point that can be generalized to include Flaherty's sponsored film *Nanook of the North*, sponsorship led to a type of self-censorship which func-tioned to set limits on what documentary filmmakers could and could not say.

## Sponsorship: the second principle of documentary

In the essays which constitute his 'First Principles of Documentary' Grierson works through various documentary forms, notably those adopted by Flaherty and Ruttmann, to arrive at a set of formal and stylistic features, encoded in his own film *Drifters*, which illustrate many of the basic features, or first principles, of documentary aes-thetics and their deployment in the service of truth claims. Within this approach it is notable that Grierson's analysis fails to include reference to any of the factors which impact on the production of documentary film, among them the central role played by sponsorship. Sponsorship – funding made available by government, academic or private sector bodies to promote a product, collect information or to create a sense of the sponsor's public-spirited commitment to certain causes or points of view – has, for much of the history of documentary film, been a dominant contextualizing feature of documentary production. The prominence of sponsorship within the documentary tradition is exemplified in the fact that 'sponsored documentary' is a category which includes the majority of documentary output. Indeed, given the significance of sponsorship to the development of documentary, the practice can, after Grierson, be termed the second principle of documentary.

Without corporate sponsorship Flaherty would not have been able to produce a film dealing with the Inuit. As he admitted in 1950, no one would finance a film dealing with the Eskimo until Revillon Frères, a French fur company, stepped in and met production costs (Flaherty, [1950] 1996: 38). *Nanook of the North* is not an advertisement for Revillon Frères in a direct sense. Rather, the film carries a number of messages that advance the interests of the sponsoring company, as in the trading post sequence in which fur is represented as a commodity which economically benefits the Inuit, and in the fact that Nanook's fur clothing is represented as an effective protection from the worst natural comments. A sales pitch for fur echoes in the background of Flaherty's silent film. Grierson instantly recognized this aspect of the film when he noted that *Nanook of the North* 'was in the first place an advertisement for furs, though it appeared in theatres all over the world as a straightforward epic of Eskimo life' (quoted in Swann, 1989: 8). Flaherty's links with corporate sponsors were extended in his subsequent films; he produced *The Land* under sponsorship provided by the US government and *Louisiana Story*, his final documentary, was made for Standard Oil of America.

Beyond the corporate sector another form of sponsorship, that of government public relations programmes (the form of sponsorship responsible for *Drifters*) was crucial to the expansion of the British documentary film movement under Grierson's direction. Stuart Legg, one of Grierson's early collaborators, reflected later in his career on the role of government sponsorship in the documentary movement by noting that the relationship between the filmmaker and the sponsor 'is at the root of everything we've done for the last forty years', admitting at the same time that the relationship was a problematic one (quoted in Winston, 1995: 58).

Civil servants did not necessarily understand or accept a film-maker's ideas or aesthetics or politics, but Grierson was particularly adept at mediating the interests and demands of sponsor and filmmaker. Over the course of his career, this skill was Grierson's greatest asset.

Grierson inaugurated a connection between non-fiction film and government funding under the auspices of the EMB, and, from 1933 to 1937, extended the link through the Film Unit of the General Post Office. He subsequently transferred the British model of state-sponsored documentary to Canada where, in 1939, he was appointed commissioner of the newly established National Film Board of Canada, a national unit for the production of government public relations films. Grierson also proposed the model to the New Zealand and Australian governments during a brief trip he made to those countries in 1941. In the United States, Pare Lorentz heard of Grierson's success in documentary production and in 1938 persuaded President Franklin Roosevelt to establish the United States Film Service for the production of government films to address the problems associated with economic depression and environmental mismanagement.

Sponsorship not only ensured the production of certain films, it frequently determined content. The unusual subject matter of *Drifters* – the herring fishing industry – resulted from the process of securing sponsorship. At the time, funding of government public relations films was approved by the Financial Secretary to the Treasury. Knowing that the Secretary, Arthur Samuel, was an authority on the herring industry, Grierson proposed a film on a topic which he was sure would appeal to, and be approved by, the Secretary. As documentary filmmaking continued to align itself through sponsorship with the demands of the civil service, sponsored filmmakers found it increasingly difficult to make films which expressed a point of view which contradicted or opposed the political stance of the sponsor (Kuhn, 1980: 30).

The formal characteristics of documentary were also subject to the demands of sponsorship, a fact ignored by Grierson in his analysis of the first principles of documentary. Later in his career, however, Grierson admitted that the requirements of various governmental sponsors meant that British documentary films of the 1930s 'ceased exploring into the poetic [avant-gardist or experimental] use of the documentary approach' (quoted in Sussex, 1972: 24). Furthermore, the rise of the Griersonian documentary form in English-speaking countries throughout the 1930s and 1940s tended in those countries to marginalize the modernist experimentations of filmmakers such as Vertov, Ruttmann and Luis Buñuel (*Las Hurdes/Land Without Bread*, 1932).[9] Indeed, works of political and formal radicalism, and agitational forms generally are largely overlooked in the majority of critical assessments of the documentary tradition and their emphasis on the Griersonian form of sponsored documentary.[10]

Though Grierson was reluctant during the 1930s to discuss the growing relationship between documentary and its chief funding source, it is clear that this relationship positioned documentary as a form of government or official information (Corner, 1996: 22). Recent criticisms of the Griersonian form have charged that Grierson's alignment of the documentary project with official funding functioned to institutionalize Grierson's foundational principles of documentary thereby denying alternative modes of documentary representation which emphasized different theoretical ideas and varying production practices (Winston, 1995). The practices of autobiographical film (examined in Chapter 7), and the recent examples of popular factual entertainment (analysed in Chapter 10), demonstrate ways in which documentary diverges from or reworks the formal approaches and content of Griersonian documentary. However, despite calls for the abandonment or revision of Griersonian forms, documentary remains committed in the main to the basic principles articulated by Grierson. Importantly, the essence of Grierson's argument, that documentary refers to images and sounds which are 'imaginatively' reconstructed in rhetorical and evidentiary narratives which lay claim to truths, persists in the face of various critical assaults on such a formulation.

## CHAPTER 3

# Constructing and Contesting Otherness: Ethnographic Film

At the close of the nineteenth century a French physician, Felix-Louis Regnault, made the following observation in the course of his research into the anatomy and physical movement of people he referred to as 'savages': 'All savage peoples make recourse to gesture to express themselves; their language is so poor it does not suffice to make them understood ... With primitive man, gesture precedes speech' (quoted in Rony, 1996: 3). By the time he published this description (in 1898), Regnault had already produced a number of filmed studies of so-called primitive people that have since been considered to be the first ethnographic films.[1] To Regnault, his films were documents which reveal, through close scientific observation, details of a 'race' of people who, plunged in darkness without adequate language, cannot represent themselves.[2] Regnault's project of representing 'inarticulate savages' in ways intended to provide 'them' with a history intersected with the original aim of anthropology, a field of study that was then developing its focus. In a broad sense, anthropology established itself at the turn of the twentieth century as a Western academic discourse which assigned itself the task of representing non-Westernized peoples.

Central to the approaches adopted within the task of anthropological cross-cultural representation are the methods of ethnography, a term which refers to the practices of fieldwork in the study of cultures and to the outcome of the fieldwork process, a report on the fieldwork experience. According to the anthropologist

Susan Slomovics:

> The classic ethnography by a social anthropologist ... would be a work in which the life of the tribe would be encapsulated into a volume, divided very clearly into certain topics: life cycle, economics, land tenure, social organization of the village notables as opposed to the various classes ... The traditional model would be to encode the account so that is implicit that you have been there, without actually stating it. (quoted in Rony, 1996: 6–7)[3]

As the last sentence of this quotation suggests, ethnography establishes a distinction between those responsible for the production and consumption of ethnographic accounts, and the subjects of ethnography who occupy a different space to the ethnologist and the reader. This dichotomy – which is reducible to 'us' (the observers) and 'them' (the observed) – constructs the ethnographic subject as 'Other', a term applied to people who are separate from one's self, whether in terms of 'race', gender, sexuality, ethnicity, time or space.[4] Within the Western perspective of ethnography, the Other has been positioned as different and, implicitly, inferior. The researcher Kenan Malik (1996: 220) has explained this process:

> Western science and philosophy ... have established a form of knowledge whereby non-Western societies and cultures are represented solely in terms of the categories of Western thought, and in which Western society acts as a standard against which all other societies are judged. This inevitably leads to the silencing of other voices. At the same time the differences between Western and non-Western cultures are rationalized through non-Western peoples being defined as the 'Others', distinguished solely through their antagonism to the dominant image of the 'self', and against whose peculiarities the self-image of the West is created. The result has been the acquisition of an aura of superiority for Western cultures and an imposition of a sense of inferiority upon non-Western ones.

The tradition of the ethnographic film, like ethnography itself, is deeply imbued with the 'us' and 'them' – self and Other – dichotomy and its attendant differential relations of power. Throughout most of its history from the time of Regnault, the ethnographic film has been constructed as a representational practice in which the culture of the non-Westernized 'Other' has been treated as a form of scientific datum subjected to the objectifying methods of Western ethnographic science. The documentary film theorist Bill Nichols (1981: 238) has brought attention to the imbalance of power evident in this practice, and the issues raised by the situation, when he states:

> Most often ethnographic films attempt to explain or describe some aspect of another culture to members of the film maker's own culture within a context informed to a varying extent by traditional anthropological and ethnographic concerns and concepts and perpetuating most of their political limitations: ideology is a word seldom used in studies of other cultures, and considerations of who defines culture and how (where do We draw the line around Them?) or, even more, of the ideological implications of representing one culture to another receive scant attention.

Situating ethnographic films within the context outlined by Nichols – the discipline of ethnography and its concerns with Otherness – this chapter examines the ways in which selected ethnographic films construct or contest categories of 'us' and 'them', and the ideological implications of such representational processes. In tracing these changes this chapter focuses on a number of key moments in the development of ethnographic film, beginning with so-called salvage ethnography, a practice exemplified by Robert Flaherty's *Nanook of the North* (1922), a film which presumes to save an ethnographic subject believed to be 'disappearing'. A subsequent development, sometimes referred to as the 'reflexive turn', in which filmmakers comment on their own methods, seeks to reveal the ways in which ethnographic film constructs its own authoritative position. *The Ax Fight* (1974), a groundbreaking film and a central work in this regard, attempts to expose the process of ethnographic interpretation, though in doing so it reinscribes the us/them dichotomy by privileging Western, scientific, modes of analysis and commentary over indigenous forms of knowledge. In a further development, Dennis O'Rourke's film *'Cannibal Tours'* (1987) interrogates Western conceptions of the primitive Other by turning the camera on European tourists. O'Rourke extends his critique within a form of *self*-reflexivity that implicates his own filmmaking in the practices of an ethnographic representation that has constructed the indigenous subject as Other. The most recent phase of ethnographic depiction examined here is the rise of a 'new ethnography' critical of traditional ethnographic representational practices. A number of developments in filmmaking in the wake of the criticisms launched by the new ethnography are considered as forms which seek to revise the existing focus of ethnographic representation.

## Savage and salvage: *Nanook of the North*

Various conceptions of racialized Otherness have coalesced in the long history of the figure of the 'noble savage'. The figure includes Shakespeare's Caliban and Defoe's Friday, for example, and the characterization was greatly extended during the phase of rapid colonization at the end of the nineteenth century. In many cases colonialism justified itself through reference to its mission to 'civilize' the noble yet savage Other, and indeed colonial definitions of the racialized Other frequently constructed a degraded savage devoid of Western civilization, on the one hand, and on the other hand a noble being living in an unsullied Eden. During the late nineteenth century, the myth of the noble savage was embellished with the idea that this Eden and its occupants were threatened by the encroachment of civilization. In what was often described as a 'clash' with civilization, the noble savage was, it was argued, threatened with extinction. One of the founders of the discipline of ethnography, Bronislaw Malinowski, writing in 1921, gave credence to the idea of the vanishing primitive when he summarized the position of the ethnographic subject in terms of loss and disappearance: 'Ethnography is in the sadly ludicrous, not to say tragic position, that at the very moment when it begins to put its work-shop in order, to forge its proper tools, to start ready for work on its appointed task, the material of its study melts away with hopeless rapidity' (in Clifford, 1986: 112).

The persistence and repetition of the narrative of the 'disappearance' of cultures has continued to pervade ethnographic writing since Malinowski. Undeniably, as the contemporary ethnographer James Clifford (1986: 112) points out, traditions are constantly being eroded and 'lost', specific languages and customs are fading and populations are regularly disrupted, sometimes subject to genocidal attacks. However, Clifford questions the assumption that with 'rapid change something essential ("culture"), a coherent differential identity, vanishes'. Clifford's most potent criticism of the 'vanishing Native' narrative is reserved for the fact that it legitimizes another, related representational practice: so-called salvage ethnography, what Clifford describes as a 'last-chance rescue operation' (1986: 112).

Salvage, or redemptive, ethnography is based on the idea that a 'primitive', vanishing culture needs to be documented by another culture before 'it is too late' and the indigenous culture 'vanishes' in the presence of the disruptive forces of colonialism and modernity. 'When we assert the need to salvage, rescue, save, preserve [a culture], we announce our fear of its destruction, our inability to trust others to take appropriate action and our sense of entitlement over the fate of the [culture]' observes the ethnographer Virginia Dominguez (1987: 131). The notion of a 'disappearing world' legitimized the confiscation of objects and artefacts from native cultures before, as the argument went, the culture disappeared. Salvage also interacted in certain nations with state control of the native people in the form of removal and wardship, policies undertaken in the name of saving the vanishing native. Salvage was not limited to colonial policies of confiscation and state control; salvage is a potent theme in much early ethnographic writing, and one that structures early ethnographic photography and filmmaking. The 1898 Cambridge Anthropological Expedition to the Torres Strait, for example, relied on photography as an ethnographic tool which the expedition's director, Alfred Haddon, deployed to document a people he believed to be in decline (Grimshaw, 2001: 23). In another example, the visual historian Rosalind Morris (1994) notes the strength of notions of salvage in the images made in the early twentieth century by filmmakers and photographers working among the people of the northwest coast of North America. The historical persistence of the salvage concept is exemplified in another way in Robert Flaherty's 1922 *Nanook of the North*, a film which reproduced the salvage project within its ground-breaking narrative techniques.

Flaherty's film depicts Inuit life not as it was lived at the time of filming, but as Flaherty imagined it to have been in some timeless prehistory. The anachronistic basis of the narrative is the core of Flaherty's salvage operation; to capture what Flaherty called the 'primitive majesty' of a culture before white contact leads to its 'decay' and eventual destruction (quoted in Huhndorf, 2000: 136). For Flaherty, salvage was a strategy motivated by saving Inuit culture from what it would become by retrieving what it once had been. To this end, Flaherty deployed reconstruction, what he called 'staging', throughout the film: re-clothing his subjects in traditional fur clothing and having them re-enact hunts of walrus and seal with harpoons not rifles, and igloo building practices which had been superseded with the introduction of modern tools. Fatimah Tobing Rony, in her analysis of 'race' and spectacle in early ethnographic films, interprets *Nanook of the North* as a 'cinema of romantic preservationalism' and analyses Flaherty's reconstructions in terms of what she calls 'ethnographic taxidermy'. Drawing on a practice that 'seeks to make that which is dead look as if it was still living', a taxidermic cinema plays on a need to reproduce and preserve the original, fixing it in place as immutable (Rony, 1996: 101). The film theorist Siegfried Kracauer captured the essence of Flaherty's 'taxidermy' when he argued that 'most Flaherty films are expressive of his romantic desire to summon, and preserve for posterity, the purity and "majesty" of a way of life not yet spoiled by the advance of civilization' (in Rony, 1996: 104). One of the clearest expressions of the notion of a culture 'unspoiled' by modern technology and civilization is Nanook's encounter with a gramophone in the film's trading post scene. Despite the fact that Nanook (or Allakariallak, who played him) possessed a sophisticated knowledge of the gramophone and was skilled enough in its operations to repair the machine, Flaherty had Nanook enact a pre-contact fantasy in which Nanook appears to be unfamiliar with the gramophone and its 'canned music'.

In contrast to Nanook, the European trader in this scene is in control of technology (the gramophone) and medicine (the dose of castor oil administered to relieve the suffering of Nanook's son, Allegoo). The trader (who is only partially framed on screen and thus removed from the objectifying ethnographic gaze that scrutinizes Nanook's every action) embodies superior European science and the notion of progress from which Nanook is excluded. Within the contrast with the trader, Nanook is positioned outside of modern history. As such, Nanook occupies the realm of 'natural history', the pre-civilized space of 'primitive peoples' (Huhndorf, 2000: 136). Isolated in this space the primitive is irrevocably positioned as Other, distanced from modern Western knowledge and ways of life. Naturalized within the narrative of disappearance and salvage is a hierarchy that inscribes Western culture as superior, and Inuit culture as inferior.

In a connected way the narrative distances Inuit culture from Western culture within its evocation of the 'noble savage'. Features of the stereotype pervade Flaherty's depiction of a 'typical Eskimo and his family' (in Rotha, 1980: 41). The family members nobly face a harsh physical environment with fortitude. Nanook, 'the Bear' is a 'great hunter' and like his wife, Nyla, 'the smiling one', is forever cheerful. The intertitles reinforce the traits popularly associated with the Inuit:

> The sterility of the soil and the rigor of the climate no other race could survive. Yet here, utterly dependent upon animal life, which is their sole source of food, live the most cheerful people in the world – the fearless, lovable, happy-go-lucky Eskimo.

The noble savage, a fearless and lovable figure, pervades Flaherty's description of Inuit culture.

According to Flaherty, 'The urge that I had to make *Nanook* came from the way I felt about [the Inuit], my admiration for them; I wanted to tell others about them. This was my whole reason for making the film' (Flaherty, 1996: 43). Elsewhere, Flaherty explained his aims by insisting that 'I wanted to show [the Inuit] not from the civilized point of view, but as they saw themselves, as "we, the people"' (in Grimshaw, 2001: 47). Flaherty's liberal and sympathetic intentions translated into a representation which carries with it, as Brian Winston (1995: 20) puts it, 'a strong whiff of paternalism and prejudice'. *Nanook of the North* was produced at a time when anthropologists were, in the words of one commentator, attempting to free 'themselves from some of the grossest of their assumptions concerning the noble savage' (Jarvie, 1983: 313). As a product of this time, *Nanook of the North*, perhaps unavoidably, reflects a number of such assumptions.

## Ethnographic observation and participatory cinema

Salvage ethnography did not cease with *Nanook of the North* (vestiges of the approach echo in the title of Granada Television's ethnographic documentary series *Disappearing World*, 1970–77[5]), nor did reconstruction disappear from ethnographic film. Though few filmmakers after Flaherty deployed the degree of reconstruction found in *Nanook of the North*, certain reconstructive practices continued to be relied on for narrative effect. A particular form of reconstruction is evident in Robert Gardner's *Dead Birds* (1963), for example, a film dealing with ritual warfare among the Dani highlanders of Papua New Guinea. The film uses voice-over to dramatically reconstruct or, more correctly, attribute thoughts in a practice which gives the impression that we are listening to a subject 'thinking out loud'. The possibility of distortion in such a method (how do we know what the subject was really thinking?) was addressed by Karl Heider in his foundational interpretative work *Ethnographic Film* (1976). Heider insists on an 'ethnographic integrity', an approach which denies the practices of a 'cinematic aesthetic' which he condemns for its editorial manipulations and, with an explicit reference to Flaherty's practice of staging, its 'intentional distortions of behavior'. For Heider, the essence of ethnographic film is captured in 'ethnographicness', a filming method that concentrates on 'whole bodies' ('Long camera shots which include whole bodies of people are preferable ... to close-ups of faces and other body parts'), 'whole acts' (the beginning, middle and end of an identifiable action), and 'whole people' (a focus on identifiable individuals, as opposed to 'faceless masses').[6] Heider's specifications, particularly his emphasis on long takes, intersected with an existing scientific mode of ethnographic observation and its close attention to daily routines.

Certain features of the formal observational techniques available in ethnographic film in the early 1970s are exemplified in David and Judith MacDougall's *To Live With Herds: A Dry Season Among the Jie* (1971), a remarkable study of the Jie pastoralists of north-eastern Uganda. The film is grounded in an observationalism dedicated to close study of the details of herding life, interspersed with extended scenes in which broader arguments are developed. Observation, in the sense of uninterrupted takes, is wedded with subtitles and commentary in scenes which cross-cut the film's linear progression. Interwoven with the lives of the pastoralists, is the encroaching presence of the representatives of Idi Amin's national government, and the resultant changes brought to the herders' way of life. *To Live With Herds* makes no overt comment on the political situation in Uganda, preferring to pay close attention to the way of life of the Jie, yet within this focus the film subtly develops an argument about contrasting forces – pastoralism and (the increasingly militarized) central bureaucratic state. The narrative is indicated in the titles of the five segments of the film: 'The Balance'; 'Changes'; 'The Nation'; 'The Value of Cattle'; and 'News from Home', a progression from a focus on Jie society, through the changes wrought by colonialism, to current political conditions in Uganda, to the market economy for cattle and, finally, a return to the Jie themselves (Grimshaw, 2001: 127).[7]

*To Live With Herds* marked a turning point in the filmmaking styles adopted by the MacDougalls. Following this film their work was marked by a shift away from a formal observationalism. The features of the newly emerging approach were suggested by David Hancock, a colleague of the MacDougalls at the University of California at Los Angeles in the late 1960s, in his outline of the working methods adopted by the UCLA filmmakers:

> We shoot in long takes dealing with specific individuals rather than cultural patterns or analysis. We try to complete an action within a single shot, rather than fragmenting it. Our work is based on an open interaction between us as people (not just film-makers) and the people being filmed. Their perspectives and concerns shape and structure the film rather than our emphasis on a particular topic or analysis of their culture which would distort or over-emphasize, perhaps, the importance of that topic to those people and that culture. (quoted in Grimshaw, 2001: 130)

The willingness of the filmmakers to involve subjects in the filming process featured as a core characteristic of the ethnographic cinema developed by the MacDougalls after *To Live With Herds*. Forced out of Uganda with the rise of Idi Amin, the MacDougalls focused their research on the Turkana pastoralists of neighbouring Kenya and began to develop a different approach to their filmmaking, one which they referred to as 'participatory cinema'. This approach carried many of the features of the observational mode, notably close attention to the details of daily life, together with an acknowledgement that filming is a process of engagement between the filmmaker and subject (the ethnographer Jean Rouch pursued a similar approach, as discussed in Chapter 5). David MacDougall (1998: 134) summarized this interaction when he stated that 'No ethnographic film is merely a record of another society: it is always a record of the meeting between filmmaker and that society.' In this way a participatory cinema is one in which the filmmaker abandons the pretext that the ethnographic filmmaker is invisible; the filmmaker appears onscreen, actively involved in the world of the subject, 'bearing witness to the "event" of the film and making strengths of what most films are at pains to conceal' (MacDougall, 1998: 134). Such a cinema is a form of collaboration between the filmmaker and subject, one which replaces a 'speaking for' the subject by the film-maker with a form of participation in which the filmmaker 'speaks with' the subjects of the film.[8] Vision or uninterrupted seeing – the centre of observational filmmaking – is replaced in participatory cinema with voice, literally, an emphasis on conversation and, metaphorically, a dialogue between filmmaker and subject (Grimshaw, 2001: 138).

The approach structures the three films the MacDougalls made about the Turkana, and is prominent in *A Wife Among Wives* (1981), the second film in the Turkana trilogy. The film opens with shots of the ethnographic filmmaker's tools (notebooks and camera) and moves to a discussion in which the MacDougalls ask a number of Turkana women for ideas for the film. One Turkana woman actualizes her ideas by filming the filmmakers, and the footage is subsequently edited into the film by the MacDougalls. In this case, the role of subject and filmmaker are (briefly) inverted in a way which draws attention to, or exposes, the ethnographic filmmaking process and the privileged interpretative role of the ethnographer in that process. Increasingly, filmmakers turned to such reflexive methods in order to reveal and question the very processes of ethnographic representation.

## The reflexive turn

Jay Ruby, a commentator on visual anthropology, has provided a useful set of observations on the nature and function of cinematic reflexivity. Writing in 1975, Ruby characterized reflexivity as 'an explicit description of the methodology used to collect, to analyze and to organize the data for presentation'. Ruby stressed that 'What is important is the absolute scientific necessity for making methods public' (1975: 107, 109). In 1980 Ruby stated that 'being reflexive means that the producer deliberately, intentionally reveals to his (*sic*) audience the underlying epistemological assumptions which caused him to formulate a set of questions in a particular way, to seek answers to those questions in a particular way, and finally to present his findings in a particular way' (in MacDougall, 1998: 88). Elsewhere Ruby states that the reflexive documentary filmmaker 'assumes responsibility for whatever meaning exists in the image, and therefore is obliged to discover ways to make people aware of point of view, ideology, author biography, and anything else deemed relevant to an understanding of the film' (in MacDougall, 1998: 88).[9] Based on this information viewers can, it has been argued, determine the appropriateness and credibility of a film's conclusions (MacDougall, 1998: 87).

Such a process of reflexive revelation was the impetus for the film *The Ax Fight*, produced in 1974 by ethnographic filmmaker Timothy Asch in collaboration with anthropologist Napoleon Chagnon. *The Ax Fight* is one of 21 films Asch made in collaboration with Chagnon dealing with the Yanomamo people of the upper reaches of the Orinoco River in South America. Asch intended each film to be an ethnographic research tool and an aid for instruction and teaching.[10] He argued that the primary aim of *The Ax Fight* was to confront the problem of bias in ethnographic interpretation, exposing it through techniques which replace the illusion of neutrality implicit in the observational stance with reflexive participation by the ethnographic filmmakers. Asch (1992: 198) insisted that:

> In a traditional *documentary* about the Yanomami Indians of southern Venezuela ... the film-maker would shoot film as an anonymous outsider, an objective observer of how the Yanomami live. Viewers of the film would have no idea who the film-maker was or how he or she was reacting to the events being filmed. In a *reflexive film*, the film-maker and anthropologist step forward and become part of the film, openly interacting with the Yanomami, letting the viewers see how questions are phrased and conclusions drawn from events. The film-makers do not become the subject of the film, but are included ... when they are influencing what is recorded.[11]

Asch and Chagnon pursue this approach in a film which seeks to expose the ethnographic construction of meaning within a focus on a particular sequence of 'chaotic' action that occurred soon after they arrived in the Yanomamo village of Mishimishimabowei-teri. *The Ax Fight* is composed of six parts. The first part is an introductory sequence which includes two maps and an intertitle which states that 'The fight began when the woman was beaten in the garden ... .' A voice on the soundtrack and a map of the location of the village give details of time and place. Another voice adds that two women are fighting with each other, adding 'Bring your camera over here, it's going to start.' The second part of the film includes the title: 'You are about to see and hear the unedited record of this seemingly chaotic and confusing fight just as the field-workers witnessed it on their second day in the village.' What follows is unedited footage of a club and axe fight in the village, and its immediate aftermath. In the third part a conversation between Asch and Chagnon is played over a blank screen. The ethnographers are heard attempting to piece together the causes and meaning of the fight. One voice (presumably Asch's) introduces the tape by saying 'Sound reel 14, wife beating sequence'. Another voice (presumably that of Chagnon) states: 'Wife beating my foot. It was a club fight.' The second voice adds, 'Two women were in the garden and one of them was seduced by her son. It was an incestuous relationship and the others found out about it and that's what started the fight.'

The fourth part opens with a title that informs the viewer that the conclusions drawn in the third part are incorrect. 'First impressions can be mistaken', states an intertitle. 'When the fight first started one informant told us that it was about incest. However, subsequent work with other informants revealed that the fight stemmed from quite a different cause.' A title that follows provides details of the circumstances leading up to the incident and explains that the fight occurred because Mohesiwa, a visitor to the village, had beaten Sinabimi, a local woman. This explanation is illustrated through voice-over commentary and slow motion footage of the action, replete with superimposed arrows pointing to the main protagonists in the fight. A lineage chart in the fifth part of the film is used to elaborate the kinship networks implicated in the conflict. The final part of the film presents, without voice-over, an edited version of the events of the fight. A concluding title reads, 'Several days after the fight some of the visitors began leaving. Tensions were temporarily relieved.'

From this 'raw data' it is possible, in the spirit of the film itself, to analyse critically the film's method of explanation. The first part of the film introduces the viewer to the elements of the film's explanatory and interpretative tools: graphics (in this case, maps), voice-over, and titles. These features are variously deployed to interpret and explain filmed action and to create a narrative trajectory in the film that leads from 'chaos' to a satisfactory resolution of events. The tools of ethnographic explanation are applied to the raw, unedited, footage in a way which replicates many of the requirements of a 'scientific' approach to filmmaking specified by Heider in his book *Ethnographic Film*. Heider argues that an ethnographic representation should minimize distortion of behaviours, and minimize 'time distortion' and 'continuity distortion'. The film should use 'natural synchronous sound' and an 'optimally demystifying' narration 'relevant to the visual materials' and provide a 'cultural and physical contextualization of behavior' leading to 'ethnographic understanding' (produced by a professional ethnographer or by a filmmaker in association with a professional ethnographer). Heider's emphasis on the pedagogical and epistemological role of the professional ethnographer is briefly subverted in the opening of part four of the film when an intertitle states that the voice-over explanation provided in part three by the professional ethnographer Chagnon was inaccurate (Chagnon's suggestion that incest was the cause of the fight was based on information provided by the anthropologist's informant, a member of the village). The unreliability of the verbal register thus points to the relevance of a combination of verbal and visual elements as the means which will provide a reliable explanation and interpretation of events.

It is via the utilization of the complete range of tools in its interpretative repertoire that the film qualifies the mistake made by Chagnon's informant and arrives at a 'scientifically correct' explanation which is reinforced in part five through the use of kinship charts. The effect of the charts is to reduce people and their lived relations to a diagrammatic representation constructed by, and deriving its authority from, anthropological knowledge. The charts employ a form of knowledge not open to the layperson, requiring a professional anthropologist to decipher the symbols (triangles, circles and connecting 'trees') used to illustrate lineage patterns. In the film's final segment, the edited version of events functions as the culmination of the narrative process of explanation presented in the preceding parts. The 'chaos' of the unedited footage has been 'scientifically' explained allowing, in the last part of the film, events to be presented in a coherent way.

In enforcing its conclusion the film relies heavily on the authoritative, interpretative and explanatory prowess of the ethnographer. The notion of reflexivity as the disclosure of method is only partially realized in *The Ax Fight*. As Brian Winston's insightful analysis of the film makes clear, the filmmakers make a number of claims about the action which, on close inspection, are not supported by the footage (Winston, 1995: 175–80). In place of a method which transparently exposes evidence and coherent conclusions, *The Ax Fight* demands that the viewer (uncritically) accept the ethnographer's interpretations. As an extension of this position, the film's conclusion derives its authority from an explanation that is privileged over and against any interpretations that may be provided by a Yanomami. In arriving at its conclusion the film reproduces the dichotomy of 'us' and 'them' through a hierarchically organized system of knowledge which situates Western anthropological thought ('us') as the superior interpretative position, and in the process unavoidably relegates 'their' thought to an inferior position.[12]

## 'Cannibal Tours': reflecting otherness

In an insight applicable to the methods of *The Ax Fight*, David MacDougall criticizes what he calls 'external reflexivity', a practice which 'attempts to erect reflexivity as a structure exterior to the work'. MacDougall (1998: 88) explains that external reflexivity

> ... proposes a frame of reference within which we are to assess the work (whether this is given in the work itself or provided separately). This metacommunication becomes the new standard, the new (and real) point of reference for scientific truth, displacing the work itself. Because it frames the frame, so to speak, it is considered to be more accurate, more valid, more scientific. It gives us an interpretation of known bias. This implies an ultimately achievable 'correct' interpretation and a way of restoring to representation its scientific objectivity.

In contrast to the imposition of an external reflexivity – a form of reflexivity constructed in postproduction – McDougall argues for a practice he calls '"deep" reflexivity' in which the ethnographer's relations with subjects and with the viewer is revealed progressively in a process of self-reflexivity, a reflection on the place of the ethnographer's presence, or self, in the film. The evocation of the filmmaker's presence does not necessarily involve constant on-camera appearances; it can be subtly suggested through small details such as off-camera comments captured on the soundtrack. A deep (self-)reflexivity reveals the ways in which the filmmaker is positioned in relation to subjects and in relation to the filmmaking process itself, thereby drawing attention to the constructed, personal and partial nature of the film's conclusions. Elements of such a practice are evident in Dennis O'Rourke's '*Cannibal Tours*' (1987), a film which incisively interrogates traditional notions of 'us' and 'them', self and Other, and reflects on the role of the filmmaker as interpretive agent of these relationships.

O'Rourke actively resists the label ethnographer, preferring to be referred to as a storyteller or essayist. He nevertheless readily admits that '*Cannibal Tours*' is ethnographic in the sense that it provides a context for an interpretation of one's *own* culture (Lutkehaus, 1989: 433).[13] '*Cannibal Tours*' follows a group of German, Italian, and North American tourists as they travel along the Sepik River in Papua New Guinea in the *Melanesian Explorer*, a modern air-conditioned cruise ship. The ship makes frequent stops at villages along the river, and in each village the tourists buy local artefacts and take photographs. The simple narrative is interspersed with interviews with the local villagers and the tourists and archival photographs of the early colonists in New Guinea. The opening segment suggests the different cultural frameworks of tourists and villagers by contrasting a wide shot of the Sepik and the shores of Papua New Guinea beyond – 'the land of cannibalism', in the tourists' terms – with sounds of 'civilization', the music of Mozart and voices from a world radio station. Signs of the now-prohibited practices of cannibalism fascinate the tourists, and the title of the film ironically underscores the search for traces of the exotic Other. O'Rourke has written of '*Cannibal Tours*' that it 'is two journeys. The first is that depicted – rich and bourgeois tourists on a luxury cruise up the mysterious Sepik River, in the jungles of Papua New Guinea ... the packaged "heart of darkness". The second journey (the real text of the film) is a metaphysical one. It is an attempt to discover the place of "the Other" in the popular imagination' (in MacCannell, 1994: 100).

The tourists reveal many of their conceptions of the Other in their reflections on the lives of the local people. One Italian tourist argues that 'nature provides [the villagers] with the necessities of life', and insists that the villagers are 'happy and well fed' and have no concerns for the future. Another tourist suggests that life in Papua New Guinea is 'slow and peaceful ... the opposite to that of Europe.' To probe the popular imagination of what Dean MacCannell (1994: 110) calls the 'touristic unconscious', O'Rourke leaves the camera running after a conversation has ceased, thereby capturing any off-hand and self-revelatory comments the subjects may make. In one such revealing moment, a young Italian woman struggles to articulate her interpretation of decapitation and castration by repeating that the acts were symbolic. 'For survival, but also symbolic. It was symbolic when they cut off the heads of the white explorers. Not with malice, but part of a symbolic tradition.' Here, as in other comments offered by the tourists, assumptions and incomplete impressions function as knowledge within which the 'noble savage' is situated as exotic Other in opposition to civilized Europe.

O'Rourke, however, wittily recodes the Other of the popular imagination. As the journey into the 'heart of darkness' progresses the roles ascribed to 'them' and 'us' are inverted; the villagers are astute and pragmatic, and the tourists become 'savages'. In their comments on their financial transactions with tourists, the villagers reveal their profound understanding of the weighted forces of market economics. In another way the villagers' pragmatism is exemplified when an old Iatmul man states that when his grandparents saw the first Western ships they shouted, 'Our dead ancestors have arrived! Our dead have come back.' Erasing the myth of the naive and superstitious savage, the man grins knowingly as he says that, 'Now when we see the tourists we say the dead have returned ... We don't seriously believe they are our dead ancestors, but we say it.' The tourists' move to 'savagery' is exemplified in a scene on board the cruise ship toward the end of the film in which a male tourist, stripped to the waist with his face painted, performs an embarrassing charade based on his notion of 'the primitive'.

The inversion of 'them' and 'us' – villager and European – is extended in the exchanges that are established in cross-cutting between comments by tourists and 'responses' by villagers. The villagers comment on the tourists' behaviour, and tourists offer numerous interpretations and comments on the villagers. In most cases the tourists' comments are countered and qualified by specific remarks by the villagers (Loizos, 1997: 88). The pattern of exchange positions the villagers' perceptions as authoritative interpretations of the strange customs of the tourists, an inversion of traditional ethnographic filmmaking practice which typically privileges Western interpretations and explanations.

Certain critics of the film have argued that O'Rourke is unfairly harsh in his representation of the tourists (see Loizos, 1997: 90), an argument that suggests that O'Rourke implicitly distances himself from the tourists' perspectives. Within the film's form of self-reflexivity a different conclusion emerges in which O'Rourke, through his presence in the film, reflects on the representation of the Other. O'Rourke is a constant presence in the film, who is heard conversing with people and is glimpsed on screen, as when his arm is seen holding a tourist's camera. His presence is also registered in a subject's gaze, as in the knowing glance to camera and direct to-camera comments by subjects. O'Rourke argues that such gazes establish a complicit relationship with his subjects – subjects are obviously aware of O'Rourke's presence, and O'Rourke facilitates this awareness by recording the gaze on camera (Lutkehaus, 1989: 431). O'Rourke's evocation of his presence through these various methods permeates the entire film, producing a kind of 'deep reflexivity' that is not applied 'externally' in the editing phase as in the case of *The Ax Fight*.[14]

The continuous inscription in the film of the filmmaker and his camera evokes parallels with the constant picture-taking by the tourists. For most of '*Cannibal Tours*' the tourists are engaged either in barter with the locals, or taking their photographs. The tourists' preoccupation with photography is queried by a villager who says, 'We don't understand why these foreigners take photographs of everything.' The fact that this comment is made to O'Rourke's camera implicates the filmmaker in the practices that trouble the villager. In another scene, O'Rourke asks a young man how he feels having his picture taken by foreigners. At that moment a female tourist appears in the frame preparing to take a photograph of the young man whom O'Rourke is filming. O'Rourke comments to the man that, 'One of them is looking at you now,' as the woman takes a photograph. Here, as elsewhere in the film, O'Rourke implicates himself as one of 'them', the picture-takers, even as he otherwise distances himself from the intrusive photographic practices of the tourists. O'Rourke acknowledged his complicity in this regard when he commented in an interview that 'virtually the whole film is informed by an awareness on my part – that I transmit to the audience – that the process of making the film, … photography itself, is an integral aspect of the film' (Lutkehaus, 1989: 429). By implicating his own photography, or filmmaking, and its alignment with touristic forms of representation, O'Rourke questions a situation in which certain individuals – tourists, ethnographers, or filmmakers (himself included) – are privileged to represent, or objectify, others (Lutkehaus, 1989: 425). Within its self-reflexive method, '*Cannibal Tours*', a filmic record of encounters with the Other, leads the viewer to reflect on ways in which the Other is encountered on film.

## The new ethnography and beyond

Throughout the 1980s a number of critiques were published of ethnography's involvement with the differential power relations that underpin the us/them dichotomy. Writers of what has been called a 'new ethnography', among them James Clifford, George Marcus, and Michael Fischer, variously argued that the discipline of ethnography has been implicated with the history of Western imperialism and colonialism. The core of this criticism resides in the charge that the power relations implicitly circulated within ethnographic representations have abetted a form of Western imperial domination of so-called Third World and 'Fourth World', or indigenous, cultures. One response to these charges has been the rise of what documentary film scholar Michael Renov (1999b) refers to as 'domestic ethnography' in which the practice of partici-pant observation abandons cross-cultural representation and focuses on the observer's own culture. Domestic ethnography is con-cerned with the documentation of familial relations, frequently engaging members of the filmmaker's own family, and in this way such works function as a form of autobiography.[15] He argues that a domestic ethnography is one which deploys a 'shared camera' in which the filmmaker and the subject interact and collaborate on the content, if not the style, of the documentary. Such an approach rewrites the traditional ethnographic separation of the roles of observed and the observer.

A further revision of these two roles is undertaken in another subgenre, so-called reverse ethnography, in which the camera, wielded by indigenous producers, is turned on Western ethno-graphic filmmaking conventions. The practice is exemplified by Rouch's *Petit á Petit* (*Little by Little*, 1960), his study of the 'strange tribe that lives in Paris', Manthia Diawara's *Rouch in Reverse* (1995), the Native American film *Ritual Clowns* (V. Masayesva, jr. 1992) and the programme *Babakiueria*, a video produced by the Aboriginal Programs Unit of the Australian Broadcasting Corporation in 1988. *Babakiueria* humorously satirizes and subverts ethnographic authority and forms of representation within a narrative recasting of Australian history in which Aboriginal Australians are posi-tioned as the colonists of a white European culture. The inversion of historical roles sees the black colonists landing on the shores of the new country. Approaching a group of white 'natives', the Aborigines ask the name of the place, to be told by their 'native' informants that it is a 'babakiueria'. The parody of colonial naming practices is complete in the name ('barbecue area'). The subse-quent 'investigation' into the 'strange culture' of white Australia is undertaken by an Aboriginal narrator who performs a role similar to the presenter of a current affairs documentary or that of an ethnographer who interprets profilmic behaviours. Mocking the discourses of an ethnography which positions the indigenous subject as an object of research, the programme 'examines' a 'typical white family', 'residing in a typical white house', in a 'typical white ghetto'.

By situating its critique within the framework of colonialism, the programme extends the connections of colonialism and ethnographic practice drawn by the new ethnography. According to certain interpretations (see Lutkehaus and Cool, 1999: 117), the imbrication of the colonialist project and ethnographic representation is most effectively redressed by indigenous filmmakers producing images of their own culture.[16] All too often, however, First World claims made on behalf of the political and representational potential of indigenous media are based on idealized and essentialist conceptions of the 'authenticity' of the 'native's voice'. Overlooked in such conceptions are the representational characteristics of indigenous film and the ways in which formal features of such films contribute to a reworking of the assumptions implicit in First World representations. With this latter approach in mind, the following chapter considers the representational features of selected indigenous documentaries within the context of indigenous media's capacity to contest aspects of the 'colonialist enterprise' in representation.

## CHAPTER 4

# Decolonizing the Image: Aboriginal Documentary Productions

According to the American anthropologist Faye Ginsburg, indigenous people worldwide share particular political circumstances. 'Whatever the cultural differences', says Ginsburg, 'such groups all struggle against a legacy of disenfranchisement of their lands, societies, and cultures by colonizing European societies' (1993: 558). Ginsburg's description usefully points to the struggle against colonialism – the conquest, control, and exploitation of a country's resources by European powers – that is a basic experience shared by indigenous populations. While the outcome of such a struggle is far from guaranteed, the struggle itself suggests the existence of enduring communities capable of speaking for themselves in vibrant and resistive ways. This contradicts those assessments in which indigenous cultures are interpreted as 'precarious', and indigenous people cast as victims of a dominant culture (see, e.g. Prins, 1997). The contrast between resistance and victimhood implicit in many characterizations of indigenous cultures is a structuring presence within assessments of post-colonial political and social experiences, and one that is echoed in certain descriptions of indigenous media. Ginsburg (1991) argues that indigenous film and video producers confront a 'Faustian dilemma': on one hand, media technologies constitute tools for cultural expression and survival yet, on the other, such technologies threaten indigenous communities with disintegration through the introduction of Western ideas which are incompatible with traditional or non-Western ways of life. All too frequently the emphasis within the 'dilemma' sketched by Ginsburg is on erosion, disintegration and loss of culture, as opposed to cultural survival and communal assertiveness through the use of electronic media.

Numerous initiatives undertaken by indigenous communities worldwide demonstrate the capacity of electronic media, and film and television in particular, to contribute to the maintenance and autonomy of native cultures. Examples of this process include, among others, the video work of the Kayapo, a Gê-speaking people of central and northern Brazil, who use video to record their traditions and their interactions with the Brazilian government. Video has become one of the ways in which the Kayapo document incursions on their land and resist activities such as dam building projects initiated without their approval. Video provides the Kayapo with an effective tool for cultural and political advocacy and Kayapo videos have been screened worldwide in attempts to gain international political support for Kayapo causes (Turner, 1992; Crawford, 1995). Cultural preservation is a central feature of the Inuit Broadcasting Corporation of Canada's far north, which went to air in 1982. IBC programmes are broadcast in Inuktitut, the language of the Inuit, and are designed to extend Inuit values and ways of life. The programmes are produced, distributed and received by the Inuit community, while other funding agencies, such as the National Film Board of Canada, have provided financial assistance for the production of a number of Inuit films (Madden, 1982). One such work, director Zacharias Kunuk's *Atanarjuat: The Fast Runner* (2001), a mixture of documentary and dramatic modes in a narrative of the lives of two brothers living in the Canadian Arctic, has been screened internationally, its success pointing to an expansion of forms of Inuit self-representation.

Within the United States, various Native American television stations, many of which are members of the Native American Public Broadcasting Consortium, produce programmes that support Native American languages and points of view. In a similar way the Hopi videographer Victor Masayesva, jr. produces videos which represent in innovative and imaginative ways aspects of Plains culture and history, thereby contributing to a growing body of work by independent Native American videographers who use video to inform indigenous visual and oral traditions (Rony, 1994; Pack, 2000). In New Zealand, the work of Maori filmmaker Merata Mita (which includes the documentaries *Bastion Point Day 507*,

1980, and *Patu!* 1981) and that of Maori film and television producer Barry Barclay (director of the television series *Tangata Whenua*, 1974, etc.) exemplify features of Maori productions which contribute to the maintenance and assertion of Maori culture (Campbell, 1987; Barclay, 1990).[1]

Such examples point to the role indigenous media can play in cultural maintenance and resistance in the presence of the continuing issues and problems raised by colonialism with its deep roots in history and its implications with governmental policies and practices. Among its many effects, colonialism as a discourse and apparatus of power produces representations which function to support the dominant culture over that of a colonized culture. Studying this situation in relation to Australia, the cultural theorist Stephen Muecke has pointed out that until recently the 'available discourses' on Aborigines in Australian film have focused either on Aboriginal Otherness, as depicted in ethnographic documents, or the 'Aboriginal problem', as constructed in numerous 'social problem' documentary films (Muecke, 1992: 179–85). Extending this point, the Aboriginal critic and filmmaker Darlene Johnson (1999) has noted the ways in which representations of Aboriginal people frequently reproduce derogatory cultural stereotypes within a form of tokenism.[2] Such discourses encode 'colonial' attitudes toward indigenous Australians, thereby extending those attitudes and predispositions throughout the mid-twentieth century and beyond. In these terms, 'colonial' images are not only those images or representations produced in the historical periods of colonial settlement or imperialist expansion; such images also circulate in the present thus perpetuating features of the colonial or imperial experience.

In an insightful analysis of the politics and aesthetics of filmmaking by Australian Aboriginal people, the Aboriginal academic, actor and activist Marcia Langton seeks to identify the ways in which Aboriginal representation 'undermine[s] the colonial hegemony' of dominant representational practices (1993: 8).[3] Central to Langton's recommendations is the need to extend access to the means of media production as a prerequisite for the practice of self-representation – the production of images of indigenous Australians by indigenous Australians (1993: 10). This chapter recognizes that increased access by indigenous Australians to the means of media production in the form of film and video cameras and television broadcast systems has produced a range of

documentary representations, which in their formal experimentation and documentation of Aboriginal identities, experiences and
histories, contribute to a decolonization of the prejudicial stereotypical images of indigenous Australians and a reworking and
expansion of documentary representation itself.[4] Within this
context, the productions analysed in this chapter include *Two
Laws/Kanymarda Yuwa* (1981), a film made by the Borroloola community in the Gulf of Carpentaria region of Australia's Northern
Territory in collaboration with the white filmmakers Alessandro
Cavadini and Carolyn Strachan, *Quest for Country* (SBS, 1993), a
work by the urban Aboriginal filmmaker Michael Riley, and the
television series *Bush Mechanics* (ABC, 2001) co-directed by David
Batty and Francis Jupurrurla Kelly. This chapter also considers
indigenous control of images, and its relationship to the practices
of documentary film and programme making, as an aspect of the
process of image decolonization. The productions included here
range from the early 1980s to the present and involve differing
representational strategies and productive arrangements pursued
within various production contexts.

## Production contexts of Aboriginal media

Aboriginal media are produced in contexts which reflect the diversity of Aboriginal populations – bush-living people and urban
dwellers – and differing production practices. The production contexts for indigenous documentary include low-power community-
based television services in remote communities, among them
those established in 1985 by the Warlpiri Media Association
(WMA) at Yuendumu in the Northern Territory and Ernabella
Video and Television (EVTV) at the Pitjantjatjara settlement of
Ernabella in South Australia. EVTV produces videotaped programmes on aspects of Pitjantjatjara culture which are broadcast to
the local community in a programming mix that includes satellite
feeds of commercial and government produced programmes.
Similarly, the WMA of Yuendumu produces a variety of television
programming dealing with local culture. From its first unedited
coverage of sporting events, the WMA has expanded to include
more formally structured programmes dedicated to ceremonial
dances, traditional implement manufacture, oral histories, information on conditions at outstations, and the recent successful
series *Bush Mechanics*.

Using the WMA and EVTV as models, the Australian government in the late 1980s created the Broadcasting for Remote Aboriginal Communities Scheme (BRACS) to provide video and radio equipment to remote Aboriginal communities for the establishment of local broadcast services. The equipment has made it possible to receive via AUSSAT, the Australian communications satellite, programmes produced by the state-funded television station, the Australian Broadcasting Corporation (ABC). Downloaded from the satellite, the programmes are rebroadcast within communities together with any locally produced programmes. The implementation of the scheme was not, however, without its problems, among them the fact that the system was introduced without a supportive framework of funding and training. Further, in certain cases, the introduction of outside broadcasts into a local community has resulted in a decrease of local production activity, or marginalized local production within scheduling formats dominated by satellite-fed broadcasts. In many ways the problems which have besieged BRACS have stemmed from a government-driven scheme which, unlike the WMA and EVTV operations, did not originate with the concerns or creativity of a specific community (Molnar, 1990; Molnar and Meadows, 2001). Despite the problems associated with its implementation, the scheme has provided remote Aboriginal communities the opportunity to produce their own video and radio programmes. In this way, the scheme holds the potential for remote Aboriginal communities to gain access to and control over production and scheduling of their own media. As Molnar and Meadows (2001: 35) point out: 'This is vital as loss of control of scheduling and programming can be equated with a loss of control of culture.'

Beyond the BRACS scheme, opportunities for the production of Aboriginal programmes have been extended through the establishment of the satellite television station Imparja, the first television station in Australia to be owned by Aborigines. Imparja, an initiative of the Central Australian Aboriginal Media Association (CAAMA), went to air in January 1988 using AUSSAT to broadcast a footprint that includes the Northern Territory, most of South Australia, and western New South Wales. One of its first and most successful programmes, *Nganampa Anwernekenhe* ('Ours'), a series broadcast in traditional Aboriginal languages, continues to examine aspects of Aboriginal culture in its various forms. Imparja has broadcast a number of feature-length documentaries, among them

*Willigens Fitzroy* (2001), the story of the struggle by the Bunuba people to halt the construction of a dam on the Fitzroy River in north-western Australia. The culturally and politically significant content of such programmes, however, often sits uncomfortably in broadcast schedules that are dominated by programmes supplied by the Sydney-based Channel Nine commercial television network. Concerns expressed elsewhere over the impact of television on remote indigenous communities have been replayed in criticisms of the negative effects of increasing commercialization of Imparja resulting from the arrangement with Channel Nine and the potential effects of this situation on the communities within the Imparja reception area (Batty, 1993: 123).

Based in urban areas, the production facilities of the national broadcasters the ABC and the Special Broadcasting Service (SBS) have contributed to the production of documentary works by Aboriginal Australians, in particular through the ABC's Indigenous Programs Unit and SBS's Aboriginal Television Unit.[5] Among the projects hosted by the Aboriginal Television Unit, the series *Spirit to Spirit* showcased the work of a number of international independent filmmakers, including *Quest for Country*, Michael Riley's journey through time and space to his cultural roots in western New South Wales. An extension of the filmmaking activities of the ABC and SBS is provided by the National Indigenous Documentary Fund (NIDF), an initiative undertaken by the national broadcasters in association with the Indigenous Unit of the Australian Film Commission and the Aboriginal and Torres Strait Islander Commission. Projects of the NIDF include, among others, *We of Little Voice* (2002), a record of the impact of uranium mining on indigenous people in South Australia, and *Ngangkari Way* (2002), which investigates the role traditional healing plays in contemporary Anangu life.

Further production contexts include self-authored independent productions and collaborations and co-productions involving members of Aboriginal communities and non-Aboriginal participants. Works in the latter category include *My Life as I Live It* (1993), an autobiography by Aboriginal activist Essie Coffey made with the assistance of white filmmakers Martha Ansara and Kit Guyatt; *Exile and Kingdom* (1993), a depiction of the Aboriginal communities of Roebourne in the north-west of Western Australia produced by Frank Rijavec and the Injibarndi, Ngarluma and Gurrama peoples; and the close collaboration between white filmmaker Trevor Graham and the Mabo family in the making of *Mabo: Life of an Island Man* (1997). The collaborative practices of such works were in many ways prefigured in the film *Two Laws* (1981), one of the first cross-cultural collaborations on a film production to be undertaken in Australia. Within the process of collaboration pursued in *Two Laws* the white filmmakers Cavadini and Strachan spent their first two months in the Aboriginal community of Borroloola in the Gulf of Carpentaria region learning aspects of Borroloola law, particularly protocols relating to behaviour in an Aboriginal society. Collaboration in the making of *Two Laws* involved technical input by Cavadini and Strachan and the verification and authentication of factual content by a broad cross-section of members of the Borroloola community. Each decision made in relation to the production of the film was discussed either at formal meetings or raised in spontaneous, often on-camera, comments by participants. In these terms, collaboration refers to a process of widespread consultation and participation resulting in a film which is most accurately characterized as a collective production.

## *Two Laws*: truth claim and land claim

*Two Laws* is an ambitious, complex and remarkable film. Its theme of the struggle for native land rights and the place of Borroloola customary law in that struggle is pursued in a film which utilizes a vigorous self-reflexivity together with dramatic re-enactment, talking heads, oral testimony, and observational sequences. The 'two laws' of the film's title refers to white law and 'the Law', the system which regulates Borroloola social interactions and relationships with the land. The Borroloola people, involved in court cases over claims to their land, recognized the legal need to document the history of their law as a way of validating their land claims. The necessity for such a document was revealed to the Borroloola people during preliminary hearings of their land claims during which it became apparent that the white judges dismissed claims which were not supported by historical records of land ownership. For the Borroloola people, the evidentiary truth claims of *Two Laws* function in a direct way in support of their historical claim to their lands.

The importance of Borroloola law to members of the community is foregrounded in the film's prologue in which representatives of the four language groups around Borroloola – Mara, Yanula,

Garrawa and Gurdandji – announce the chosen title for the film and discuss the meaning of white and black law. The prologue also features the white filmmakers being introduced to the community, and brief discussion of the processes that will be used in making the film. The prologue thus establishes two themes – the place of law and land in the Borroloola community, and the processes of collaborative filmmaking – which are elaborated and connected in the remainder of the film within and through a variety of innovative formal strategies. Part One of the film, 'Police Times', centres on the themes of dispossession and brutality. The segment focuses on an incident in 1933 when a police constable, Gordon Stott, arrested a number of Aboriginal people for killing a bullock. Through oral testimony and dramatic re-enactment members of the community narrate the events in which Stott beat those arrested as he marched them in chains from their various lands to Borroloola.

Part Two, 'Welfare Times', depicts life for members of the community under the welfare system of the 1950s and includes a re-enactment of welfare handouts of clothing. The theme of removal and dispossession which was introduced in Part One reappears at the end of Part Two in dramatizations of the forced removal of the community of Borroloola to Robinson River as a result of plans by the Mount Isa Mining Company to mine Borroloola lands. The loss of lands together with the place of Borroloola law in claims to the land emerges in parts three and four as the film's central preoccupations.

The focus of Part Three, 'Struggle for Our Land', is a stylized re-enactment of a Land Claim Court in 1976 in which the Borroloola people attempted, unsuccessfully, to reclaim large tracts of their lands, all of which were contested by mining and fishing interests. The court scene, staged in a non-naturalistic way on an airstrip, depicts the differences in evidentiary claims made by the 'two laws'. Whereas evidence presented under white law includes written documents and maps, Aboriginal evidence is presented in the form of a gudjika, a traditional ceremonial song which encodes a history that is not contained in white written documents. The question of the adequacy of written interpretations of Borroloola history had been touched on in the introduction to Part Two in two contrasting comments. An on-screen text comments on a piece of white law: 'The year 1953 was the beginning of the Welfare Ordinance. Its aim was to direct and encourage the re-establishment of the Aborigines, that they would eventually be assimilated as an integral part of the Australian community.' Appended by the film-makers to this statement is the line: 'Which means that they wanted us to be like white people.' The last line is the Borroloola response to the writing of history by whites, a way of 'talking back' to the official white perspective, a strategy which is pursued in a similar way within the performance of the complex gudjika and its confrontation with the written evidence presented in the Land Court.

Part Three also documents a confrontation between a Borroloola man and a white worker who has chopped down a number of trees of special significance to the Borroloola people. The resultant discussion of rights to the land raises the privileged position accorded to written leases as tangible evidence in claims to owner-ship. Extending the theme of land rights and land usage, part three contains a scene which dramatically illustrates the outcome of disputes in which control of the land is granted to mining inter-ests. A Borroloola man stands next to a river held sacred by the Aborigines as a Rainbow Serpent dreaming site which has been despoiled by effluent dumped by Mount Isa Mines, the successful claimants to the land.

The final part of the film, 'Living with Two Laws', opens with a depiction of a traditional brolga dance. The dance connects to the gudjika of part three, the assertion of Aboriginal law, and in this context the dance is a 'statement about practicing black law, about practicing ceremony' (Cavadini, Strachan, 1981: 74). The brolga dance is juxtaposed with other culturally important activities, such as an initiation ceremony, a women's dance, and life on the out sta-tions. Such a positioning, argue Cavadini and Strachan (1981: 74), places the dance within and against broader contemporary social and cultural activities of the Borroloola people.

*Two Laws* not only documents the history of Borroloola law, it also depicts the existence of Borroloola law in the present, specifi-cally, as it operates in relation to the making of the film. Borroloola law – the rules governing social relations in the Borroloola com-munity – is structured into the film itself. Cavadini and Strachan (1981: 67) note that:

> ... when we got down to filming there was automatically only one posi-tion for the camera and one position for the sound recordist – because everyone has their place in a highly structured spatial arrangement.

Men sit in one position, women in another, and each individual sits with particular relatives. So the determinations had to do with the tribal structure in which the film fitted as opposed to being outside it.

The law not only structured spatial positions and camera angles, it also determined the lens to be used and the type of shots to be made in the film:

> ... the choice was made to shoot the entire film with a wide-angle lens. It was the one that people responded to and liked. With a wide-angle lens you can include much more in the shot than with a standard lens, but it's not so appropriate for close-ups. If someone wants to make a statement, others have to be present to make that possible – to confirm or contradict it. Sometimes there was disagreement between people, but it's presented as a group discussion as opposed to one individual being the authority. (Cavadini and Strachan, 1981: 67)

Cavadini and Strachan point here to the fact that the use of a wide-angle lens can capture the group decision-making process – the action of people confirming or contradicting evidence. The evidentiary bases of the film (which are, primarily, established in the form of oral testimony and re-enactments) are accompanied by moments of self-reflexivity, which function in support of Borroloola law. The pattern of self-reflexive revelation deployed in the film owes little to Western traditions of filmmaking. Cavadini and Strachan (1981: 67) noted that few films have been seen in Borroloola, and generally, the people were unfamiliar with filmic practices. Filmmaking for the Borroloola people is a matter of social function, and in this way, the film's many self-reflexive moments serve a particular social purpose. People talk of the production of the film on camera and look directly at the camera; clapper boards and sound recording equipment appear in the frame; prior to re-enactments people introduce themselves and during re-enactments people comment on the historical details they have relied on for the scene; in one scene a man addresses the camera directly to thank the audience for listening to his speech; and the film documents the discussion and the accompanying agreement that the information to be depicted in the film is correct. The various examples of self-reflexivity function as a guarantee that nothing is hidden, transparently exposing the processes involved in the film's production to reveal that the information contained in the film is verified by all members of the community as a correct interpretation of Borroloola law.

By presenting itself as a legitimate record of Borroloola law the film becomes, in effect, a legal document which can be used as evidence in support of the Borroloola claim to their land. Importantly, the presentation of evidence is achieved in filmic terms of the Borroloola people's own choosing (MacBean, 1988: 225). The documentation of an Aboriginal community is here removed from the often prurient gaze of ethnographic cinema and television journalism within a collective process of self-representation undertaken for social ends.

## Formal innovation in Aboriginal television programmes

Various works produced by Aboriginal filmmakers deploy experimental or avant-gardist aesthetics to create what Marcia Langton calls 'culturally useful meaning' capable of contributing to a revision of colonialist depictions of indigenous Australians, their histories and experiences (1993: 85). The works of Tracey Moffatt are exemplary in this regard. The formal experimentalism of her film *Nice Coloured Girls* (1987), for example, reworks not only the representational practices of dominant cinema but also many of the conventions of 'Aboriginal film' (Shohat and Stam, 1994: 326). Reflecting this position, Moffatt refuses restrictive categorizations of her work, 'I want to be known as Tracey Moffatt, interesting film-maker', she says, not 'Tracey Moffatt, Aboriginal film-maker.' Moffatt adds, 'Yes, I am Aboriginal, but I have the right to be avant-garde like any white artist' (quoted in O'Regan, 1996: 327). *Nice Coloured Girls* melds a fictional narrative dealing with relations between contemporary urban Aboriginal women and white men with documentary accounts of interactions between Aboriginal women and white men at the time of European contact. The film mixes realism and antirealism and involves reconstructions using stylized sets and subtitles which ironize the parodic and excessive performance styles. Through its multiple experimentations, *Nice Coloured Girls* presents an image of irreverent and resourceful Aboriginal women which is 'in sharp contrast to the colonial construction of the Aboriginal female body seen as a metaphorical extension of an exoticized land' (Shohat and Stam, 1994: 326).

While the complexity of Moffatt's work 'fits the satisfactions demanded by the cinephile and gallery-based appreciative audience' (O'Regan, 1996: 327), different approaches are often demanded of documentary works produced for television. The medium of television tends to restrict aesthetic experimentation in its emphasis on accepted, conventional formats. The Aboriginal documentary filmmaker Frances Peters-Little has acknowledged this fact though she, nevertheless, maintains a commitment to a revision of the content and formal techniques of television documentary as a way of leading to the production of indigenous representations that hold the potential for self-analysis, political critique and the revisions of cultural stereotypes (in Urla, 1993: 102). Peters-Little suggests that the stereotypical representation of indigenous Australians in dominant forms of documentary representation 'may have something to do with why many indigenous artists are moving away from documentary and into fiction or drama films. We are sick of the documentary format; we've seen so many of them about us, especially in news and current affairs. So, unfortunately, what we've done is associate documentary with just another form of stereotyping film.' Peters-Little adds that 'It's just that we haven't explored how to be more adventurous with documentary. We've got the opportunity as Aboriginal filmmakers to change documentary' (quoted in Urla, 1993: 102).

The films of Peters-Little suggest some of the features of such a reconsideration and reworking of content, styles and forms of documentary film and television. In her work *Oceans Apart* (ABC, 1992),[6] for example, Peters-Little depicts the lives of three 'light skinned' Aboriginal women who were raised in urban white society, and their attempts in their adult lives to reconnect with their black families.[7] The focus contravenes the pervasive stereotype of images of Aborigines living uncomplicated 'traditional' lifestyles in desert regions and Peters-Little extends the critique of stereotypes by deliberately deploying an expressive style which contrasts with the 'nostalgic' or 'scientific' formal qualities of ethnographic films about indigenous people.

*Oceans Apart* ignores the familiar television journalistic format of an 'investigation' into the lives of its subjects and opens itself to an observationalism that measures its visual pace – a long take of a train slowly heading toward the viewer and another of a woman walking on a pier – thereby replacing the frequent cuts and short takes of television journalism. The move away from the conventions of television journalism is further reflected in the use of a pop music soundtrack (played by Peters-Little) which includes songs that indirectly comment on the women's experiences. The personal, intimate and complex feelings associated with 'passing' as white and living in a white society and the felt need to reconnect with Aboriginal ways of life are relayed in interviews and, more often, voice-over reflections which, in their meandering presentation, abandon the direct line of questioning and tightly edited replies that would typically accompany the representation of the topic in a conventional current affairs television report.

The formal innovations of Michael Riley's 23 minute film *Quest for Country* contributes to the reworking of television documentary suggested by Peters-Little, and in doing so extends the innovative forms and content of indigenous self-representation which Marcia Langton argues are integral to the process of decolonizing the common stock of images of Aborigines (1993: 85).[8] The theme of Riley's film – return to an ancestral homeland – embodies a critique of the colonial history of displacement and exile of indigenous peoples. Within this context, Riley's journey from Sydney to his traditional homeland in Dubbo in the western region of New South Wales, provides the basis of an Aboriginal perspective on European settlement of the continent, subsequent white expansionism, and its attendant impact on the land. The latter topic is exemplified in a memorable scene in which Riley is depicted standing in a field of tall grass. As the shot widens he is seen outlined against a huge power station which dominates the horizon. Riley's voice-over reflections on the differences between white and black approaches to the land and nature are off-set by flashcuts to a series of images produced by whites at the time of settlement. While providing specific information concerning contact between settlers and Aborigines and differing attitudes to the environment, the sepia images visually contrast with the vibrant colours of the Australian landscape observed from the automobile in Riley's journey.

As he travels westward to his home country (the land of his family) the programme focuses on various features of the landscape – mountains, plains, trees, and notably, sky. Images of clouds and empty blue sky become a device linking and unifying successive scenes. The central argument – white encroachment on the land – is supplemented by the continual return to images of clouds and sky which push the film away from traditional realist forms of documentary representation into the realm of poetic evocation of nature in a way that is reminiscent of certain avant-garde works and the detailed depictions of natural phenomena in Godfrey Reggio's *Kooyanisqatsi* (1982). The evocation of infinite space in the frequent cuts to sky and limitless horizons is literally 'grounded' when Riley reaches his destination and the film focuses on the intimate space of his family home and the surrounding country-side. Members of Riley's family point to meaningful markers on the landscape: his father talks of the significance of a large tree to the local community and his aunt wanders through the ruins of a family house, reminiscing on her family's history. The mode of poetic evocation and its emphasis on the visual (historical images and spectacular scenes of nature) is superseded in these scenes by a form of observation that is attentive to the words and stories being narrated by members of the family. The two modes of representation (the visual spectacle of poetic evocation and an auditory enhanced observationalism) construct two spatial levels – open space and localized space. Together, the two spaces connote a landscape that is at once abundant and varied, and personal and familiar. In this way the depictive strategies and content of *Quest for Country* simultaneously oppose a reductionist view of landscape as an object of industrialism and emphasize the valuable experience of place and location ('home') within and against colonial forces of dispersal.

## *Bush Mechanics*: parodying documentary sobriety

One of the most fully worked recent examples of innovation in documentary styles and form is *Bush Mechanics*, a four-part television series co-directed by David Batty and Francis Jupurrurla Kelly which was produced by the Warlpiri Media Association and the National Indigenous Documentary Fund.[9] Batty, a non-Aboriginal Australian, had collaborated with the Warlpiri Media Association on a number of occasions, most notably in the production of the ten-part children's television series *Manyu Wana* ('Let's Have Fun'). In the mid-1980s, Jupurrurla Kelly pioneered television production at the Warlpiri community of Yuendumu, resulting in the first television programmes to be broadcast from an indigenous community in Australia. Jupurrurla Kelly was assisted in technical aspects of his early productions by the American media ethnographer Eric Michaels, who wrote extensively on the Yuendumu experiment in television. In his essay 'For a Cultural Future: Francis Jupurrurla Makes TV at Yuendumu', Michaels refers to Jupurrurla Kelly as a 'sophisticated cultural broker' who uses videotape and electronic media technology to document aspects of Warlpiri law, ceremony and relations to the land (1984: 105).

The style of the early programmes from Yuendumu was, as Michaels notes, unusual and inventive. Michaels (1984: 38) describes the way in which Jupurrurla Kelly introduced each programme within the broadcast schedule: 'Jupurrurla ... is a big reggae fan, so for his schedule he begins with reggae music and focuses the camera on his Bob Marley T-shirt draped over a chair. After a while he refocuses on the compère's desk, walks around and into the shot, announces the schedule and any news, then walks out of the shot, turns off the camera switches on the VCR. This procedure is repeated for each tape.' A similar 'home grown' quality informs *Bush Mechanics*, a work which is determinately parodic. According to the cultural theorist Homi Bhabha (1994), parody and mimicry are expressions of the ambivalent relationship between the colonized and the colonizer through which it is possible for the colonized subject to insolently yet subtly 'talk back' to the colonizer, inverting and rewriting dominant speech and actions. In these terms, mimicry and parody are decolonizing strategies deployed by members of a colonized culture to subvert and menace the authority of dominant discourses (Griffiths, 1995: 240). The cultural critic Coco Fusco (1993: 84) informs this point when she argues that 'resistance within colonial contexts is rarely direct, overt, or literal; rather it articulates itself through semantic reversals, infusing icons, objects, and symbols with different meanings'. The representational strategy was exercised to effect in *Babakiueria*, a work which criticizes and revises ethnographic interpretations through its parodic inversions of ethnographer and subject. In *Bush Mechanics*, a light-hearted 'decolonizing' parody effectively mocks the contents and approaches of non-fictional 'lifestyle' televisual formats dedicated to automobile maintenance and the reverential and 'sober' quality of much documentary representation.[10]

*Bush Mechanics* blends a core of documentary observation and information with moments of dramatic re-enactment in a humorous depiction of the mechanical skills of five Aboriginal 'bush mechanics', do-it-yourself automobile repairers who use anything at hand to mend broken car parts. The programme was produced in the township of Yuendumu and each episode features a different journey made by the mechanics from Yuendumu across Australia's Central Desert region: to a local community to perform at a rock concert (in episode one), to Alice Springs to collect a nephew from jail (episode two), to a nearby township to play football (episode three), and a trip to Broome on Australia's west coast (episode four). Each journey provides numerous opportunities for the mechanics to apply their automotive repair skills to the battered old cars they drive. In the first episode, for example, 'Motorcar Ngutju' ('Good Motorcar'), the mechanics refashion the car in various creative ways to reach their destination. When the car's undercarriage begins to fall apart they chop down a young tree which, trimmed of its branches, is wired to the underside of the vehicle to hold the suspension and exhaust system in place. The trip continues although the car's rusted roof is next to collapse, a result of the weight of the baggage that has been loaded on top of the car. The problem is fixed by cutting the roof free with an axe and the baggage is then reloaded on what was the roof, which is towed behind the car as a sleigh.

Each episode commences with a long shot of Jackamarra, a Warlpiri elder, standing before culturally significant features of the landscape. In one episode, the landmark is a rusted body of a truck which first brought whites to the area. Jackamarra then recounts the history of black/white contact on Warlpiri land through his recollections of his own encounters with white people and their strange ways. Jackamarra's role as Warlpiri historian and the conventional realist mode of talking head in which he is depicted is contrasted with that of Jupurrurla, a magical figure who suddenly appears to provide advice to the mechanics. In these scenes documentary exposition and observation give way to magic realism and its emphasis on the fantastic within naturalistic settings. The latter mode is extended in the use of flash cuts and slow and speeded motion reminiscent of an MTV-style aesthetic. Batty and Kelly first used similar effects in *Manu Wana*, a series shot on 16 mm film with post-synchronized dialogue. Like that series, parts of *Bush Mechanics* are shot on a hand-held Bolex camera, with much of the audio track (talk and ambient sounds) dubbed in post-production.

Beyond the generalized mockery of conventional documentary representation, the series parodies a flourishing genre on Australian television of Outback adventure and travel. The Leyland brothers – Mike and Mal – popularized the form in the early 1960s in the independently produced documentaries *Down the Darling* (1963) and *Wheels Across the Wilderness* (1966). By the 1980s the Leyland brothers had produced almost 300 television programmes in this vein. *Walkabout* (ABC, 1970) and *Peach's Australia* (ABC, 1975), presented by Rolf Harris and Bill Peach respectively, advanced a trend which continues today in numerous Australian television travel programmes featuring segments on Outback 'adventure holidays'.[11] These programmes typically emphasize 'correct' ways to 'experience' the Outback (e.g. frequently referring to the need to carry extra water and spare vehicle parts) through traditional modes of exposition in which the narrator doubles as host of the programme.

Behind these references, the content of *Bush Mechanics* alludes to John Heyer's remarkable story-documentary *The Back of Beyond* (1954). Heyer's film is a reconstruction of the working lives of people who live on the Birdsville Track in central Australia. The film is a romanticized view of life in the Outback, replete with resilient characters who stoically survive the harsh landscape in a narrative centred on Tom Kruse, who delivers mail and supplies along the Track in a ramshackle old truck. Kruse is accompanied at times by Malcolm, an Aborigine who recounts his past in the area. Eric Else, in his book on *The Back of Beyond*, wrote that the 'social ethic of *The Back of Beyond* is that of *Night Mail*' and that in this way the film is 'probably the last of the great romantic documentaries' in the mould of pre-Second World War Griersonian work (1968: 56).[12] Heyer's film was the first in what has become a prominent narrative convention in Australian cinema – the 'road movie' – in which characters are drawn together through the device of a journey by motor vehicle.

*Bush Mechanics*, in turn, ironizes the 'road movie' structure and documentary conventions of *The Back of Beyond*. Whereas the 'customized' motor vehicles of *Bush Mechanics* are direct descendents of the heavily modified mail truck in Heyer's film (and the stripped-down vehicles of the *Mad Max* films), *Bush Mechanics* revises the secondary role of Henry and Malcolm in *The Back of Beyond*. In *Bush Mechanics*, indigenous Australians are the central focus of information and action. More particularly, *Bush Mechanics* rewrites and 'Aboriginalizes' the Griersonian mode of *The Back of Beyond*, abandoning the stentorian voice of God voice-over and the romanticization of what Grierson called 'upstanding labour' in a narrative which mixes traditional Aboriginal knowledge and contemporary automobile repair 'advice' within a representational aesthetic derived from sources as varied as MTV and magic realism.

## Controlling the image

The creative impulse for *Bush Mechanics*, and earlier productions by the Warlpiri Media Association, stemmed from the direct participation by the people of Yuendumu in the production of documentary television. A number of Aboriginal and Torres Strait Islander commentators have argued that direct participation in the form of indigenous control of images by and about indigenous people is a necessary requirement of a truly decolonized media (see e.g. Bostock, 1990; Saunders, 1994; Torres, 1995; Morris, 2001; Janke, 2003). Control in this sense operates through the widespread implementation of policies and protocols designed to ensure various representational rights for indigenous Australians. Such rights include ownership of stories and other creative sources originating from indigenous communities, the trusteeship of archival images, and access by indigenous people to the filmmaking process (including arrangements for the payment of royalties and the need for the informed consent of the subjects depicted in films and television programmes and multimedia projects). The extension of legislative protection of indigenous culture in the form of amended copyright provisions that recognize the full dimensions of indigenous intellectual property is another aspect of control of indigenous creative works. As new media and pay television expand their demand for 'content' the need increases to extend copyright provisions to all aspects of indigenous creative sources.

Various protocols have been devised to address questions of the ownership, control and access to images by and about indigenous Australians. Eric Michaels' essay 'Primer on Restrictions on Picture-Taking in Traditional Areas of Aboriginal Australia', first published in 1986, was an early contribution to cultural policy in this area. In his essay Michaels was wary of drafting guidelines that would become prescriptive rules. Instead, Michaels raises awareness of issues likely to cause concern for Aboriginal communities, among them secret/sacred materials, class and gender restrictions, and mortuary restrictions (Michaels, 1994). Since Michaels' essay was published other reports have identified issues involved in indigenous control of media productions and representations. A report by Mackinolty and Duffy (1987) considers editorial and distribution control of indigenous works, factors pertaining to employment in media productions on Aboriginal land, environmental issues relating to such productions, and legal issues, including contracts and copyright relating to filmmaking. These recommendations were extended and informed in the report *The Greater Perspective* (1990), subtitled 'guidelines for the production of film and television on Aborigines and Torres Strait Islanders' prepared by Aboriginal filmmaker and broadcaster Lester Bostock for the Special Broadcasting Service. Bostock's guidelines emphasize interactions between indigenous and non-indigenous Australians based on consultation and liaison and an awareness of culturally appropriate behaviour and languages. By influencing behaviours and understandings at the production phase, the guidelines seek to inform approaches to the representation of content. Not coincidentally, Bostock's protocols were devised in the wake of the release of *Crocodile Dundee* (1986), a film which includes a number of ill-informed and offensive depictions of Aboriginal culture. Similar objections were raised by indigenous groups against the film *Australian Rules* (2002), highlighting the continuing need for the implementation of such guidelines (Williams, 2002: 7).

The effects of the presence and absence of ethically and culturally informed approaches to documentaries featuring indigenous Australians is illustrated in the cases of two documentary programmes made in 1986 and 1992 involving the Warlpiri people. In 1986, the ABC produced a programme titled *Fight Fire with Fire* dealing with the establishment of satellite-based television in the Warlpiri community. Disturbed by the contents of many earlier films made about the community, the Warlpiri people insisted on the right to preview any film or programme made in the community. The condition was denied by the ABC. The community refused to approve the programme without seeing the final cut and sought an injunction against the programme until a screening was arranged. In the face of the threat of further legal action initiated by the Warlpiri, the ABC previewed the programme in Yuendumu, and the community approved its contents clearing the way for the programme to be broadcast on national television. At the time, the ABC lacked a policy regarding the representation of Aboriginal traditions, and guidelines for appropriate procedures for filming in traditional communities. The absence of such protocols and guidelines was felt by both the local community and the ABC in this case (Michaels, 1994).

In contrast, respect for the autonomy of Aboriginal traditions resulted in a very different outcome for another production. *Jardiwarnpa*, a programme directed by Ned Lander for the Special Broadcasting Service in 1992, was the successful outcome of a Warlpiri initiative to produce a high-quality representation of the community's traditional fire ceremony. The fact that the content is

normally restricted from general viewing highlights the careful
and detailed negotiations that were pursued in the commissioning
process for this programme. Such negotiations involved the community's right to preview the unedited programme and legal contractual agreements concerning copyright and production investment.
The establishment and conduct of protocols and legal agreements
ensured that the *Jardiwarnpa* production avoided many of the pitfalls
which befell the ABC programme (Langton, 1993).

Here as elsewhere in the field of documentary representation of
indigenous people, the 'Aboriginalization' of documentary –
access by indigenous communities to the means of documentary
production – becomes an aspect of the strategic process of decolonizing the image. The need to 'decolonize the documentary
image' points, on the one hand, to the fact that documentary has
been implicated with the historical, political and cultural practices
of colonialism and, on the other hand, to the ways in which indigenous documentary contests the contents and conventions of documentary film and television. In this way, 'indigenous documentary'
emerges as a series of procedures, practices, policies, and protocols –
among them, the perspectives studied in this chapter – which hold
the capacity to remake documentary representation.

## CHAPTER 5

# The Truth of the Matter: Cinéma Vérité and Direct Cinema

Cinéma vérité – a form associated with developments in France – and direct cinema – work associated with the United States – have, since their inceptions in the early 1960s, constituted profound influences on documentary filmmaking.[1] Cinéma vérité, 'film truth', drew on Vertov's description of a kino pravda, a cinema or film dedicated to representing truth in ways not achieved in the fictional cinema. Direct cinema, a misnomer in terms of the fact that most work in the category comprised journalistic reports produced for television, aimed to reveal the truths of human existence residing behind the surface facts. Film historian Eric Barnouw (1983: 255) summarized the forms by describing what he saw as their essential differences:

> The direct cinema artist aspired to invisibility; the ... *cinéma vérité* artist was often an avowed participant. The direct cinema artist played the role of the involved bystander; the *cinéma vérité* artist espoused that of provocateur. Direct cinema found its truth in events available to the camera. *Cinéma vérité* was committed to a paradox: that artificial circumstances could bring hidden truth to the surface.

Against such a description, another film historian, Richard Barsam (1992: 303), emphasized the similarities of the two forms. Barsam noted that cinéma vérité and direct cinema share objectives and characteristics: 'Both cinéma vérité and direct cinema are similar in that they are committed to ... the advantages produced by the use of lightweight equipment; to a close relationship between shooting and editing; and to producing a cinema that simultaneously brought the filmmaker and the audience closer to the subject.' Barsam's description of overlap and intersection between cinéma vérité and direct cinema forces a reconsideration of the putative differences between the forms. Indeed, a history of the two forms suggests that the polarities listed by Barnouw reflect claims made by cinéma vérité and direct cinema practitioners on the efficacy of their respective methods, claims not necessarily borne out in practice. These claims stem from the different factors in France and the United States that contributed to the development of portable synchronized sound cameras, the technology that made possible the innovative filmmaking practices referred to as cinéma vérité and direct cinema. In the United States, demand for such technology issued from television journalists dismayed at the static quality of much television reportage, who sought ways to 'get close to the action' while remaining committed to journalistic objectivity and observational practices. In France, social scientists, particularly ethnographers, looked to new ways to record their subjects. From within these differing traditions practitioners developed varying theoretical claims for their work – cinéma vérité, it was claimed, provoked subjects into action while direct cinema, it was argued, filmed life as it enfolded before the camera. These differing aspirations – provocation and observation – continued to inform the theories of cinéma vérité and direct cinema, even as their practices converged on key points: cinéma vérité was provocational *and* observational; direct cinema was observational *and* interventionist.

For the practitioners of direct cinema and cinéma vérité questions of theory and issues of practice centred on the crucial issue of 'truth', which in this context refers to the camera's capacity to depict or reveal authentic moments of human experience. Truth in these terms hinges on the question of behaviour modification, specifically, the degree to which behaviour is altered in the presence of the camera. This issue informed the development of both cinéma vérité and direct cinema, feeding demands from within television journalism in the United States and the social sciences in France for a new camera technology that could be used to capture truth. This chapter examines the factors contributing to the development of new camera technologies as the informing context within which the distinctive representational forms of cinéma vérité and direct cinema were established. The claims and practices circulated by practitioners of direct cinema and cinéma vérité based on this technology are also examined. The analysis focuses on the differing formal qualities and methods of two films, *Chronicle of a Summer* (*Chronique d'un été*, 1961), a foundational work of cinéma vérité made by Jean Rouch and Edgar Morin, and *Don't Look Back*, a prominent example of direct cinema made by D.A. Pennebaker in 1966. Both films raise questions concerning the place of performance within observational and interactive modes designed to reveal truth. The analysis considers this issue and the ways in which a performative element structures the newer, post-observational forms of documentary representation.

## Technology and supervening necessities

New camera technology occupies a privileged place in histories of cinéma vérité and direct cinema. Prior to the late 1950s, film production was largely dependent on a studio rigged to accommodate heavy 35 mm cameras linked by cables to huge sound recorders. The technology restricted location shooting, and the requirements of a large boomed microphone connected to a stationary camera frequently denied the spontaneity and movement demanded by a growing number of documentary filmmakers. The invention of a mobile camera synchronized to a sound recorder was an innovation that permitted multiple applications and filmmaking experiments.

The utility of the new technology is, however, emphasized in a number of written accounts of direct cinema and cinéma vérité to the point where in many descriptions the technology is interpreted as *the* factor that made possible the new work. A crude technological determinism operates in such accounts, one which, in effect, argues that new technology created new documentary forms. Such a conclusion overlooks important non-technological factors, what Brian Winston (1996) calls 'supervening necessities' and what Allen and Gomez (1985) call 'generative mechanisms', which facilitated the emergence of the new technology. In the United States the supervening necessity that led to and informed direct cinema was television, in particular the requirements of television news reportage. In France the supervening necessity took the form of the practical and academic demands of the discipline of ethnography.

In the late 1950s television journalism in the United States consisted, typically, of still and moving images accompanied by a didactic voice-over. A number of filmmakers and producers, displeased

by a form that resembled that of 'illustrated lectures', looked for
new ways to present information within the documentary format
(Winston, 1995: 157). One such innovator, Robert Drew, inspired
by the tradition of photojournalism exemplified by *Life* magazine,
sought a camera technology which would enable him to capture
events as they unfolded. In early 1960 Drew's employer, the
Time–Life company, provided Drew and his colleagues funds to
develop equipment for this purpose. Drew had assembled at
Time–Life various associates who shared his enthusiasm for creating an innovative form of television journalism. Drew's team
included a number of talented young filmmakers, many of whom
went on to noted careers in direct cinema production, among
them Richard Leacock, D.A. Pennebaker, Albert and David
Maysles, and Gregory Shuker.[2] Near the end of the 1950s, after
a series of experiments with camera and sound equipment, Drew and
Leacock developed a lightweight, portable camera with synchronized
sound based on a modified 16 mm camera. Accompanying the
innovations in camera and sound technology, new sensitive film
stocks permitted shooting in low lights, thus replacing the need to
illuminate the subject with multiple spotlights. The 16 mm film was
loaded in magazines which could be replaced in seconds, thereby
reducing the downtime spent reloading the camera.

The new equipment was first used to film *Primary* (1960), a programme by Robert Drew, Terry Filgate, Richard Leacock, Albert
Maysles, and D.A. Pennebaker which follows John F. Kennedy and
Hubert Humphrey as they campaigned in Wisconsin for the 1960
Democratic presidential nomination. *Primary* was screened on a
number of television stations owned by Time–Life and impressed
executives at the ABC television network who saw the potential of
the new form as a way to compete with the rival CBS and NBC news
operations (Winston, 1995: 153). The ABC network contracted
Drew and his associates to produce further synchronized-sound
documentaries, including *Yanki No!* (1960), an account of Castro's
Cuba, *Crisis: Behind a Presidential Commitment* (1963), a study of the
confrontation between the Kennedy federal administration and
Governor George Wallace of Alabama over the desegregation of
the state's universities, and *The Chair* (1962), which deals with the
legal appeal of a man sentenced to death by electric chair. Through
the use of the new technology, the films Drew and his associates
produced for ABC broke new stylistic ground by permitting the
filmmaker a degree of proximity to events unmatched by earlier

news reports. Such an innovation did not, however, lead the film-makers to abandon established journalistic traditions and, indeed, the form of direct cinema developed by Drew and his associates was deeply implicated with the established discourse of journalistic objectivity. In the early 1960s Leacock, for one, referred to his filming practice as 'film-reporting' and to himself as a reporter (in Bachmann, 1961), an identification that counts in large part for his subsequent insistence on the place of objectivity within observational direct cinema filmmaking. The emphasis on a journalistic objectivity was reinforced by other direct cinema practitioners, many of whom collaborated with Leacock in the production of news films for Time–Life and the ABC network.

Running concurrently with technological developments in the United States, in France a film and sound engineer, André Coutant, developed a portable, self-blimped (mechanically quiet), 16mm camera which was marketed commercially in the early 1960s as the Eclair. The camera enabled sound to be recorded free of interruptive camera noise on newly developed battery-powered magnetic tape recorders synchronized to the image track of the camera. Coutant's impetus to develop a portable camera stemmed from the demands of social scientists for a workable tool for ethnographic purposes. Such a tool, it was argued, would reduce or banish a baleful subjectivity which many ethnographers felt had crept into the anthropological literature and ethnographic field notes, thereby subverting the basis of the objective discipline of anthropology and its subdiscipline ethnography.[3] For many ethnographers committed to a visual anthropology the motion picture camera was an instrument that would bring cultural reality into objective focus. The demand for objectivity entered ethnographic filmmaking in various ways. Certain ethnographers, Margaret Mead and Gregory Bateson among them, relied on 'record footage', the filmic equivalent of field notes, as a useful source for research. The unscripted, unedited, unstructured nature of such footage reinforced its acceptability as a neutral and impartial record of actions and events. Editing was to be avoided as a potential source of bias. Karl Heider's set of rules in his book *Ethnographic Film*, quoted in Chapter 3, includes the dictum that ethnographic filmmakers depict 'whole bodies and whole people in whole acts', a prescription that seeks to install an objective filmmaking practice by reducing or denying editing and its traces of subjective decision-making (1976: 7).

Despite such injunctions, other ethnographers recognized the limitations of the camera as an objective recording device. Certain ethnographers noted that the ideal of objectivity was frequently compromised by the presence of the camera that altered a subject's behaviour even as the filmmaker attempted to remain distanced and impartial. A number of critics argued that detached social observation is impossible given that the ethnographer inevitably brings prior knowledge and a subjective point of view to bear on the profilmic world. Colin Young (1975: 67–8) extended this point in his description of a filmmaking practice in which the ethnographer accepts that a camera alters a subject's behaviour and thereby openly and actively intervenes within the filming process. Within this method it is understood,

> That the normal behavior being filmed is the behavior that is normal for the subjects under the circumstances, including but not exclusively, the fact that they are being filmed. If we observe, as a matter of fact, that our filming CHANGES the behavior, then we have to decide whether or not that change is relevant to the total portrait we are trying to make. In one set of circumstances, the subject might have to be abandoned or postponed. In another, the alteration introduced by the camera might have to be accepted ... [and if so] then the ... participation of the filmmaker in the events ... might turn out to be the most revealing method to adopt.

Pursuing a similar stance to that described by Young, the ethnographer Jean Rouch abandoned the pretence of objectivity and, using the newly developed camera technology, actively participated in the events he filmed. Rouch's practice in *Chronicle of a Summer* largely defined the tradition of what the subtitle of the film refers to as 'an experiment in cinéma vérité'.

## *Chronicle of a Summer*: the provocational camera

A seminal film in the history of documentary film in general and cinéma vérité in particular, *Chronicle of a Summer* was made in Paris in the summer of 1960 by Jean Rouch and his colleague, the sociologist Edgar Morin. Rouch had established a career filming among peoples of Africa and wanted to make a film about 'the strange tribe that lives in Paris', as he described it in his film *Petit a Petit*. In this way, Rouch and Morin conceived a film that was to be, according to Morin (1985: 6), an 'experiment in cinematographic interrogation ... "two authors in search of six characters" ... a sort of psychodrama ... which through filmed conversations of a spontaneous nature would get in touch with fundamentals'. The six subjects were all friends of Morin: Marceline, a survivor of Auschwitz, Jean-Pierre, a philosophy student, Landry, a student, Regis, a political science student, Marilou, an Italian woman living in Paris who has had a succession of ill-fated love affairs, and Angelo, a union militant. With the participation of these subjects, the film examines life in a modern city in the mid-twentieth century. The questions motivating the filmic 'experiment' are those which the filmmakers ask Marceline in the film – 'How do you live?', 'What do you do with your life?' – and which Marceline asks passers-by on a Paris street: 'Are you happy?'. The questions raise a number of issues concerning the place of work and the ability to find a meaningful occupation in a complex modern mass society, and whether happiness, or personal fulfilment, is achievable in such a society.

Various aspects of these themes are addressed within the film's three parts. The first section introduces the subjects whose experiences will form the basis of the experiment. Rouch and Morin also appear in the film asking questions on-camera of the subjects. The opening sequence in which Marceline asks people if they are happy extends the interactive component beyond the questions asked by Rouch and Morin. Marceline's encounters with bemused passers-by and their refusal or inability to answer her question betrays a lack of happiness and satisfaction in the lives of people living in the large modern city. This theme is explored by Rouch and Morin in their conversations with Angelo, Marilou, Marceline, Jean-Pierre and the married couple, Jacques and Simone Gabillon. The emphasis on job satisfaction and work is extended in the first section in a day in the life of Angelo, a car worker at Renault. The detailed observational sequence replaces talk – the frequent conversations of the other scenes of the first segment – with the noise of the factory. Concerns about meaningful work and happiness are here focused on the mechanized routines, regulation and discipline of modern factory life. Angelo's response to the situation expresses itself in a militancy that is alien to Marilou, who is introduced near the end of the first segment. Marilou's experiences have resulted in introspection and her current emotional turmoil – she appears to be on the edge of a nervous breakdown.

Marilou's life typifies yet another response to the questions of work, happiness and satisfaction explored in the first part of the film.

The second section of the film begins with a meeting in which Morin seeks to open the film to current political issues, thereby going beyond the focus on what Rouch called the 'personal' stories of the lives of its subjects. To this end, Morin tries to initiate discussion on the French colonial war in Algeria, which was then in a critical phase. Marceline's recollections of her experience of deportation during the Second World War, the other major segment of this section of the film, extend the reference to warfare raised by Morin. The third section of the film depicts the summer vacation period and follows Landry, the 'African adventurer', in St Tropez investigating the 'strange tribe' of Europeans at play in the south of France. Near the end of the film Rouch and Morin gather the subjects together for a screening of a rough cut of the film's footage and seek their comments on the filmmaking process. The film ends in the Musée de l'Homme, Rouch's employer, as Rouch and Morin discuss the film and attempt to anticipate its critical reception.

Within its various approaches and innovations, the experiment that is *Chronicle of a Summer* exemplifies central aspects of the method and formal components the filmmakers refer to as cinéma vérité. A notable feature of the film is its various editorial manipulations, which Rouch called 'a whole series of intermediaries'. Rouch acknowledged that he and Morin 'contract time, we extend it, we choose an angle for the shot, we deform the people we're shooting, we speed things up and follow one movement to the detriment of another movement' (quoted in Eaton, 1979: 51). The film bears the marks of the filmmakers' presence in other ways, most obviously in the fact that both Rouch and Morin appear in the film. In certain shots the camera appears reflected in windows and mirrors and occasionally a microphone boom can be seen in frame, a radical reformulation of conventional fictional and documentary filming methods which seek to deny traces of the cinematic apparatus. For Rouch the camera is to be acknowledged and foregrounded as a way of inspiring action. Rouch explained that he quickly 'discovered the camera was ... not a brake but let's say, to use an automobile term, an accelerator' which pushes 'these people to confess themselves' (Eaton, 1979: 51).

The essence of cinéma vérité as Rouch conceived it is a method that does not film reality as it is, but 'truth' as it is provoked, stimulated, modified or catalysed (all terms Rouch used in his writings)

by the very act of filming. 'Not to film life as it is, but life as it is provoked', he argued (Eaton, 1979: 51). In one way, being provocative
is the simple act of placing the camera before subjects, an act
which inspires a response which the camera captures. In another
way, provocation can be confrontational and challenging, a practice reflected in Morin's technique of questioning which, on certain occasions, becomes a form of 'bullying' (at one point in the
film Rouch refers to Morin as 'the bully'). Morin's method is
depicted in a segment at the beginning of part two in which he
seeks to turn the discussion toward the French war in Algeria:

> Rouch: We've reached the point where the film, which up to here has
> been enclosed in a relatively personal and individual universe, opens
> up on to the situation of this summer of 1960.
> Voices: Yeah, yeah ...
> Rouch: So, shall we go ahead?
> Morin: Yes, but I'd really like to know what they think [of the war].
> Morin advances the topic by addressing the participants: 'Okay, let's
> go ... if I were a student ... old enough to do military service, I'd be
> thinking about events in Algeria ... You don't give a damn about this
> issue, about the war in Algeria, do you?'

In place of Morin's aggressive form of provocation, Rouch was
willing to try alternate, subtler, forms of questioning in his attempts
to provoke responses and gain insights. Rouch's method is exemplified during a lunch at the Musée d'Art with Marceline and a
group of African students. As the conversation turns to the topic of
anti-Semitism, Rouch directs the attention of the African students
to the tattoo on Marceline's arm and asks what they thought of it.
The students, with their differing historical experiences compared
to the Europeans, do not recognize that the tattoo had been
forcibly inscribed on Marceline by the Nazis. From the basis of their
own experience of tattooing, the students interpret Marceline's
tattoo as a bodily adornment, with one student asking Marceline if
it was her telephone number. This scene effectively depicts separate
historical experiences and differing cross-cultural interpretive
strategies. For Rouch the encounter demonstrated the capacity of
a provocational intervention, in the form of his directives and
questioning, to produce 'evidence' of a remarkable reality (Feld,
1989: 239).

In each case, such interventions reflect the 'guiding hand' of
Rouch and Morin as they construct situations and propose lines of

discussion. The various forms of provocation do not, however, deny subjects an active role in decisions concerning the film. A basic strategy employed in *Chronicle* is one which Rouch referred to elsewhere as 'shared anthropology', a practice in which subjects actively collaborate with the filmmaker in a form of participatory cinema (as discussed in Chapter 3). In *Chronicle of a Summer*, the resultant 'dialogue' between the filmmakers and the subjects is illustrated in the fact that certain scenes suggested by the participants are included in the final cut. One such sequence is Marceline's emotionally powerful and profoundly moving reminiscences of the loss of her father in the Nazi Holocaust and her own deportation to Auschwitz, a sequence which Rouch points to as exemplary of the essence of cinéma vérité – the revelation of subjective feelings and thoughts which is equated in the film to truth. Given Rouch's emphasis on this scene within the cinéma vérité method it is quoted here at some length:[4]

> *The image of the Place de la Concorde appears, almost deserted. It is August 15th, morning. From the centre of the square, Marceline is coming towards us, slowly. She's walking with her eyes lowered. We hear her voice speaking slowly and sadly:*
>
> 'And Concorde is empty, too … as it was 20 years ago, or was it 15 … I don't quite remember, now … "Pitchipoi", my dad said, "you'll see, we'll go there, we'll work in the factories, we'll see each other on Sundays". And you answered my questions, and said, "You are young, you'll come back, but I definitely won't." '
>
> *She hums,* Ti ta ti ta ta ti la la, *and walks more quickly. The camera tracks in front of her, looking back at her.*
>
> 'And now, here I am, there, now: Concorde … I came back, you stayed there … (she sighs). When I saw you, we had already been there six months. We threw ourselves into each other's arms, and then …'
>
> *Wide shot Marceline, who continues to walk.*
>
> 'That dirty SS man who hurled himself on me, who hit me in front of you … You said "But she's my daughter, my daughter." Achtung! He threatened to give you a beating too … you were holding an onion, and you thrust it into my hand and I disappeared …'
>
> *Another setting. A crossroads. Marceline keeps walking, and gets further away from us. We hear her humming* 'The Big Swampy Meadows.' *She sighs.*
>
> 'Daddy … when I saw you, you said to me "And mummy? Michel?" You called me your little daughter, and I was almost happy …'
>
> *We can recognize the arches of Les Halles, the markets. The camera, which is again in front of her, quickly distances itself from her, and Marceline is soon nothing but a small silhouette alone in the vast emptiness of Les Halles, gloomy*

*and huge, while we hear her voice.*

'To be deported with you, loving you so much ... daddy, daddy, how much I would like to have you here now ... I lived there thinking you would come back ... when I came back, it was hard ... hard ... (she sighs). I could see everyone on the platform, mummy, everyone. People kissed me ... my heart was a stone ... it was Michel who moved me. I said, "Don't you recognize me?" He said to me "If I can believe it ... I think you are Marceline" ... oh, daddy ...'

Soon after this scene was filmed Rouch and Morin screened it for Marceline, who in the words of Rouch speaking in an interview, 'said that none of that concerned her! Now what did that mean? She meant – "I'm an excellent actress and I am capable of acting that!" But that's not true. Morin and I are persuaded that when she said those things, it was the real Marceline, terribly sincere, who was speaking of all that – exactly as she felt it, as she was' (quoted in Macdonald and Cousins, 1996: 270). Rouch's claim is based on his notion of the provocative potential of the camera. Rouch insisted that:

> contrary to what one might think, when people are being recorded, the reactions that they have are always infinitely more sincere than those they have when they are not being recorded. The fact of being recorded gives these people a public. At first, of course, there is a self-conscious 'hamminess'. They say to themselves 'People are looking at me I must give a nice impression of myself.' But this lasts only a very short time. And then, very rapidly, they begin to try to think – perhaps for the first time sincerely – about their own problems, about who they are and then they begin to express what they have within themselves. These moments are very short, and one must know how to take advantage of them. That's the art of making a film like *Chronique d'un Été*.... (quoted in Macdonald and Cousins, 1996: 269)

Marceline was obviously aware of the camera (it was she who suggested the scene), though in Rouch's philosophy the camera holds the capacity to reveal or, to use Rouch's much-quoted word for the process, provoke, sincere and authentic reactions. As Rouch's observation highlights, cinéma vérité works with the assumption that people are always adopting roles, constantly performing impressions of themselves. However, as Rouch argues above, the camera can also inspire honest emotions and thoughts. In this way Rouch understood cinéma vérité to be a practice which documents a performance *and* which has the capacity to take the subject (and the viewer) beyond or through performance to an authentic and truthful revelation of being.

Within the context of a work of provocation the film also contains a number of moments of a different representational order in which the camera observes behaviour, not provokes it. In many of the dinner table scenes, for example, the camera lingers on the face of a guest listening to another guest speaking. In these shots observation replaces any emphasis on the responses provoked by the filmmakers or other guests. A notable example of 'pure' observation occurs in the Renault factory segment and its attention to the faces and hands of workers as they go about their tasks, seemingly unaware of the camera. The camera's presence is downplayed here, an effect achieved in the fact that certain shots used within the scene were made with a telephoto lens which unobtrusively captured action from a distance.[5] For Rouch and Morin cinéma vérité aimed to capture 'the authenticity of life as it is lived', the 'truth' of life behind the performance (Morin, 1985: 4). To this end the camera was deployed as both provocateur and observer. Rouch did not subscribe to the critical distinction between cinéma vérité and direct cinema which suggested that the former was exclusively provocational and the latter refrained from provocation. Rouch considered the direct cinema filmmakers to be also engaged in 'cinéma vérité' (Rothman, 1997: 87), an assessment that did not, however, sit well with direct cinema filmmakers.

## A fly on the wall and a can of worms: direct cinema and the practice of observation

Direct cinema filmmakers in the United States were critical of the participatory and reflexive approaches employed in *Chronicle of a Summer*. For Leacock and other practitioners of direct cinema, Rouch's film moved toward 'theater' and supplied 'answers' as opposed to objectively reporting events (in Feld, 1989: 258). Leacock felt that *Chronicle of a Summer* did little more than document its own filming (1963: 18). According to the early practitioners of direct cinema, filmmakers should not intervene in the filmmaking process – that is, they should not be in frame, and keep contact with subjects to a minimum. The filmmaker should not manipulate the documentary mise-en-scène for the purposes of the film. Direct questioning of subjects on camera, or directives to subjects on or off camera, were to be avoided. Voice-over commentary was also disparaged. Leacock (1996: 253) summarized the essence of these injunctions as: 'No interviews. No re-enactments. No staged scenes and very little narration.' The philosophy or theory of direct cinema also emphasized that editing should ensure that the order of events in the final film followed the sequence of events as they were filmed. Though there was considerable variation in their work, practitioners of direct cinema in the United States and the United Kingdom in the 1960s upheld a theory of observational 'purity' which maintained that the filmmaker should be an unobtrusive observer or, in the phrase popularized to describe the method in the United Kingdom, a 'fly on the wall'.[6]

The theory was, however, zealously overstated and its exaggerated claims contradicted in practice, as numerous critics have pointed out. The deflation of direct cinema's claims to unique observational status reveals it to be a form which in its interventions and manipulations and interpretations of its subject matter is closer to the practices of cinéma vérité than was often acknowledged. As film theorist Noel Carroll has noted, 'critics and viewers turned the polemics of direct cinema against direct cinema' by pointing out 'all the ways that direct cinema was inextricably involved with interpreting its materials'. Carroll summarized the situation by commenting that '[d]irect cinema opened a can of worms and then got eaten by them' (1983: 7).

In an illuminating essay, Jeanne Hall (1991) explicates various ways in which the theoretical claims made for direct cinema were contravened in practice. Regarding the claim by direct cinema filmmakers that they did not use interviews, Hall notes that Robert Drew and his colleagues routinely conducted interviews, and then edited the interviewer's questions out of the final cut. Other moments, such as a subject's look to camera, were cut in order to preserve the illusion of an unmediated scene. Elsewhere in the films made by Drew and his team subjects talk directly to the filmmaker on camera, thus contradicting the notion of the filmmaker's unobtrusive presence. The direct cinema filmmaker was, it was argued, a neutral observer who did not take sides or espouse a particular point of view. Contradicting the claim, Hall identifies various instances of polemic and argument within direct cinema. The programme *Yanki No!*, for example, begins with the announcement 'This is a film editorial', and concludes with an open plea for increased aid to Latin America. *The Children are Watching* (1960), an early programme by the Drew team dealing with racial segregation in the South, refrains from announcing itself as an editorial, though its criticisms of segregation are openly polemical.

Assertions that the filmmaker was unobtrusive were reinforced in claims that a person involved in a crisis was unlikely to be aware of the presence of the ever-present camera. The result, allegedly, would be the revelation of the subject's true nature captured on film. This logic was translated into a number of direct cinema films which chose as their subject matter situations liable to result in crises. The dramatic potential created by impending or unravelling crisis was exploited within the so-called crisis structure or crisis moment of various films made by Drew's team. The technique was pursued in *Crisis: Behind a Presidential Commitment* and *The Chair*. *Primary* defers to the technique by choosing to follow presidential candidates involved in a hectic round of electioneering. Richard Leacock, one of the team responsible for shooting the film, argued for the efficacy of filming subjects involved in critical situations when he stated that as he filmed John Kennedy in a hotel room 'I retired into a corner and got lost, sitting in a big comfortable arm-chair with the camera on my lap. I'm quite sure [Kennedy] hadn't the foggiest notion I was shooting' (in Winston, 1995: 150). The statement points to a problem inherent in the assumption that a subject will, in certain situations, be too preoccupied to register the presence of a camera. In this particular case Leacock denies the fact that it was highly unlikely that Kennedy, who at that time in his career was already a practised and astute politician fully aware of the power of the media, would 'forget' or overlook the presence of the camera and its operator.

The discrepancies between the theory and practices of direct cinema are further evident in *Salesman*, a film made in 1969 by Albert and David Maysles. *Salesman* is a record of the daily routines of four itinerant Bible salesmen which focuses on Paul Brennan ('The Badger') as he makes his door-to-door rounds among the Catholic communities of New England and Florida. Direct cinema's commitment to documenting reality without interference on the part of the filmmaker is compromised in a scene in *Salesman* in which a friend enters her neighbour's kitchen to find it is occupied not only by her neighbour but also by an unfamiliar salesman and two filmmakers. The absence of any look of surprise on the face of the woman as she enters the room strongly suggests that the scene was re-enacted for the camera.[7] The myth of the unobtrusive filmmaker is further exposed through reference to a photograph used to promote *Salesman*. The image depicts Paul, seated in the living room of a (potential) customer, displaying a leather-bound Bible for the customer's inspection. Another photograph taken at the same time, though not as commonly reproduced, shows Albert and David Maysles holding a camera and tape-recording gear as they stand close to the seated Paul and his customer.[8] The looming presence of the two men, replete with camera and sound recording equipment in the cramped confines of a small living room belies the assumption of a fly on the wall. In this case, the startling presence of the filmmakers is more accurately characterized as an elephant on the table!

## *Don't Look Back*: performing the documentary

Another form of direct cinema – the rock concert film, the so-called rockumentary – raises further issues relating to the direct cinema presumption of the non-disruptive presence of the camera. The rockumentary, a popular and commercially successful documentary subgenre, is, according to the influential film historians Kristin Thompson and David Bordwell (1994: 668), 'The most widespread use of Direct Cinema.'[9] Despite its broad circulation, rockumentary has received scant critical attention in analyses of documentary film.[10] This situation is a curious one given that many of the most notable works in the subgenre, including *Don't Look Back* (1966), a film which inaugurated the meeting of rock and documentary, *Monterey Pop* (1968), and *Gimme Shelter* (1970), were made by filmmakers associated with the early phases of direct cinema – D.A. Pennebaker (*Don't Look Back* and *Monterey Pop*) and the Maysles brothers (*Gimme Shelter*). In making these films the directors did not necessarily abandon their theoretical commitment to notions of detachment and neutrality, though, increasingly, the films they made in the rockumentary subgenre stretched the contradiction between the theory and practice of direct cinema. The Maysles brothers' *Gimme Shelter*, for example, relies heavily on reconstruction of events and the inclusion of reflexive moments to construct its narrative of the Rolling Stones' 1969 tour of the United States and the disastrous concert at Altamont. More particularly, the presence of performance in the rockumentary complicates the emphasis by direct cinema filmmakers on pure observation.

As with other works of direct cinema, a rockumentary presumes to be an objective record of an event, in this case musical concert performances and off-stage actions. As a species of direct cinema which focuses on performance, the rockumentary begs a number of questions concerning the effects of the camera on a subject's behaviour. The notion of a subject's 'virtual performance' (Nichols, 1991: 122) inspired by the camera is something that direct cinema, with its emphasis on unreconstructed action, seeks to minimize or banish. This point is of particular relevance to Pennebaker's *Don't Look Back*, a film which features multiple levels of performance. *Don't Look Back*, a record of Bob Dylan's triumphant 1965 concert tour of the United Kingdom, includes a number of Dylan's onstage performances amidst scenes of life away from the spotlight. The intriguing aspect of *Don't Look Back* is the degree of attention the film gives to depicting the exploits of Dylan and his entourage in 'off stage' environments such as hotel rooms. Such scenes constitute another level of performance in which Dylan continues, in effect, to perform for the camera away from the stage.[11]

The film's prologue, which was suggested to Pennebaker by Dylan, exemplifies Pennebaker's willingness to abandon pure direct cinema by foregrounding off-stage performance as one of the film's central concerns – not as something to be minimized or banished, but as an activity to be encouraged and highlighted. The segment features Dylan, standing in an alleyway in London flipping though large cue cards inscribed with hand-lettered words of his song 'Subterranean Homesick Blues', which plays on the soundtrack. During the sequence Dylan stands facing the camera flipping through the cards, the first inscribed with 'BASEMENT' (in the song Dylan sings 'Johnny's in the basement mixing up the medicine ...'), continuing with others which bear various lyrics from the song: 'LOOK OUT!', 'WATCH IT!', 'HERE THEY COME!', 'LEADERS???' and so on. Dylan discards the cards one by one as the song continues to play. Dylan's act is replete with knowing looks to the camera which also depicts the alleyway in the background, empty except for the brief appearance of a bearded figure carrying a staff (the poet Allen Ginsburg). At the end of the segment, as the song is fading on the soundtrack, another man (Dylan's friend Bob Neuwirth) enters the frame, nods at Dylan, and the two walk away in opposite directions, with Dylan heading down the alley without looking back.

The prologue is a fully contained segment within the broader film, and it approximates what later became the 'rock clip', short interpretative works produced to accompany rock songs on television in formats such as those on MTV. (Indeed, Dylan's manager, Albert Grossman, had conceived of Pennebaker's film as an opportunity to produce promotional clips for Dylan's songs.) The segment positions Dylan 'centre stage' within a self-conscious performance. In these terms the prologue can either be considered out of place, even inappropriate, within the context of observationalism, or, alternatively, an indication that performance – an abandonment of the pretence of naturalism – will supersede the demands of a direct cinema committed to naturalism and observation. It is clear as the film progresses, and as Dylan continues to act for the camera, that Dylan's proposal to include the segment, and Pennebaker's agreement to do so, signals an emphasis on the performative which extends beyond the realms of the stage. William Rothman, in his lengthy and dense analysis of *Don't Look Back*, suggests that the purpose of the prologue is to announce that the film is not merely a 'documentary'; it is, instead, a 'collaboration in which filmmaker and subject are co-conspirators'. In this way, the prologue functions as a marker that the body of the film will also be a 'performance by co-conspirators' (Rothman, 1997: 149). This is not to suggest that Pennebaker consciously set out to 'defraud' or deceive the viewer. The 'collusion' between Dylan and Pennebaker does, however, point to a manipulation, or transgression of the codes of direct cinema. The prologue, as with the rest of the film, constitutes Pennebaker's willingness to abandon 'pure' direct cinema, and to give reign, with Dylan's participation, to performance – both on and off stage.

Another indication of this willingness occurs during an interview between Dylan and a Jamaican correspondent for the BBC, one of the many interviews in the film. The interviewer asks, 'How did it all begin for you, Bob?'. Dylan mumbles inaudibly and the film cuts to footage of a young Dylan singing 'He's Only a Pawn in Their Game' at a civil rights rally in Mississippi. As the scattered crowd at the rally applauds his performance, another cut introduces Dylan onstage during the 1965 tour singing 'The Times They Are A-Changin'.' The cuts from contemporary action to the past depicted in archival footage, back to contemporary action, disrupts the temporal and spatial continuity that narratively orders observationalism, replacing it with the non-narrativized presence of performance. Elsewhere, Dylan's musical performances are structured into the narrative as he heads north to Manchester and back to London though, ironically, the narrative lacks the 'honesty' and 'integrity' of the Mississippi performance, a function of Dylan's constant performing off stage. Within these performances there is no way to get 'access' to 'the real' Dylan.

The rockumentary convention of 'backstage' has developed in reaction to such a difficulty, offering supposedly unmediated glimpses of the 'real' person behind the performance. The convention, operative in a range of rockumentaries including *Woodstock* (1970), *Gimme Shelter*, *The Last Waltz* (1978) and Pennebaker's *Monterey Pop*, exploits the hand-held camera of direct cinema and its capacity to film in confined and poorly lit spaces such as dressing rooms, concert hall corridors, the back seats of limousines, and hotel rooms. Erving Goffman, in his sociological and psychological study of selfhood, *The Presentation of Self in Everyday Life*, examines various behaviours undertaken in particular social environments, among them 'backstage', the physical space behind or off stage in which a performer can relax and 'step out of character' (Goffman, 1969: 98). Such an understanding informs the convention of backstage as it operates in the rockumentary where, as Jonathan Romney argues, it is

> the most potent of all concepts designed to separate performer and fan. It is a space of privacy, a world behind the curtain in which the *real being*, the ineffable precious essence of the performer's self, supposedly lies shielded from sight…The audience is not normally permitted behind the sacred veil, but it is a convention of the music documentary to include scenes which take us backstage and offer us tantalizing glimpses of the reality behind the show… [Such scenes] offer us a fantasy 'Access All Areas' pass, one of those areas being the artist's very soul. Above all, they promise access to the truth, for backstage is imagined as a far more 'real' space than the stage in which the artists do their work. (Romney, 1995: 83)

The convention creates a distinction between the public space of the stage, where a performer presents a persona constructed for the purposes of entertaining an audience, and the private spaces off-stage in which the mask of the performer is dropped and the person behind the performer is revealed. *Don't Look Back* includes a shot which clearly indicates a separation of stage and backstage – a shaky tracking shot following Dylan and his companions as they flee a concert hall by running along corridors, up and down staircases, past fans in the street, and into a waiting limousine which will take them to the secluded space of a hotel room. (The shot, which mirrors a famous shot made by Albert Maysles for *Primary* in which Kennedy is followed into an auditorium of waiting well-wishers, has since became a rockumentary cliché parodied in *This is Spinal Tap*, 1984, in a scene in which the fictional band gets lost in a similar set of corridors and stairs.)

While *Don't Look Back* replicates the two domains of onstage and backstage, the film does not fully reproduce what are in other rock documentaries the attendant meanings of public and private space. We are permitted backstage, but not granted access to the 'real being', in Romney's terms. Off stage, Dylan continues to perform, particularly in the presence of the many interviewers who appear in the backstage spaces. At certain times, Dylan seems to take delight in the interviews, and at other times, he appears to be annoyed by interviewers, but both reactions seem to be calculated. Dylan appears as a masterful role player, an obfuscationist, indulging in word games and gambits, willing to spin stories which are clearly fabricated at the interviewer's expense. In one particular interview, with Horace Judson, the London-based arts correspondent for *Time* magazine, Dylan launches a verbal attack on Judson and steps out of the role of interviewee by asking Judson unanswerable questions. The scene is unsettling – Dylan, the man of peace indulging in verbal aggression – and it is difficult not to wonder whether it was another example of Dylan's performance. Judson felt that the scene was contrived as an entertaining sequence for the film to compensate for the fact that the recorded interview had gone flat (Sounes, 2001: 175).

In other, less overtly dramatic moments, the film captures, if not Dylan acting for the camera, then his awareness of the camera's presence revealed, however fleetingly, in glances at the camera. Having thrown a hotel assistant out of the room, telling him to go to his 'fop manager', Dylan looks to-camera. On another occasion, while playing music and talking with Alan Price of the Animals, Dylan starts a song and then looks directly at the camera, annoyed, it seems, that Pennebaker is at that moment still filming when, for once, Dylan would prefer he wasn't (Pennebaker, 1990: 27). In these moments, and particularly during his interactions with interviewers, the camera reveals or inspires performances which are, in effect, an acknowledgement of the camera's presence. The camera does not capture the man 'behind the shades' (Heylin, 1991); as Pennebaker (1971: 192) pointed out, Dylan 'knew that the camera was recording [him] in a way which [he] elected to be recorded. [He was] enacting [a] role ... very accurately.'

*Don't Look Back* effectively documents a consummate performer, and extends the opportunities (in the prologue and throughout the film) for Dylan to perform. Pennebaker is implicated in this process not as neutral observer but as co-conspirator colluding in Dylan's performances. By privileging and, in effect, licensing Dylan's off-stage 'performances' for the camera *Don't Look Back* complicates the direct cinema rhetoric of detached observationalism and the claim that the presence of a camera does not modify a subject's behaviour. In this way *Don't Look Back* points to the essential paradox that underlines the direct cinema claim: the notion of a subject 'acting naturally' in the presence of the camera.

## Post observationalism

The rockumentary has continued as one of the most commercially successful cinema release documentary forms (one which also features in the large-screen IMAX format; *Rolling Stones: At the Max*, 1991, is one such work). Various films which followed *Don't Look Back* contributed further revisions to a basic observationalism. The Maysles brothers *Gimme Shelter*, for example, marries observation with a Rouchian reflexivity in a scene near the end of the film in which the filmmakers appear in frame to replay footage for Mick Jagger and Keith Richards of the Stones' Altamont concert (at which a fan was killed by a member of the Hell's Angels, an event that is evident in the footage). Prior to the rise of docusoap and gamedocs and their reworking of observationalism (see Chapter 10), the rockumentary contained some of the most radical disruptions of the observational mode.

Beyond the rock documentary a 'purer', more conventional in terms of observational practice, form of non-interventionist direct cinema persisted. Notably, productive output in this line has tended to outstrip works informed by cinéma vérité's reflexive approach (though, confusingly, the terms 'ciné vérité' and 'vérité' have come to be used interchangeably with 'direct cinema' to refer to work in the field). In the United Kingdom, Paul Watson's *The Family* (BBC, 1974) and Roger Graef's 13-part television series

*Police* (BBC, 1982) made significant contributions to a 'direct cinema' approach.[12] In the United States, the 12-part series *An American Family* (PBS, 1973) drew large audiences to its detailed daily observations of the Loud family of Santa Barbara, California. In episode one of the series the producer Craig Gilbert speaks in voice-over, introducing the series and its concerns.[13] The segment was one of the first instances of exposition melded to sequences of observation and it anticipated a subsequent increasing move toward the incorporation of narration within the context of observation. Other prominent observational works from the United States include the theatrically released *Hoop Dreams* (1994), *Crumb* (1995), *The War Room* (1994) directed by Pennebeker and Chris Hegedus, and *StartUp.Com* (2001), which was directed by Hegedus and produced by Pennebaker. In Australia the observational films of Robert Connolly and Robin Anderson (*Rats in the Ranks*, 1996, *Facing the Music*, 2001) and Dennis O'Rourke ('*Cannibal Tours*', 1987, *The Good Woman of Bangkok*, 1992, and *Cunnamulla*, 2001), like *Crumb*, openly incorporate off-camera comments by the filmmaker and, at times, moments of direct questioning of the subject by the filmmaker.

The increasing integration of aspects of exposition within an observational context has broadened to the point that many works, particularly those in the docusoap format, commonly rely on interviews and voice-over to provide additional information as part of a practice of revising what a number of directors see as the limitations of conventional observational methods. Another development in this regard has been an increasing admission of performative 'set pieces' in works which playfully revise observation through references by subjects to the presence of the camera and its effect on their actions. Corner cites *Sylvania Waters* (BBC/ABC, 1992)[14] in this regard, a work of what he calls 'neo vérité', which dispels a detached observationalism in the first episode when the son of the household introduces the viewer to the 'characters' the viewer is 'going to get to know'. Here the 'intensity of the vérité gaze' applied to a small familial group elicited a histrionic performance from participants (Corner, 1996: 51). A knowing and open recognition by subjects of the filmmaker's presence is a persistent feature of contemporary forms of neo vérité such as *The Osbournes* (MTV, 2002).

In a similar vein, subjects in the docusoap often offer asides to the camera, thereby implicating the viewer in action which is self-consciously performed for the camera. It is within and through performative methods that docusoaps and other forms of popular factual programming (see Chapter 10) constitute a significant recent revision of observationalism. Performance and observation interact to a heightened degree in contemporary gamedocs such as *Big Brother*, for example, in which an unrelieved observational gaze inspires and warrants a performative element. Observation is here extended to a form of provocation reminiscent of its operation in cinéma vérité. Where the makers of *Chronicle of a Summer* regularly gathered subjects together (typically over dinner) to draw out their responses, *Big Brother* routinely invites subjects into a 'diary room' for a focused session of questioning. In one way, the increasing prominence of performance within particular observational contexts tends to render moot, or at least mitigates, the early debate concerning the role of the camera in revealing or provoking essential, *unperformed*, 'truths' of human behaviour. In another way, however, an acknowledgement of the place of performance in contemporary documentary representation points to a reinvigoration of the debate concerning the possibility of filming people who, though openly aware of the camera's presence, display 'natural' or 'authentic' behaviour.

## CHAPTER 6

# The Camera I: Autobiographical Documentary

'I thought it was real'; 'I try to keep track of the days'; 'dear diary'. The styles and language of written autobiography are familiar to us. The expression of the self – through use of the first person 'I' – characterizes a written form which reflects and focuses various 'personal' or subjective issues and agendas. A move from written autobiography to filmed self-representation has extended the possibilities for the depiction of 'first person' topics and created new styles and forms available for such representation. In turn, new camera and sound technology has further contributed to the growth of the autobiographical mode. The camcorder diary, for example, is now a popular and expanding form of self-authored work which has impacted on the visual language of the autobiography, creating new visual styles that situate the viewer in an intimate relationship with the subject of the autobiography. Other issues beyond new camera technologies have impacted on the development of autobiographical film and video. The rise in various Western countries in the late 1960s and 1970s of social movements committed to promoting personal issues of sexuality, gender, 'race' and ethnicity have, by popularly expressing and thereby foregrounding these issues, contributed to the expression of self and identity in autobiographical forms of filmmaking.

The 'imaginative singularity' which we call our self (Smith, 1988: 101) is expressed in and through our thoughts and feelings. The intensely personal and individual subjective sense of self is not, however, inherent; we learn or develop such a sense of self as we grow and interact within society. In this way, our subjectivity, rather than being inherently ours, 'a property that we own' (O'Sullivan, *et al.*, 1989: 232), is constructed from the numerous contending identities that are constituted by relations with others in particular social environments (Woodward, 1997: 39). These identities are expressed in various ways – 'student', 'woman', 'worker', 'mother', 'daughter', 'sister' and so on. As individuals interact in a community specific aspects of identity are privileged; in one context 'mother' may be emphasized, in another environment it may be 'worker' which is stressed. Thus, identity is not a unified category based on an unchanging, immutable or 'essential' identity. Rather, identity, in the singular, can be understood as a fluid and multiple condition composed of the sum of various identities which are defined through interaction with others whose identities are similarly changing.

Autobiographical texts attempt to represent, and thereby contribute to the construction of, an author's identity. One theorist of the autobiographical form, Paul Eakin (1992: 67), emphasizes the centrality of identity to the autobiographical project when he argues that both print and visual autobiographies take the 'constitution of identity … [to be] the genre's characteristic, even defining goal'. Within the informing context of the construction of personal identity, this chapter examines self-authored film and video through reference to selected autobiographical works produced over the past 20 years. The works examined include *Sherman's March* (1985), by Ross McElwee, a film in which McElwee complicates the idea that the autobiographical text is a simple reflection of the authoring self by adopting a persona through which he 'performs' an identity. A different kind of work, Rea Tajiri's *History and Memory* (1991), a record of her Japanese American family and their experience of internment during the Second World War, connects personal memory and identity to social history within a form of experimental autobiography. Finally, questions of self-authorship, identity, and the visual grammar of camcorder autobiography are examined through reference to works in the video diary genre.

## *Sherman's March,* performance and autobiography

Documentary has traditionally presented itself as work capable of objectively reporting the world. The documentary emphasis on objectivity has aligned documentary with other soberly objective methods, particularly those of science and journalism which have typically been applied to the exploration, explanation and documentation of others – the poor, the disadvantaged, the politically disenfranchised, or the 'exotic' (Ruby, 1978: 7–8). Autobiographical documentary constitutes a profound rewriting of such approaches. The assertion of subjective and personal points of view and the representation of one's self, family and culture, forces a significant revision of an objective, externalizing, documentary practice.

Prior to the relatively recent expansion of the autobiographical mode in its various film and video formats, certain strands of personal and autobiographical non-fictional filmmaking existed alongside the canonical works of an objective documentary tradition. Home movies, and their documentations of family and individual concerns, have long been a repository of personal and subjective filmmaking. The rise of cinéma vérité in the early 1960s offered another form for the expression of subjectivity. As pointed out in the previous chapter, Jean Rouch's cinéma vérité techniques deployed the camera as a way of provoking personal and private revelations from the film's subjects. Rouch's cinéma vérité was not, however, an autobiographical cinema – Rouch's subjects, not Rouch himself, revealed their intimacies on film. Working with many of the interactive positions established by Rouch, Ross McElwee's *Sherman's March* extends Rouch's cinéma vérité into the realm of the autobiographical.[1]

Ross McElwee's *Sherman's March* carries the lengthy subtitle *A Meditation on the Possibility of Romantic Love in the South during an Era of Nuclear Weapons Proliferation*. Together, title and subtitle encapsulate strands of a narrative which simultaneously records McElwee's travels through the South in the steps of the Civil War general William Tecumseh Sherman, his anxieties and fears of nuclear war, and his romantic relationships with a number of women he meets on his journey. Each of these strands is amplified through a variety of references into major themes within the film. Sherman and his military career, for example, feature in numerous direct and indirect ways. McElwee visits Civil War battlefields and fortifications and reads from Sherman's journals, identifying with various aspects of Sherman's experiences. McElwee notes that Sherman liked to paint portraits of women and he recognizes that his film is a portrait of a number of women. Further, McElwee directly evokes Sherman's presence by identifying with Sherman's physical appearance and many of his character traits, pointing out that, like Sherman, he is an insomniac prone to bouts of melancholy. In one scene, McElwee becomes Sherman's Southern alter ego by dressing in the uniform of an officer in the Confederate Army to attend a costume ball.

References to Sherman's career and visits to various Civil War battlefields open the theme of warfare which is broadened in a number of allusions to nuclear conflict. McElwee encounters armed survivalists readying themselves for a nuclear war with the Soviet Union, antinuclear protesters and people hoarding food in preparation for impending nuclear attack. On a number of occasions throughout the film McElwee recounts a childhood nightmare of nuclear holocaust inspired by witnessing the detonation of a hydrogen bomb while on holiday with his parents in Hawaii. As he states in the film, the nightmare is a reflection of his emotional condition, an indicator that his 'love life' is not going well.

The 'possibility of romantic love' is established immediately after the film opens as McElwee explains in voice-over that his current girlfriend, Anne, has left for a former boyfriend. Returning to his family home in Charlotte, North Carolina, and from there heading south tracing Sherman's march to the sea, McElwee encounters a childhood friend, Mary, who is modelling in a local fashion show; Pat, an aspiring actress, whom he follows to Atlanta; Claudia, who is planning to live in the mountains with other survivalists; Winnie, a linguist working on her PhD on an island off the coast of Georgia; Jackie, an old girlfriend who is active in the movement against nuclear weapons; Deedee, an administrator at a girl's school introduced to him by his friend Charleen; Joy, a nightclub singer; Karen, a friend from high school, now a lawyer and Pam, his music teacher in Boston. Though seeking 'romantic love' McElwee's attempts to understand the women he meets typically end in his frustration at his inability to maintain a lasting relationship.

McElwee's failures in this regard are reflected in his reference to his 'psychosexual despair' and his allusions to his damaged masculinity. At a Highland games gathering he comments wistfully on the virility and strength of the men participating, characteristics which he seemingly lacks (Arthur, 1993: 129). The actor Burt Reynolds, his 'old nemesis', appears as a figure of masculinity whom McElwee is restrained from approaching. Sherman's military successes stand in opposition to McElwee's indecision and apprehension and romantic failures. Interestingly, these comments on his masculinity, at once comic and pathetic, serve, ultimately, to subvert, rather than assert and validate patriarchal male identity. Although McElwee's film raises the issue of the relationship between the camera and male power, McElwee's masculinity is displayed as vulnerable, insecure, and far from confident in ways which thus mitigate the assertiveness of the male gaze. Against Sherman's heroism, McElwee's mock-heroism is bathed in masochism, the result of unreciprocated affections (Fischer, 1998: 338). A telling scene in this regard shows McElwee sleeping alone in a tree house on an island off the Georgia coast, attacked by 'bloodsucking cone-nose' insects while nearby Winnie sleeps with another man.

In his own synopsis of the film McElwee draws attention to a different set of concerns which overlay the themes outlined here:

> It is a non-fiction documentary story in which I shape narratively the documentary footage I've gathered during a serendipitous journey through the South. My film is a story in so far as it adheres to the auto-biographically narrative line of a return home followed by a mutedly comic quest in which, repeatedly, boy meets girl, boy chases girl, boy loses girl. It is documentary in so far as all the people, places and situations appearing in the film are all unscripted and unplanned. (quoted in Schwartz, 1986: 13)

McElwee's description highlights the border area of fact and fiction, story and documentary, which the film occupies. The references here to story and romantic quest centring on a comic male figure (shades of a character in a Woody Allen film) are placed against statements concerning the film's status as a documentary. As the narrative progresses the film moves away from a documentary style into openly performative moments in which McElwee adopts a specific persona, thereby pointing to autobiography as an act in which the author 'performs the self'.

*Sherman's March* opens with a piece of traditional expositional filmmaking. Across a map of the southern states of the United States an animated arrow crawls south and then northeast, tracing the route of Sherman's Union Army as a voice-over (which, in a nod to McElwee's cinematic predecessors, is spoken by Richard Leacock, a founder of direct cinema) provides a commentary on the army's march through the Southern states. At the end of the segment McElwee's voice is heard off-camera asking 'want to do [the narration] once more?'. The admission of McElwee's authorial presence within the self-reflexive disruption of established expository conventions suggests a film that is willing to expose its own methods by way of enhancing its self-revelations.

In the following scene McElwee walks back and forth across the space of a New York loft apartment as he recounts in voice-over his recent past – his trip from Boston to visit his old girlfriend, Anne, who has since returned to her former boyfriend, and his plans to make a documentary on Sherman's military campaign. McElwee is here taking the viewer into his confidence, explaining the situations that led to his decision to make a documentary on Sherman, introducing us not to the documentary, but to his current predicament and his thoughts on making the Sherman film. Through this method *Sherman's March* is positioned as what has since become a popular documentary form – a film about the making of the film. Such works promise to take us 'behind the scenes', a method which, as with its use in rockumentary, suggests access to aspects of identity normally reserved from the prying camera. McElwee reinforces this suggestion through an interactive form and provocational method which resembles Rouch's cinéma vérité. Indeed, McElwee like Rouch conceives of the camera as a catalyst, one which 'sparks a response from people I'm filming. It takes me places I wouldn't ordinarily go, not just geographically, but emotionally and psychologically with the people I'm filming and with myself' (quoted in Lucia, 1993: 37). According to McElwee, 'You're after something with the camera. You're often not even sure what it is moment to moment' (quoted in Lucia, 1993: 34). Beyond a certain similarity of method, however, Rouch's cinéma vérité and McElwee's film are different in many ways, not the least in the level of self-revelation achieved in the varying approaches to the subjects. Whereas Rouch is able to draw out Marceline's wartime experiences, for example, the depths of the subjective feelings of the women are revealed, ironically, in the fact that they elude McElwee's attempts to represent them.

Though McElwee may use the catalytic potential of the camera in a way suggested by his sister ('to meet women'), the women he encounters are, interestingly, only partially realized in the film. McElwee somewhat voyeuristically films women in intimate moments such as dressing and applying makeup, but their intimate selves remain beyond his attempts to document them. Jackie sits in a boat with her back to McElwee and refuses to discuss her pain over their relationship; Winnie, too, backs away from disclosing her feelings as to why she left McElwee. Other friends and lovers merely depart, without explanation. During a tense personal exchange with McElwee, Karen asks him to switch the camera off, a request that suggests that her most honest feelings and expressions are made off-camera. This is an especially difficult moment, not only because McElwee ignores Karen's request and continues to film. McElwee recognizes that, as he suggests in the film, 'filming has become the only way I can relate to women'. In these terms, to stop filming Karen at this moment would mean he could not relate to her (though to continue filming as he does, he is faced with Karen's silent disapproval).

Like the other subjects of his film, McElwee himself is only partially revealed in *Sherman's March*. In one way 'Ross McElwee' disappears within the character of Sherman; McElwee identifies with Sherman to the point that he interprets his insomnia and melancholy in terms of Sherman's, not his own, character. In another way 'Ross McElwee' remains hidden behind a particular comic persona that he constructs for himself in the film. Aspects of this persona are established within what he calls the 'almost literary voice-over' through which he chooses to present certain information about himself. McElwee stated that:

> ... the Ross McElwee who's presented in the film is not a completely rendered Ross McElwee. I don't say everything about myself that I could be saying. I don't tell you everything that's on my mind. I'm creating a deadpan persona. Perhaps I create a heightened sense of depression, heightened in an attempt to attain some sort of comic level. I'm creating a persona for the film that's based upon who I am, but it isn't exactly me. (quoted in MacDonald, 1992: 282)

By adopting and enacting a persona, McElwee pushes his film towards the realm of performative documentary, those works constructed around a performance by the filmmaker (Bruzzi, 2000: 154). In such works the filmmaker's performance becomes the focus of attention replacing, to a degree, the ostensible topic being represented. An early example of this approach is Michael Rubbo's witty film *Waiting for Fidel* (1974). Rubbo originally conceived of the film as a portrait of Fidel Castro; however, through his inability to make contact with Castro, the film reflexively focuses on Rubbo and his numerous attempts to interview the Cuban leader. In the United Kingdom the performative mode has been adopted by Nick Broomfield (*Heidi Fleiss: Hollywood Madam*, 1995, *Kurt and*

*Courtney*, 1998, *Biggie and Tupac*, 2002, and others) and in the United States by Michael Moore (*Roger and Me*, 1989, *Bowling for Columbine*, 2002, and other works).

McElwee's performance, and the distinction between the 'two Ross McElwees', subtly subverts the assumption that autobiography provides direct access to the author's 'real' identity, while at the same time it points to the complexity and mutability of individual subjectivity that refuses reduction to a singular unified identity. The purposive and self-conscious reflection on self enacted within McElwee's performance also draws attention to the fact that while autobiographical films appear 'natural' and spontaneous they are often very carefully constructed works produced for specific public consumption (Dovey, 2000: 41, 45). McElwee's performance, like Dylan's in *Don't Look Back*, and like the 'virtual' performances (Nichols, 1991: 122) of subjects in docusoaps and contemporary 'gamedocs' such as *Big Brother* (discussed in Chapter 10), points to the centrality of self-conscious performance within a documentary tradition that stretches back to Flaherty's 'stagings'.

## *History and Memory*: experimental autobiography

The cinéma vérité approach adopted by McElwee in *Sherman's March* is transcended in 'post-vérité' works of 'new autobiography' (Renov, 1989 and 1999c), among them Rea Tajiri's innovative autobiographical portrait *History and Memory*. Formally, Tajiri's video is a hybrid of documentary and experimental elements, and its autobiographical focus is informed by the recent historical concerns with identity mentioned at the opening of this chapter. From the 1970s onwards a number of groups within society have demanded the right to speak on their own behalf. The women's movement and the gay rights movement, for example, have brought a range of 'personal' issues – including gender, sexuality, 'race' and ethnicity – to widespread attention. In turn, these issues have been politicized within the struggle by women, gays and people of colour to express freely and publicly aspects of identity. The resultant so-called identity politics (which have been rallied under the slogan 'the personal is political') have revised existing political structures and been expressed in new forms of political and media representation. In many cases the forms of visual representation constructed around the issues emerging from this context have, as in the case of Tajiri's work, drawn on both documentary and avant-garde cinemas.

In the United States, the avant-gardist New American Cinema, a term used to refer to experiments undertaken in the 1960s by a group of loosely aligned filmmakers, explored new forms in the representation of selfhood. Exemplary of the new connections, the personal films of Stan Brakhage and the diary films of Jonas Mekas, central practitioners of the New American Cinema, combined formal experimentation with autobiographical documentations in ways which influenced and informed filmmakers throughout the 1970s in America and elsewhere. Recent autobiographical documentaries have also drawn on avant-gardist traditions to reveal varieties of ethnic and women's experiences. Laura Marks (1994) uses the term 'hybrid cinema', a form concerned with the histories of minority social groups, to refer to such work. Hybrid cinema is constituted within a mixture of documentary, fiction and experimental genres which, Marks argues, characterizes the film production of cultures and peoples in the process of creating identities (1994: 245).[2] In her analysis of the newer forms of documentary representation Julia Lesage (1999: 311) argues that what she calls feminist experimental autobiographical films and videotapes concentrate on the lives of women of colour in works which reformulate relations between 'women's mind, body, emotions and history – especially family history'.

The emphasis in the accounts of both Marks and Lesage on the expressive and evocative documentation of (changing) identities as a central component of recent visual autobiography is extended in the 'memory work' undertaken in *History and Memory*. Annette Kuhn in her book *Family Secrets: Acts of Memory and Imagination* (1995: 4) argues that memory work has the potential to integrate public and private spheres thereby incorporating and linking history and memory:

> ... as far as memory ... is concerned, private and public turned out in practice less readily separable than conventional wisdom would have us believe ... [I]f the memories are one individual's, their associations extend beyond the personal. They spread into an extended network of meanings that bring together the personal with the familial, the cultural, the economic, social and the historical. Memory work makes it possible to explore connections between 'public' historical events, structures of feeling, family dramas, relations of class, national identity and gender, and 'personal memory'.

Rea Tajiri explores the connections outlined by Kuhn within a work which integrates documentary and avant-gardist traditions of filmmaking, the personal and the familial, individual and communal concerns, by counterposing memory and history and the dense layers of textual articulation in which both are encoded. The tape mixes a variety of sources – including reconstructed scenes, written text, photographs, extracts from feature fictional films, wartime government documentaries, and home movies – to construct a history of the experiences of Tajiri's Japanese American family during the Second World War. The family story narrated through the diverse sources is one of displacement, internment and resettlement, which begins in 1942 with the family's removal from their home in California and their internment in Poston, Arizona. Despite the fact that her father was serving in the US Army, Tajiri's family, together with 110 000 persons of Japanese descent, was interned for the duration of the war on the basis of government fears that Japanese Americans posed a threat to the United States fighting a Pacific war with Japan.[3]

It is the experience of displacement and internment that motivates Tajiri's attempt to understand her family's past and her own place in that history. Tajiri comments on this process in voice-over:

> I began searching for a history, my own history, because I had known all along that the stories I heard were not true and parts had been left out. I remember having this feeling when I was growing up, that I was haunted by something, that I was living within a family full of ghosts. There was this place that they knew about. I had never been there, yet I had a memory of it. I could remember a time of great sadness before I was born. We had been moved, uprooted. We had lived with a lot of pain. I had no idea where these memories came from, yet I knew the place.

In a complex and highly structured way, *History and Memory* draws on differing forms of 'evidence' to re-create history and to retrieve the memory of the past Tajiri knows only as a haunting absence. The history of the era is recorded in film sources which include Department of War Information films and clips from newsreels. Such 'official' versions of history are extended in popular representations of the period such as John Sturges's 1954 fictional film *Bad Day at Blackrock*.

Against the well-documented popular and official records of the era, Tajiri relies on fragments and shards of memory to construct a counterhistory of displacement and internment suffered by a

generation of Japanese Americans. In the absence of a photographic and filmic record of life under internment (the US government banned the unauthorized use of cameras in the camps)
the objects and drawings produced by her mother and grandparents in the camp are recycled in Tajiri's work as unique records of
her family's experiences during this time. Standing in contrast to
the images of official and popular history, memory is encoded in
the printed words which appear on the screen. The tape opens
with an evocation of a scene that was not documented visually and
hence which only exists in memory and the words used to describe
it. The tape begins with a scrolling text that describes a scene
viewed from above:

> ... slowly, very, very slowly the ground comes closer as the tops of trees
> disappear. The tops of the heads of a man and woman become visible as
> they move them back and forth in an animated fashion. The black hair
> on the heads catch and reflect light from the street lamps. The light
> from the street lamps has created a path for them to walk and argue.

The text continues, informing the viewer that the scene which
has just been described is that witnessed by the spirit of Tajiri's
grandfather who observes Tajiri's mother and father argue about
their daughter's unexplained nightmares twenty years after the
bombing of Pearl Harbour. Past and present interact in this evocation of three generations of the family. It is a scene which can only
exist in memory, and one which is, since Tajiri was too young to
remember it herself, reconstructed from hearsay. The scene brings
into focus many of the central elements of the tape: family, memory, (reconstructed) recollections, images whose referents can
only exist in memory or in the form of reconstructions. Soon after
the opening scene Tajiri recounts another 'memory' which she
knows only through other people's recollections:

> I don't know where this comes from, but I just had this fragment, this
> picture that's always in my mind. My mother, she's standing at a faucet,
> and it's really hot outside. And she's filling this canteen and the water's
> really cold and it feels really good. And outside the sun is just so hot, it's
> just beating down. And there's this dust that gets everywhere and
> they're always sweeping the floors.

The image is that of the mother in the Poston internment camp.
Tajiri's 'fragment' is accompanied by a brief visual image – not an

image of Tajiri's mother, but an image (since no original exists) of Tajiri re-enacting her mother filling a canteen at the dusty and dry internment camp. In the search for the meaning of this powerful and provocative 'ever-absent image' (as it is described in the voice-over), Tajiri will reconstruct her family's memories and in the process find herself and her identity as a member of a family which is aligned with a wider Japanese-American community whose members also share the experiences of displacement and internment.

Tajiri's determination to reconstruct her family's history is intensified by her mother's wilful forgetting of her painful past. All that her mother remembers of the period of wartime internment is 'why she forgot to remember'. Tajiri cleverly evokes the 'image' of a suppressed memory when she states, in references to the internees: 'There are things that only people who were there saw', a statement which is accompanied by a blank screen. In her attempt to re-create her mother's experiences Tajiri supplements scraps of memory by visiting the camp at Poston in which her mother was forcibly interned. As a record of this visit, Tajiri inter-cuts her own photographs of the disused and decaying barracks in Poston with clips from the film *Bad Day at Black Rock*, a story of the search for clues to the murder of a Japanese-American man named Kimoko. Tajiri deploys the search for Kimoko in Sturges's film as a metaphor for the missing histories of her family and the other Japanese Americans held in Poston and other such camps. Tajiri comments in voice-over: 'Kimoko's disappearance from Black Rock was like our disappearance from history ... Somehow, I could identify with this search, this search for an ever-absent image and the desire to create an image where there are so few.'

Tajiri's desire to find an image of this particular past is extended through the inclusion of an extract from the Hollywood internment drama, *Come See the Paradise* (A. Parker, 1990). The clip is screened against stills and propagandistic footage from the war period as Tajiri's nephew reads his openly critical newspaper review of the film. In the juxtaposition of word and image the Hollywood film is situated as another work that is incapable of adequately representing the missing history of the Japanese-American experience during the war. The notion of disappearance and absence suggested by the images from *Bad Day at Black Rock* and *Come See the Paradise* is extended in the fact that the family home was removed during the war – 'requisitioned' for use by the US Navy – an ignominious event that compounded the family's sense of dislocation. The disappearance of the house, and with it, aspects of the family's memories, functions as a metonym for the erasure of the history of Japanese-American experiences during the Second World War.

At the end of the video, as Tajiri surveys the arid land around the Poston camp, she states in voice-over:

> I've been carrying around this picture with me for years. It's the one memory I have of my mother speaking of camp while I grew up. I over-hear her describing to my sister this simple action: her hands filling a canteen out in the middle of the desert. For years I've been living with this picture without the story, feeling a lot of pain, not knowing how they fit together. But now I've found I could connect the picture to the story. I could forgive my mother her loss of memory, and could make this image for her.

In her search for the record of her family and that of the Japanese-American community, Tajiri retrieves and reconstructs once lost memories, and in the process comes to understand her past and the collective past of generations of Japanese Americans. As the voice-over highlights, the tape becomes a gift for her mother and to herself in which the pain of a neglected past is assuaged. The video is also a documentation of Tajiri's realization of her sense of self in her identity as daughter and *sansei* (third-generation Japanese-American). In this way, Tajiri's tape is a document not of a fixed identity, but of an identity in process – Tajiri's cumulative and progressive working toward an understanding of the familial and collective past and 'who she is' in relation to this past. In doc-umenting this process the tape also documents the basis of autobi-ography – the *desire* to record identity. Alexandra Juhasz explains this formulation by noting that, 'The point is not that by shooting a video you lock yourself, your identity, into one place, but rather that you work on it, that you are self-consciously aware that there needs to be an identity there' (1999: 208).

## *Video Diaries*: problematizing self-authorship

In contrast to the complexity of the interaction of image and identity operating within the independently produced gallery-exhibited videotape *History and Memory*, television has traditionally offered few spaces for autobiographical work (Dovey, 2000: 110). Recent changes in technology, productive practices, and access to broadcasting have altered this situation to a degree, creating opportunities for an expansion of representations concerned with documenting aspects of self and identity. Specifically, increased access to television programming, coupled with the arrival in 1985 of cost-effective moving image technology in the form of the camcorder, have extended the intersection of image and identity on television through the broadcast of autobiographical work in the 'video diary' format.[4]

In the United States a number of such works have been broadcast within the Public Broadcasting Service series *POV* ('point of view'), a slot established for self-authored programmes which, as the title of the series suggests, are openly subjective. Works within this category are marked by the first person voice of the testimonial and the confessional modes in the form of the 'personal essay' documentary (Aufderheide, 2000: 215). First person video developed in the United States from a basis in social activism and investigation in which video was used as a tool to document social problems. *POV* was established to support work of this type, subsequently shifting its emphasis to the personal essay documentary, many of which examine pressing personal issues within the context of a focus on aspects of identity. *POV* documentaries have included *Silverlake Life: The View from Here* (1993), a video diary by Mark Massi and Tom Joslin dealing with their last days in their fight with AIDS, Alan Berlinger's *Nobody's Business* (1996), a portrait of his father, the third in his trilogy of family history, and *A Healthy Baby Girl* (1997) by Judith Helfand, an autobiographical account of cancer.

*POV* extended its commitment to first person documentary through the *ECU* ('extreme close up') project, which, in turn, developed into the PBS video diary series *Right Here, Right Now* (2000). The series provided non-professional videomakers access to the equipment and services needed to produce and broadcast their diaries. Prior to the series, access in the United States had primarily been a practice associated with cable television, particularly in the form of community-produced programming broadcast on local cable stations (Engelman, 1990; Blau, 1992; Kellner, 1992; Aufderheide, 2000). In both the PBS series and the example of community programming, 'access' implies a situation in which people previously excluded from media production obtain the means of producing their own media which, in a further way, present a diversity of views to that otherwise available in the dominant media.[5] In the case of *Right Here, Right Now* access to the relevant technology enabled the production and broadcast of a number of video diary records of various significant experiences, including teenage motherhood, coping with hearing loss and the experience of growing up in two cultures. The rise of interest in first person work was exemplified in 1993 when the publicly funded Independent Television Service, established by Congress in 1989 to promote diversity in public broadcasting programming, noted that proposals to produce personal essays made up the largest single category of submissions received by the service at that time (Aufderheide, 2000: 216).

In the United Kingdom, the BBC's Community Programmes Unit has provided a space for the exhibition of autobiographical work, notably in the form of video diaries broadcast within the *Video Diaries* series. First broadcast on BBC2 in April and May of 1990, the series proved enormously popular and led to another camcorder-based series *Teenage Diaries* (1992). The *Video Diaries* format has been emulated in other countries, including Australia's *First Person* series of autobiographical works, which was first broadcast in 1996. Among the programmes broadcast under this banner are *Killing Time*, one man's account of his 17 years (half his life) spent in jail, and *Body and Soul*, a record produced by Bernice, a transsexual living in rural Australia. The first two series of Britain's *Video Diaries* (the second series of 10 programmes was broadcast in 1991 and 1992) included among other works, photographer Jo Spence's record of her life with leukaemia; soccer fans travelling to Italy to attend a World Cup match; the life of a prisoner convicted of armed robbery and South African exiles returning to their homeland. Subsequent series were equally diverse, including the diaries of an Antarctic adventurer, a disabled Member of Parliament and a young musician suffering from Asperger's syndrome.

In each case the representation of an identity is, through the broadcast of the diary on national television, displayed before a wide audience. The irony of individual, private moments expressed nationally points to the way in which identity in the era of camcorder videos and broadcast television connects directly with the public collectivity that is the nation. This is not to argue, however, that the *Video Diaries* concept supports the thesis of the collapse of public and private spheres in the electronically mediated domain. The circulation of the diaries suggests, instead, the realization of an effective private sphere within the mediated domain that is the public sphere.

The intersection of private and public, individual and collective, associated with the *Video Diaries* series is also apparent in the further irony that these 'autobiographical', nominally self-authored works, are the result of a collective process of production. The production practices associated with the autobiographical mode in the era of access television underline the way in which *Video Diaries* problematizes basic notions of autobiography by raising questions concerning the degree of autonomy that diarists are able to command in the authorship in production of the works. Jeremy Gibson at the Community Programmes Unit alluded to the degree of professional intervention in the postproduction phase of a video diary when he commented that 'Your ego, and your attitude and approach can come across from the rushes in a very off-putting way that an outsider wouldn't like. It's our job to identify that and try and turn the diarist to take a less egocentric approach...' (quoted in Wayne, 1997: 65). Jon Dovey (1994: 165) highlights the place of the professional in the production process when he comments:

> Crucially, access programming is made under the editorial control of the accessee or author, who has the final say; not the producer, series editor, commissioning editor or any of the numerous supremos in the media hierarchy the programme-makers usually have to satisfy. For this power to be in any way meaningful, the authors should have control over the whole process of representation. In practice this is rarely possible...

As Dovey points out, each video diary is the result of collaboration between the amateur video diarist and various people possessing professional skills in video production. Peter Keighron (1993: 25) notes that professional input occurs throughout the production process of each video, particularly the editing stage, which is heavily informed by the technical assistance provided by the producers. The intervention by a professional broadcaster in the post-production process threatens in this case to erode the understanding that autobiographical works are self-authored. The video-maker's personal points of view are present in the final edited video, though the degree to which the work is the result of self-authorship is, arguably, compromised in the context of television.

Ironically, the 'anti-professional' or amateur quality of the video diaries compensates to a degree for any compromises to the authenticity of the works resulting from the involvement of professionals. Amateurism is encoded in a visual style which operates in association with the first person point of view to position a work as a self-produced, less manufactured, more truthful expression of the autobiographical impulse. The visual language of authenticity is articulated within effects which bear the traces of amateurism, including low resolution shots, images in which the subject may appear off-centre, variations in lighting, imbalances in sound levels, voices from behind the camera heard on the soundtrack, a narration composed of on-the-spot reactions spoken on camera by the diarist, and editorial cuts produced in camera which do not necessarily align scenes. Such a language has, as Patricia Zimmermann (1995) has pointed out, traditionally been associated with the self-produced low-resolution home movie/video that in its virtually exclusive focus on familial relations, establishes and reinforces a connection between amateur video and subjectivity. In this way, questions concerning the degree of self-authorship in the works screened in the *Video Diaries* series are displaced by the host of meanings attached to the term 'amateur video' and its associated visual style which functions to legitimate and authenticate the autobiographical, subjective, component of the works.

## *Video Fool for Love*: the visual language of camcorder autobiography

The visual styles expressed within the *Video Diaries* series contribute to a certain recognizable language within the camcorder diary format which is now deployed in a variety of contexts to signal authenticity and the personal mode. One of the more significant contributions to the mode is the feature length *Video Fool for Love*, a camcorder diary kept by Robert Gibson, a professional film editor living in Sydney. *Video Fool for Love* (1995) is reminiscent of McElwee's *Sherman's March* in its self-portrait of the romantic entanglements undertaken by a self-described 'serial monogamist'. Gibson, though, is more explicit (and narcissistic) in his self-revelations and confessions than McElwee, including in his tape, for example, a scene in which he proposes marriage sitting naked in a bath, and a segment in which he talks to camera as he enters an operating theatre to have his vasectomy reversed.

Gibson's willingness to document the most intimate aspects of his life approximates Dennis O'Rourke's similar act of excessive self-exposure in his film *The Good Woman of Bangkok* (1992). O'Rourke's controversial autobiography depicts his act of purchasing the services of a Thai prostitute, Aoi, whom he films during their months together. In many of the sequences involving Aoi, O'Rourke is also positioned in frame, the dual subject of the film. Nearly a third of the shots of Aoi are made as Aoi, seated, speaks into a mirror which reflects O'Rourke standing behind her filming the scene. The method constantly positions O'Rourke as the authoring presence who structures and manipulates the representation. O'Rourke acknowledged his degree of intervention in the structuring process of the film when he called his film a 'documentary fiction film', one which relies on certain techniques of the traditional documentary but which, as O'Rourke puts it 'nevertheless, clearly asserts its own aesthetic – one which is recognisable as being related to the fiction film' (O'Rourke, 1997: 212).

In a similar way, the appearance of 'spontaneous' moments and a life that is messy, even chaotic, is achieved within Gibson's film through a tightly structured narrative that bears elements of the fictive. Unlike 'slice of life' video diaries, Gibson's film recounts a story, replete with characterization, causation and plot. At the beginning of the film Gibson is in love with the impetuous April, whom he films – as with all those who enter his life – relentlessly. Their relationship is one of emotional outbursts followed by lengthy sulky silences. This pattern of behaviour is an intimation of what follows: April leaves Gibson, travelling to London to be with friends. Two days after April's departure, Gibson falls in love with Gianna, though he soon follows April to London and proposes to marry her. When April travels to Europe, Gibson returns to Sydney and Gianna moves in with him. Having discovered the situation, April plans to disrupt the romance. Gibson evokes April's destructive wrath through television footage of the Gulf War, then in progress, and symbolizes April's attack in the form of Scud missiles striking Iraqi targets. To defend themselves from April's vengeful onslaught, Gibson and Gianna decide to marry – as Gibson documents what becomes an increasingly troubled and disintegrating relationship with Gianna. The film ends with Gibson finding a new lover, Cindy.

Gibson fills his romantic narrative with particular 'characters'; his voice-over comments describe Gianna as his 'holy grail', Caterina, Gianna's friend whom he suspects of plotting against him is the 'black witch', and his new lover Cindy is his 'guardian angel'. Despite Gibson's reductive verbal identifications, the images reveal identities which overflow any strict categorization. In an astute reading of Gibson's film, Jon Dovey (2000: 74) outlines

the dimensions of various identities defined in and through relations with others present within the work when he states:

> within the terms of his own fabulous narcissism, [Gibson] presents
> himself as *at once* loving, arrogant, romantic, sexist, duplicitous, vulner-
> able, idiotic, addicted, confused, jealous, violent, conciliatory,
> happy … As to the other main characters in the film, April and Gianna,
> they again are portrayed in a constant state of flux: nobody stays the
> same, feelings change … The film offers a view of the subject that is at
> once emotive and sentimental in the necessary manner of the 'human
> interest' story, but which, in contrast to the conventional genre, refuses
> to offer the comfort of unified, coherent accounts of subject identity.
> The typical video diarist is messy, contradictory, difficult, opinionated,
> narcissistic *with* a good story to tell.

The mutable and contradictory identities represented in *Video
Fool for Love* reflect what Dovey nominates as the film's central
feature, its 'formal fluidity' (2000: 73). This feature is evident in
the way Gibson treats his footage as completely malleable, to be cut
and re-cut, and inserted in different scenes, or used in an associative way to construct and complete a scene. The latter method is
exemplified in a scene in which Gianna and Gibson talk of the
night they visited the tally room during a national election. Gibson
then 'flashes back' to the incident by cutting to footage they both
filmed that night. Though released in 1995, Gibson's diary is composed of taped footage shot from 1983 onwards. As such, the diary
contains segments of varying image and sound quality, each segment reinforcing the passage of time (a central feature of a diary)
and Gibson's changing personal experiences.

The fluidity with which the footage is treated is extended
through the camcorder's portability – a camera that can be
handed from one person to the next – resulting in images shot by
Gibson and images of Gibson shot by others, a mark of difference
between a camcorder video work and the less portable and less
user-friendly film camera. Gibson also holds the camcorder at
arm's length to film himself in close-up, a popular characteristic
technique in the video diary format. Dovey notes that the shot
creates 'high levels of identification with the film-maker. Aiming
the camera at yourself, using your own body to record your own
body, you, the diarist, whisper into the lens.' The effect is a different form of connection with the viewer than that achievable in
traditional representational techniques: in the shot's 'separation

of foreground and background I am given to understand that as an individual viewer I have been chosen for privileged information which the rest of the scene is not party to. I am being brought much closer, intimately closer, to the diarist and his or particular subjective experience' (Dovey, 2000: 72–3).

While *Sherman's March*, a work which inaugurated many of the techniques adopted by Gibson, includes a number of scenes in which McElwee, sitting alone late at night, talks directly to the camera, such scenes are statically arranged and bespeak a certain amount of preplanning. In these ways McElwee's to-camera dialogues resemble the 'talking heads' mode of expository documentary (albeit that McElwee is, in each case, speaking in a low whisper). Gibson's to-camera pieces, in contrast, spontaneously capture various moments (as when he films himself on a hospital trolley awaiting his vasectomy reversal operation), replete with ambient sounds and background action. The effect intensifies viewer identification with the diarist, and opens the diary up to otherwise unrecorded and unrecordable thoughts, contextual details and effects. Drawing on such techniques, Dovey (2000: 76) points to a number of significant qualities of *Video Fool for Love* which, he argues, mark it as a paradigm of the first-person-based camcorder documentary form: its focus on individual relations in domestic settings; a form of self-reflexivity focused on the work's authenticity (a process exemplified in Gibson's self-conscious comment to Gianna in his film, 'I'm trying to turn us into a media event'); and the shocking effects achieved through a voyeuristic and unrestrained self-exposure.

In these ways, the paradigmatic features of the camcorder diary displayed in Gibson's work, and the visual language in which they are expressed, suggest an emergent 'grammar' of the expanding diaristic mode (Dovey, 2000: 71). The grammar of the video diary, coupled with the range of forms and practices displayed in the work of McElwee and Tajiri, constitute a set of formal features and productive practices which begin to situate first-person records of identity as a central form within the established field of documentary film, video and television. From this position, autobiographical documentary examines a range of subjective issues within the field of what are, otherwise, the objective concerns which conventionally occupy documentary representations. As such, autobiographical documentary reflects the rise of 'the personal' to a place of prominence in contemporary social life, a situation which, in turn, points to the continued expansion of autobiographical forms.

## CHAPTER 7

# Finding and Keeping: Compilation Documentary

The compilation filmmaker is a collector and an editor who creates an object – a film or television programme – from a variety of so-called found footage. Footage that can serve as the basis of the compilation film includes, among other sources, newsreels, television programmes, government produced films, instructional films, home movies and fiction films. From among these diverse sources the compilation filmmaker constructs a work that in its 'pure' form is composed entirely of archival footage, devoid of interviews and voice-over narration. The pure form of compilation film has been encoded in definitions such as: 'the compilation film is a documentary made solely from already existing footage. The filmmaker may never use the camera, functioning primarily as an editor, presenting and analysing new footage (made by others for other purposes) through juxtaposition and ordering of material in the editing process' (Sobchack and Sobchack, 1987: 355). This definition, with its emphasis on a film constructed solely from existing sources, reflects the approach to compilation film taken by film historian Jay Leyda (1964) in one of the few book-length studies of the form in which he characterized the process of compilation as one in which 'films beget films'. Though many definitions foreground 'pure' works which contain only archival footage as the pre-eminent form of compilation, found or archival footage has been recycled in other compilation works. Notably, the interweaving of archival footage with interview footage and a voice-over narration is a common feature of contemporary compilation forms on television.

Speaking of the abundance of images in the mass-mediated world of the late twentieth century, one observer has commented 'that the job of future documenters may be more in the nature of editing than of creating' (Court, 1995: 58). The observation points to compilation film, and its practices of editing pre-existing footage. In another way, the comment assumes that the multitude of images circulating in the 'image domain' is readily accessible and available to the compilation filmmaker. This is not always the case; compilation films are produced within a context that involves issues of availability of, and access to, source footage. This context informs compilation filmmaking in various direct ways, not the least by determining which topics will be covered and how they are treated. In the absence of relevant footage to illustrate a subject important topics may go unaddressed or, alternatively, a lack of necessary footage has led to an increasing reliance on generic shots – footage which symbolically connotes a referent (this process is discussed below).

The availability of footage and access to footage impact on the compilation filmmaking process in further ways. For example, the makers of the compilation film *The Atomic Café*, a witty recoding of US government footage dealing with Cold War fears of nuclear attack, faced the problem of an abundance of footage on the topic. To produce *The Atomic Café* the filmmakers screened an estimated 10 000 films and had an editing ratio for the footage they purchased of 200 to one (one foot of film was used for every 200 feet of footage purchased). The compilation filmmaker Emile de Antonio faced problems of access to footage in the production of his compilation history of the Vietnam War, *In the Year of the Pig*. Much of the footage de Antonio required for his film was held in French military archives and de Antonio (quoted in Crowdus and Georgakas, 1988: 166–7) admits to one of the more extreme measures he took to 'obtain' relevant footage from the strictly controlled military source:

> I … got access to the French army's film library, the greatest collection of Vietnam footage that exists – it goes back to 1902 … There's this beautiful shot in *Pig* of something you can't get in [the US]. It's Ho Chi Minh with Admiral d'Argenlieu, the French commissioner of Vietnam, aboard the battlecruiser *Richelieu*. It's … a really symbolic scene, because [in the midst of Vietnam's anticolonial war with the French] … Ho leaves the ship, with the French saluting, [and] takes a

cigarette out of his mouth and, in that casual way of his, flips it over the side. I had to have that shot, so I said to [a French sergeant assigned to supervise de Antonio in the archive], 'Listen, I'm going to steal this. Would you mind going out, because I don't want you to be implicated in all this.' So I just cut that shot out of the roll of 35 mm negative and stuck it in the pocket of my raincoat. I realized that since they knew who I was now, there was a good chance that the guys with the guns at the gate would stop me, and I could have gotten five years for that in France, but I thought it was worth it. Making films is risk taking.

The presence of increasing restrictions imposed by the provisions of global copyright laws placed on access to images have led to other, more sustained versions of image pilfering. So-called culture jamming compilation filmmakers confront the problem of access to and control of images through practices of image piracy purposefully designed to draw attention to the increasing commercialization of the image domain. Availability and accessibility, then, involve a range of practices in the production process of compilation films beyond that of editing. These practices include, as the examples here suggest, the thorough reviewing of archival sources (such as those maintained by government and scientific bodies, television stations and film studios and commercial 'stock footage' collections), the cost of purchase from stock footage collections, other methods of obtaining relevant footage and the risk of prosecution under national and international copyright laws associated with the re-use of appropriated footage. To paraphrase de Antonio, making compilation films is an intricate, frequently expensive and risky business which belies the suggestion of serendipity implied by the term 'found footage'. Within the context of issues of availability of, and access to, recyclable footage, this chapter examines formal features of selected compilation films as they are rallied in the construction of historical interpretations and argumentation. The chapter focuses on the works mentioned above: Emile de Antonio's *In the Year of the Pig* (1969), a mixture of archival footage and interviews, and the 'pure' compilation film *The Atomic Café* (1982), and works produced through the practices of image piracy. The compilation works addressed here do not deploy source footage merely to complement an historical thesis, rather they apply source footage within the construction of new histories. The differing approaches to the use of archival source footage are set out in the following section.

## Uses of archival footage

Early historical television documentaries often relied on the denotative function of source footage to reinforce the exposition established in a voice-over or to complement comments made by witnesses or experts. Examples of the practice include the National Broadcasting Company's (NBC) television series *Victory at Sea* (1952–53), a 26-part history of naval combat during the Second World War, which deployed war footage in support of points made in the voice-over. Columbia Broadcasting System's (CBS) *The Twentieth Century* (1957–64) and NBC's *Project XX* or Project 20 (1954–74) series of special presentations adopted the approach in their respective examinations of aspects of the history of the twentieth century. In addition to the accuracy of a representation – its verifiable relationship to the narrated events – a variety of criteria govern the selection of footage to be included as illustration, including the matching of lighting, and alignment of movement in the frame (narrative drive is reinforced by action moving in the same direction in each frame; troops moving left to ride in one frame, for example, and right to left in the next disrupts such movement). The clarity of the image may be another factor in selection. Damaged, scratched or water-marked film evokes a degree of historical authenticity in the suggestion that the film survived the vicissitudes of the era it represents. The markers of authenticity are enhanced by the use of black and white footage as opposed to colour footage (Sandusky, 1992: 12–13).

Working with these criteria, footage is edited into a pattern of voices and images in a film or programme to construct a thesis or in support of a pre-existing thesis about the socio-historical world. In those cases where appropriate footage cannot be found, the thesis may be altered or, as noted in the introduction to this chapter, aspects of an argument are left unaddressed. In this way, Jerry Kuehl, producer of Thames Television's *World at War* (1974) series acknowledged historical omissions in the programme's coverage of the rise of the Third Reich:

> relations between Church and State were very important to the leaders of the Third Reich, and, it goes without saying, to ordinary Germans too. But very little film was ever made which even showed National Socialist leaders and churchmen together, let alone doing anything significant. So considerations of Church and State were virtually omitted from our films on Nazi Germany....(quoted in McArthur, 1980: 14)

As Kuehl's comment reveals, the producers worked with a historical thesis ('relations between Church and State were very important to the leaders of the Third Reich') and sought footage to
support the thesis. In this case, a conventional historical argument
is constructed and confirmed as the outline of a programme or
series which is supported and reinforced by available footage.

Archival footage is not always deployed in this way. Source
footage has also been used to foreground historical contradictions
through which new or unprecedented historical arguments
emerge. Within the so-called expressive or critical use of archival
footage (Arthur, 1999–2000: 64; Bruzzi, 2000: 22), unmatched
images are counterposed to create new meanings. The method
relies on the denotative function of the images, the meanings of
which are, however, critically reworked within their oppositional
reframing. This method, the basis of the compilation films studied
in this chapter, was pioneered in the 1920s by the Soviet filmmakers Dziga Vertov and Esther (Esfir) Shub in works intended to be
both instructive and agitational.

Shub's film *The Fall of the Romanov Dynasty* (1927), a work produced to mark the tenth anniversary of the overthrow of the
Russian imperial family, demonstrates the method within its innovative deployment of source footage, among which includes the
home movies of Nicholas II. From what was largely pro-Czarist
footage, Shub constructed a pro-Bolshevik narrative critical of the
decadent excesses of the Czars. The operative principle of Shub's
editorial technique was juxtaposition. Working with the found
footage Shub juxtaposed images to 'achieve effects of irony, absurdity, pathos and grandeur', as film historian Jay Leyda notes (in
Bruzzi, 2000: 22). The juxtapositions operate in association with
intertitles to produce what Eisenstein referred to as a 'montage of
collision' – the editing of dissimilar images to produce new, unan-
ticipated meanings (as discussed in Chapter 2). In one sequence in
*The Fall of the Romanov Dynasty*, for example, Shub cleverly juxtaposes footage of members of the Russian court dancing on board a
pleasure cruise ship with images of peasants working in fields to
produce ironic effects. The contrast of images is reinforced in the
intertitles which introduce the dance by stating: 'Their Honours
Were Pleased to Dance with Their Highnesses.' The footage of the
shipboard dance is interrupted by the intertitle 'Until They
Perspired'. At the end of the dance the women wipe sweat from
their faces and Shub cuts to footage of peasants digging a ditch,

one of whom scratches himself in a visual echo of the dancers' gestures (Winston, 1995: 167).

Brian Winston has pointed out (1995: 167) that Shub was also able to transform a whole event through the application of an intertitle: across a religious ceremonial parade Shub included the words 'The Priests' Moscow', thereby reframing the ceremony as evidence of collusion between the Church and the Czarist regime. Shub admitted the historical specificity of the source footage, not necessarily seeking to match lighting textures or movement in the frame. In the case of *The Fall of the Romanov Dynasty*, differences in technical standards between the home movie footage and the other footage included in the work draw attention to the home footage and the fact that few people in Russia at the time, other than the excessively rich, could afford to operate moving image technology. *The Fall of the Romanov Dynasty* pays close attention to the content of the images, not expressly to unearth previously hidden historical details, but to locate images that could be used to analyse and critique conditions from a revolutionary (in both meanings of the term: innovative and Bolshevik) point of view. Using unstructured 'bits of reality' (Leyda, 1983: 224) the juxtapositional technique produces a new, structured work which attains documentary status in its critique and analysis of historical conditions. Shub wrote in her autobiography that:

> The intention was not to provide the facts but to evaluate them from the vantage point of the revolutionary class. This is what made my films revolutionary and agitational – although they were composed of counter-revolutionary material … Each of my compilation films was also a form of agitation for the new concept of documentary cinema, a statement about unstaged film as the most important cinematic form of the present day. (quoted in Winston, 1995: 167)

The concept of documentary as an 'unstaged film' clearly set Shub apart from her contemporary Flaherty and his dedication to extended reconstruction. Shub's revolutionary cinema was also at variance with Flaherty's romantic individualism and its legacy to Western documentary filmmaking. Winston (1995: 168) interprets Shub's legacy not only in terms of her contribution to the development of compilation film, but also through reference to her position as a role model for politically engaged filmmakers. Both legacies coalesce in the figure of the politically motivated compilation filmmaker Emile de Antonio.[1]

## *In the Year of the Pig*: 'radical scavenging' and radical history

Emile de Antonio (1918–89) produced a number of films concerned with events within US history. His compilation films include among others *Point of Order* (1964), which utilizes television footage to examine the McCarthy hearings of the late 1950s, *America is Hard to See* (1971), de Antonio's most conventional compilation work, which examines Senator Eugene McCarthy's unsuccessful bid for the 1968 Democratic presidential nomination, *Millhouse: A White Comedy* (1971), a scathing satirical analysis of the political career of Richard Nixon, and *In the Year of the Pig*, an interpretation of the Vietnam War from French colonial rule through US invasion of the country, to the Tet offensive of 1968. In the latter work, de Antonio was not concerned with representing the war; his intention in the film was to examine the causes and effects of US involvement in the war.

A number of television documentaries had dealt with the war in ways which failed to achieve the type of analysis de Antonio sought to undertake. The television special *Christmas in Vietnam* (CBS, 1965) and the films *The Anderson Platoon* (1966–67) and *A Face of War* (1968) focused on the actions of individual US soldiers in the war, an approach that has been endlessly replicated in the stream of US fiction films dealing with the Vietnam War. Within this representational focus, the US soldier (GI) is positioned as the principal, if not exclusive, agent of political interpretation and historical understanding. '[The US soldier's] experience of the war, always weightier and more authoritative than ours and circumscribing any experience we can have', notes film scholar David James, 'is proposed [in these representations] as the moment of authenticity and knowledge … upon which the war can be evaluated and validated' (1989: 198). The focus limits analysis of the war to the level of personal knowledge, thus restricting broad analysis of topics such as the reasons why the United States was involved in Vietnam and the political effects of the war on the Vietnamese. The documentary *Why Vietnam?* (1965), produced by the US State Department (the title an echo of the Pentagon's Second World War *Why We Fight* series) presented US involvement in Vietnam from a standpoint of official US policy toward the war. Upholding the debatable claim that the United States was drawn into the war after its warships were attacked in the Gulf of Tonkin, the film repeats the arguments made by President Johnson that the United States was involved in the war to assist 'a free people defend their sovereignty' against Ho Chi Minh's 'reign of terror' (James, 1989: 202). The absence of analysis of the issues and events asserted in the film denied an informed historical understanding of the war. De Antonio, however, held television news most accountable for its absence of interpretive critique of the conflict:

> There is nothing as bad that's happened concerning the war as the networks' coverage of it, because it seems as if they're covering the war whereas in fact they're not. The networks have made the American people comfortable with the war – because it appears between commercials. There's never the question asked, 'Why are we doing this? What is this war about?' It's never suggested by anything that occurs on television that we should even be interested in that type of question. Television is a way of avoiding coming to terms with the fact that we're in this war. (quoted in Waugh, 1985: 251)

*In the Year of the Pig* functions to readdress television's lack of analytical coverage of the war and, unlike *Why Vietnam?*, and its unified and univocal history structured around the notion of US 'liberation' of Vietnam, de Antonio's film constructs a provocative history of the US invasion of Vietnam from multiple and competing discourses (James, 1989: 206). The film's visual images were assembled from extensive searches of various sources in a process of what de Antonio referred to as 'radical scavenging' (quoted in Weiner, 1971). Images were obtained from archives in East Germany, Hanoi, the offices of the Vietnamese National Liberation Front in Prague, the archives of United States and British television companies, notably the ABC and the BBC, and other sources, including the French army, the offices of United Press International, and newsreel footage shot by the film company Paramount. De Antonio weaves interviews he conducted with a number of contemporary figures with archival footage in which politicians and others comment on the war. The assembled collage of voices includes observations by, among others, Ho Chi Minh, Lyndon Johnson, Robert McNamara, Daniel Berrigan, Generals Paul Le May and William Westmoreland, US scholars Paul Mus and David Halberstam and French scholars Jean Lacouture, author of a biography of Ho Chi Minh, and Phillippe Devilliers, the editor of an academic journal devoted to the study of southeast Asia. The film adds to the auditory register of spoken comments through various musical and sonic overlays. In this way, for example, a US Department of Defense film, 'Communist Guerrilla Becomes U.S Ally' is accompanied by an excerpt from a Mahler symphony. The soundtrack also features several tunes played on traditional Vietnamese folk instruments, which are used in one scene, ironically, to perform a version of 'The Marseillaise' over images of French military defeat at Dien Bien Phu.

The complexity of the interrelationship of the film's visual and auditory discourses is exemplified in the film's opening sequence. Seemingly chaotic images and non-synchronous sounds become, within de Antonio's approach, powerful pieces of evidence of the methods employed by the United States in the conduct of the war. Within the opening segment de Antonio links Vietnam to other American wars and in the process criticizes attempts to justify and legitimate the war in Vietnam through such comparisons. References to the Civil War, located in the opening image of the soldier from that conflict and in a subsequent image of a Civil War memorial, are interspersed with words from the Revolutionary War: 'When I heard of the revolution, my heart was enlisted.' Such allusions to 'honourable' wars are accompanied by references, contained in a series of images, to the inordinate violence involved in pursuing the war in Vietnam: a still image of a GI's helmet inscribed 'make war not love', images of scared Vietnamese fleeing a destroyed village, footage of a monk who has set himself alight to protest the war, and a still image of a soldier loading a helicopter gunship with shells, his body almost completely obscured by the ammunition. Accompanying the visual images is the sound of helicopters – a sound popularly associated with the Vietnam War and one that is used in the film as an aural motif – that suggests the auditory overload of the war itself and the 'noise' of verbal commentary associated with the war, examples of which are incorporated in the film in the form of comments by US Vice President Hubert Humphrey and President Lyndon Johnson. Coming as they do after images of the violence suffered in the conflict by the Vietnamese, statements about the United States as peacemaker (Humphrey) and the ethnocentric focus on an America which punishes itself with self-criticism (Johnson) are particularly offensive.

After the introductory montage the film turns to an analysis of French occupation of Vietnam. Pre-Second World War footage shows French colonialists abusing rickshaw drivers, a scene which de Antonio described as 'the equivalent of a couple of chapters of dense writing about the meaning of colonialism' (in Lewis, 2000: 99). The history of the Vietnamese struggle continues in the following scenes in which de Antonio outlines the rise of Vietnamese nationalism under Ho Chi Minh, and the French re-occupation of Vietnam after Japanese control during the Second World War. The end of French rule is signified in footage from a Soviet reenactment of the Vietnamese victory at Dien Bien Phu.

The following sequences examine US support for South Vietnamese president Ngo Dinh Diem amid evidence of the corruption of the Diem regime. American policy-makers discuss full scale US military involvement in the Vietnamese war amid an analysis of events in the Gulf of Tonkin. The next section examines the US military conflict in Vietnam, focusing on the war in the countryside and the (racist) impressions of US soldiers and generals of their adversary. De Antonio contrasts these estimations of the enemy with images of the US ally, South Vietnamese premier Nguyen Cao Ky, and his authoritarian rule. The final sequence contains a number of comments on the war by US observers, among them the journalist Harrison Salisbury of the *New York Times*, who describes the effects of US bombing on North Vietnam. The last words in the film are by the scholar Paul Mus, whose comments are directed at the American audience for the film: 'You are not the first people who destroyed villages in Vietnam, unfortunately. And so, they are used to that, and it's a great tradition that the village is not lost even when it disappears from the surface of the ground.' The observation intimates that Vietnamese fortitude and perseverance will outweigh America's military power, a suggestion extended in an image in the closing montage sequence of wounded American soldiers in Vietnam awaiting evacuation. The final sequence includes the same image of a Civil War statue of the young man who died at Gettysburg featured in the beginning of the film, here used in negative. Through a reversal of the image de Antonio sought to subtly evoke the notion that Vietnam was the reversal of the Civil War, 'that our cause in Vietnam was not the one that boy had died for in 1863' (in Crowdus and Georgakas, 1988: 168).

De Antonio readily acknowledged that his work is opinionated: 'I happen to have strong feelings … and my prejudice is under everything I do' (in Rosenthal, 1980: 211). His open abandonment of the presumption of objectivity was mirrored in his condemnation of the seemingly neutral and objective stance of direct cinema, a style which he called a 'joke' and a 'lie' for its refusal to make manifest its inherent 'prejudices' (in Rosenthal, 1980: 211). He argued that his approach, in contrast, was one of 'democratic didacticism', a method which presents aspects of an argument while constructing a conclusion which is ineluctable (in Waugh, 1985: 244). By acknowledging his didacticism de Antonio sought to diffuse the negative connotations of the term while reworking the position in ways which, he argued, do not condescend to his audience. De Antonio (in Waugh, 1985: 244–5) expanded on his method by stating that:

> I have been a teacher. My work is didactic ... I only want to think that [*In the Year of the Pig*] is more complicated, has more levels of meaning than there are in a slogan or in a purely didactic message. I don't believe that such a message has any more sense than to shout in the street 'Down with war!' ... The goal of a truly didactic work is to go beyond that and to suggest the 'why'. I like to describe my own feelings as democratic with a small *d*, which means that if you don't want to teach things to people but to reveal things to them, you will permit them then to arrive at the same conclusion as yourself. That's a democratic didacticism, without having to say 'firstly, secondly, thirdly'. And that's why I insist on the word 'reveal'.

De Antonio's 'democratic didacticism' is, in this way, democratic in the sense that the viewer is asked to interpret information without reference to explanations imposed in a voice-over. De Antonio argued against what he interpreted as the manipulative and 'fascist' technique of voice-over:

> I've always thought that it's wrong to explain things to audiences. The material is there, and interpretations can be made. I mean, I could have stopped the film and inserted outside explanations, but I'm really not terribly interested in that. I disagree with that approach from every point of view aesthetically and even politically. I think it's a mistake to show everything. (in Waugh, 1985: 244)

The film scholar Thomas Waugh has called the verbal the 'dominant logic of the de Antonio film'. The depth of content provided through the interviews in de Antonio's film contrasts with the often facile and brief interviews of television journalism and avoids the reign of personal reminiscence that stands in for historical analysis in many interview-based reports (Waugh, 1985: 249). Whereas, commonly, archival images are sequentially ordered by a

voice-over narration, in de Antonio's film comments by an interviewee establish a contrapuntal and critical relationship with the
images, judging and recoding them (Waugh, 1985: 249). De
Antonio acknowledged that spoken comments form the basis of
the film around and against which he organized archival images:
'Words are very important in [*In the Year of the Pig*] and all of my
work, that's how I do the editing: I start with the transcription of
the soundtrack and put all those pages up on the walls of the big
editing rooms where I work and begin to assemble the pages
before the film: that's how the structure begins' (in Waugh, 1985:
249). This methodology differs from a strict adherence to a pre-
planned script and a ready-made thesis to which the documents
must conform.

Attention to the word does not, however, result in an uncritical
acceptance of the opinions of interviewees. Comments by individuals are juxtaposed in ways which call into question the perceptions and claims of different commentators. It is a strategy which
reveals that no one witness holds the definitive interpretation of
events. Within this strategy the film 'cross-examines' interviewees
within a process in which the verbal statements made by one commentator are juxtaposed with the observations of another interviewee. The process is exemplified in interviews relating to the Gulf
of Tonkin incident. Statements by the United States Secretary of
Defense, Robert McNamara, that the US warship Maddox
returned fire only when attacked by North Vietnamese patrol
boats are contested by testimony given by a sailor from the Maddox
who denies that the North Vietnamese attacks took place. The
process of 'questioning' is extended in those places within the film
in which images are used as evidence to undercut the veracity of
verbal statements. In one scene, for example, the claim by US Vice
President Hubert Humphrey that Communist prisoners are not
being ill-treated is juxtaposed with images of a captive Vietnamese
man being kicked and beaten.

Elsewhere the film enters a complex process of exposing the evidential inadequacies of both film footage and verbal comments.
The process is exemplified in the film's attitude to Ho Chi Minh,
who in many ways occupies the ideological and emotive centre of
the film. While the visual and the verbal domains coalesce in a
hagiographic representation of Ho, at the same time such modes
of representation are revealed as incapable of fully realizing the
North Vietnamese leader. Throughout the film Ho remains silent.

In a sequence near the beginning of the film Ho's words emanate, in a form of ventriloquism, from Paul Mus. It is part of de Antonio's approach that Ho remains an enigma, a historical figure who cannot be contained by characterizations achievable via archival film and contemporary interviews.

Through various means, then, the film's interrogative process results in the destabilization of the evidentiary status of both verbal comments and visual images. History, as a stable interpretation of past events, is not located in either the verbal or visual realms of de Antonio's film, but in the dialectical relationship of the verbal and visual operating in the film as a whole. De Antonio's method – one which forms the practical basis of a fully realized compilation film practice – exceeds both the juxtaposition of archival images and the counterpointing of testimony and images. Within de Antonio's film the illustrative and evidentiary capacities of multiple images and sounds are questioned and reworked to produce a history which contests the official record of US involvement in the war encoded in many of the sources that de Antonio criticizes, recontextualizes and recodes.

## Re-presenting history: *The Atomic Café*

De Antonio's criticisms of direct cinema as a 'lie' and a 'joke' that hides its own prejudices behind a veneer of objectivity were extended in other filmmaking and critical quarters. According to certain criticisms, observational filmmaking failed to engage history adequately.[2] Following de Antonio's lead, many filmmakers in the 1970s and 1980s relied on archival footage and direct address by interviewing subjects as a method of retrieving historical experiences denied within observational representation. In works such as *Union Maids* (1976), *With Babies and Banners* (1978), *The Wobblies* (1979), *The Good Fight* (1984) and *Seeing Red: Portraits of American Communists* (1984), archival footage is used in association with verbal testimony to retrieve suppressed or submerged histories of labour struggle and Left experiences.[3] The deployment of archival footage in this way runs contrary to its popular usage in support of mainstream or dominant interpretations of the past. In the case of histories such as *Union Maids* and *With Babies and Banners*, with their focus on women's labour struggle, the method employed resulted in a major shift in historical representation. 'Writing women into "history"', as Judith Newton has observed, meant that 'traditional definitions of "history" would have to change' (1988: 100). Traditional constructions of history as a teleological narrative involving the exploits of 'Great Men' was reconceptualized in these films in a 'history from below' focused on the struggles of women and people of colour. The method involved a critical interrogation of official records encoding a dominant history and a turn to oral testimony and recreations of women's experiences routinely excluded from mainstream historical narratives.

Such an approach is rigorously applied in Connie Field's *The Life and Times of Rosie the Riveter* (1980), a history of women workers in heavy industry during the Second World War. The work contrasts the 'official' or mainstream record of the past located in archival footage with evidence provided in the oral testimony of five women who worked in various heavy industries in the early to mid-1940s. The title of the film refers to a wartime illustration by the artist Norman Rockwell for the cover of the popular *Saturday Evening Post* for 29 May 1943 which depicts a woman holding a rivet gun while eating a sandwich from a lunch box inscribed with the name 'Rosie'. The illustration and a popular song of the period about 'Rosie' became representative of women in the US workforce during the latter years of the Second World War. Interviews in Field's film with five women construct biographies of their lives prior to the war and the prejudicial attitudes they encountered in their wartime occupations. The film's various sources, among them newspaper headlines, popular songs and, principally, the oral testimony of the five women, contain what Foucault (1996: 122–32) called in a different context the 'popular memory' of an era which is frequently denied within a focus on 'official' sources of historical knowledge such as census statistics, bureaucratic reports and, in this case, government produced 'informational' films.

Field's film abandons voice-over narration and relies on extensive interviews with the selected subjects together with archival footage culled from government films to complicate history and to question the notion that events can be contained in a univocal narrative. The two discourses – archival footage and oral testimony – speak of the events within a process in which the two sources are contrasted and counterpointed. The women's experiences of sexist and racist discrimination are recounted in interviews which form the film's central discursive focus against which the archival footage is situated as propagandistic and mendacious. *Rosie the*

*Riveter* problematizes the notion of evidence through the inclusion of testimony which contests the denotative status of the footage. Within the contrast of image and voice, archival footage is profitably included as evidence not of the experience of working women during the Second World War but as a reflection and register of an 'official' history and its ideological record of the times.

*The Life and Times of Rosie the Riveter* does not, interestingly, uniformly contrast archival footage and oral testimony. While the government propaganda footage is consistently undercut by the women's testimony, newsreel footage is presented in a positive and productive way to provide a visual accompaniment to the women's reminiscences. John Corner, in his discussion of the different ways in which the official images are deployed in the film, points out the inadvertent comic force of much of the propaganda footage and the inconsistency of the arguments that it attempts to maintain (1996: 137). The film's use of newsreel footage raises a different set of issues. The newsreel footage is not relied on as illustration; it does not directly signify the specific conditions described in the testimony. Rather, the newsreel footage is used descriptively, evoking general features of wartime conditions to accompany the women's comments. In this way, the archival footage functions to provide a set of images that suggest certain social conditions.

A version of the practice of incorporating images which function descriptively occurs in those cases in which there is no footage available to illustrate an event. In such situations so-called generic shots are used to re-create historical conditions. Generic shots are those which approximate or symbolically represent experiences. Film historian Paul Arthur (1999–2000: 65) illustrates the use of generic shots through reference to *Union Maids* (1976), a history of women in the labour movement constructed from archival footage and oral testimony. In the example quoted by Arthur, a witness to a Depression-era strike describes the arrival of armed police called to dispel a labour protest, and mentions that one of the policemen carried a sawed-off shotgun. To satisfy the demands of visual illustration of the speaker's testimony a generic shot is used of a policeman at a protest. However, Arthur points to a problem with the use of this particular image. Reading the image very carefully he notes that the policeman is carrying a tear gas gun and canisters, not a shotgun as stated by the witness.

According to Arthur, the contradiction amounts to a fabrication that blocks or revises the use of found footage as evidence (Arthur,

1999–2000: 66). The argument is extended in other cases involving generic shots. In *War Stories* (1995), for example, a documentary dealing with the role of New Zealand women in the Second World War, the director, Gaylene Preston, illustrates one woman's reminiscences through use of black and white footage of a jeep on a beach. Preston shot the footage, as she readily acknowledges, in colour for another film and recycled it in *War Stories* (Beattie, 1996: 8). Based on the example from *Union Maids*, Arthur (1999–2000: 66) argues, in a conclusion that implicates the practices of *War Stories*, that the 'guarantees of authenticity ostensibly secured by archival footage are largely a myth'. Arthur's conclusion, not inconsiderably, points to a crisis of representation in which, effectively, archival footage is stripped of any evidentiary function. Arthur here usefully highlights the ways in which meanings can be constructed through the use of footage that is of a discursively different order to the associative footage, though overstates his case that such practices subvert an entire tradition of documentary compilation. While raising questions related to particular uses of footage the practices do not in themselves destroy the documentary compact and traditions which reinforce the provenance of archival footage. (A more resolute and sustained assault on the referentiality of the image and questions of provenance occurs in mock compilation documentaries such as Peter Jackson's *Forgotten Silver*, referred to in Chapter 1.)

Arthur further illustrates the use of generic shots through reference to the opening of *The Atomic Café*, a film by Jayne Loader, Kevin Raffety and Pierce Raffety, a film which constructs a history of Cold War years by satirically recoding US government propaganda films from the 1950s intended to allay communal anxieties of nuclear attack. The sequence Arthur refers to deals with the atomic bombing of Hiroshima, and includes snippets of an interview with the captain of the bomber which dropped the bomb on the city, mixed with footage of street scenes in Japan, and shots of a bomber in flight. Tension is constructed through the combination of scenes which narrativize the impending destruction of the city. The sequence includes several low-angle shots of a Japanese man framed against a clear sky, innocently gazing upward, as the sounds of a plane are heard on the soundtrack. In its context within *The Atomic Café* the image represents an inhabitant of Hiroshima being alerted to the approach of bombers. However the image is derived from a source (most probably a fiction film) not of the same status as the other footage in the sequence. Clearly the footage could not have been recorded in Hiroshima at the time of the attack and have survived the blast and is included in *The Atomic Café* to create a meaning and elaborate a point of view – that of those under the bomb – typically denied in official US accounts of the bombing. Arthur concludes that the shots suggest the wide range of non-denotative functions of found footage which carry the capacity to critique and revise the conventional reliance on compilation footage as illustration and transparent evidence.

*The Atomic Café* is a 'pure' compilation film which draws on an incredibly rich archive of US government information films from the 1950s and eschews interviews or additional narration, though some of the source footage does carry its own commentary. The film, which took five years to produce, is heavily indebted to the compilation films of Emile de Antonio, whose comments the film-makers echo in their assessment of voice-over narration. Jayne Loader commented that 'so-called Voice of God narration, ubiquitous in documentaries destined for PBS [the US Public Broadcasting Service], is insulting to the audience. If you believe in the intelligence of your audience, you don't need to tell them what to think and how to process the material they're seeing.' However, as Loader added, 'making a documentary without a narrator is not an easy process. It's much easier to get your point-of-view across with a voice-over than to find precisely the right images and sounds and put them together in such a way that they communicate what you want to say' (Loader: 4).

On its release a number of critics claimed that the film's only response to the official position promoted in the archival film is 'profound skepticism' (Boyle, 1982; Seitz, 1982). Though imbued with the blackest of humour derivable from the absurd remarks contained in the footage, the film transcends condescension and incredulity in its willingness to address the frightening and 'unthinkable' proposition at the centre of the propaganda: 'what is it like to experience nuclear attack?' Thinking the unthinkable has been pursued in the dramatized documentaries *The War Game* and *The Day After* (1983) in chilling scenarios of mass death and destruction. In contrast, *The Atomic Café* exposes attempts by the US government to persuade citizens that by following simple procedures they will safely survive a nuclear war. The absurdity of the proposition is compounded by the fact that in the immediate post the Second World War era, one which witnessed the annihilation by nuclear weapons of the majority of the populations of the Japanese cities of Hiroshima and Nagasaki, the government would expect its citizens to believe its nuclear propaganda. Just as the US government sought to convince its audience of its position on nuclear weapons, so too the filmmakers of *The Atomic Café* seek through skilful editing of official footage to establish a preferred reading which subverts the government's position, thereby criticizing Cold War thinking for its naiveté while simultaneously mounting a powerful critique of contemporary (Reagan era) policies of nuclear proliferation (Bruzzi, 2000: 38).

The perspective provided by temporal distance from the events described underscores the irrationality of the notion of surviving nuclear holocaust and reinforces the black humour derivable from such a grim and absurd idea. In a scene toward the end of the film, the filmmakers insert footage extracted from an 'informational' film in which members of a family gather in the wake of a nuclear attack in their minimally damaged living room as the calm and assured father suggests that his children clean up the broken window glass. The viewer can, of course, find it humorous that the effects of nuclear attack can be easily brushed away and, further, the post-1950s withering of the patriarchal family underscores the film's joking reliance on the assertive presence of the patriarch as head of the 'nuclear' family. The humour and insight here derives from an historical perspective which overdetermines the images of the family, investing them with meanings derivable only from the distance of the early 1980s. In this way the film profitably constructs a dialectic of past and present which reflects on current conditions as it reframes past events. The historical revisionist approach is, then, pursued as a politically committed contribution to informing the present.

However, the particular application of the montage method to enact this process exposes certain limitations of the film's revisionist project. An example from near the end of the film points to the problem. Archival television news footage features a reporter describing the impending execution of Julius and Ethel Rosenberg following their convictions for providing US nuclear secrets to the Soviet Union. The sequence ends with images filmed from a moving car of a new suburb, its freshly built homes lined up street after street. The contrast of 1950s suburbia and the execution of the Rosenbergs suggests political quietism and passivity in the presence of nuclear destruction (symbolized by the Rosenberg's cause)

and McCarthyist witch hunts which branded the Rosenbergs communists. The meaning of the montage – acquiescence in the face
of various forms of political threat – is established through reliance
on the denotative features of the original footage. The method
here does not interrogate the archival footage, rather, it merely
deploys it uncritically as illustration of what the film accepts as
authentic historical conditions. Further, the method fails to pose
certain questions, in particular whether the 'history' so illustrated
is a complete or 'authentic' picture of the period.[4] Did all of
America demand the deaths of the Rosenbergs? (A brief clip
included in *The Atomic Café* of a news report dealing with the
impending execution features a pro-Rosenberg demonstration,
which is immediately replaced by more extensive clips of people
demanding their execution.) Was the entire population of the
United States in the 1950s locked into a relentless drive to build
and populate suburbias? Were the 1950s totally devoid of political
action? An exclusive reliance on propaganda footage designed to
reinforce consensus and to deny the presence of dissent leaves little space for representations of political protest and opposition to
the nuclear threat.

## Cultural plagiarism and the production of counterhistories

In a description of the production and reception of *The Atomic
Café*, Jayne Loader suggests quite reasonably that the film's popularity raised the profile of, and increased demand for, archival
footage thereby contributing to the growth of the stock footage
industry (1996a: [6]). The comment did not anticipate, however,
the rising costs of obtaining stock footage. The compilation filmmaker will frequently spend the majority of a film's budget purchasing so-called stock footage from commercial vendors, and in
an era of global copyright few alternatives exist for access to
archival footage beyond payment for the rights to use selected
film. However, filmmakers working in the tradition of avant-garde
compilation work have readily ignored copyright restrictions and
reworked images gathered from a variety of sources, including
footage copied directly from television, into parodic and politicized
comments on consumer society.

Exemplifying the alternative uses of plagiarized footage, the
avant-garde filmmaker Bruce Conner used television footage of

the shooting of President John Kennedy, together with other recycled images, to comment in his film *Report* (1967) on issues surrounding the assassination. The film replays the television coverage, stops it, restarts it and projects images upside down and in reverse. The objective of Conner's reworking of the source footage is to draw attention to the mass media coverage of the event and his treatment parodies television's obsessive documentation of every aspect of the Kennedy assassination as a news 'story'. Conner's intention is not to reveal the motives behind Kennedy's killing (an exercise that, typically, slides into varieties of conspiracy theory, as evidenced by Oliver Stone's attempt to do so in *JFK*, 1991), but to subject the footage from television coverage of the event to an analysis which reveals meanings and ideological dispositions implicit in the footage. Conner's method reads the footage 'against the grain', not as evidence of a presidential assassination, but as an indicator of the morbid popularization of a tragic event and the ideological positions of television networks which promote tragedy for ratings.[5] For artists such as Conner, compilation filmmaking is not, as Paul Arthur notes, 'the combining of "pure", unaffiliated fragments in order to construct new meanings with alternative historical perspectives, but rather the interrogation... of collusive strands of embedded ideology in extant materials' (2000: 62).

In Conner's *Report* and his film *A Movie* (1958) – a collagist reflection on mass-mediated depictions of human disasters based on footage culled from television, old Hollywood films, ethnographic films and information films – Conner makes little attempt to deploy footage in the manner of television documentaries, in which the source of the archival footage is erased or minimized within a seamless and smooth visualization of the rhetorical drive established in voice-over. By drawing attention to the sources from which the footage was extracted, the politicized avant-garde compilation filmmakers comment on the ways in which original contexts inflect footage with meanings (e.g. the commercial thrust of Hollywood and television, the construction of Otherness in certain ethnographic films) which are revealed and analysed within the recontextualization of the images in new compilation works.[6]

The commercial conditions under which footage is produced and archived and the extension of copyright of images and sounds have led beyond the appropriative methods of avant-garde compilation filmmakers to even more flagrant practices of cultural plagiarism aimed at openly violating the laws pertaining to sound and image reproduction. The practices of media piracy and so-called culture jamming extract and 'sample' images and sound from various sources. Here the act of 'finding' footage, a seemingly passive act, becomes appropriation, an active intervention in the field of media representations and copyright. Examples of such activist interventions include *The Nation Erupts* (1992), a videotape of the Los Angeles riots and rebellion of 1992 which uses appropriated images from commercial television news and historical footage interspersed with amateur camcorder footage to provide an interpretation of events in Los Angeles which opposes and revises that presented in mainstream media coverage. For his video *Spin* (1994), Brian Springer extracted and edited images from over 600 hours of downloaded satellite feeds (unedited videotape footage transmitted to television stations by satellite) for an analysis of the ways in which political debate and discourse is packaged and presented in the United States. Craig Baldwin's film *Sonic Outlaws* (1995) enacts the slogan 'Copyright Infringement is Your Best Entertainment Value' as it documents the activities of audio and video activists through pirated footage and sound extracts. 'Scratch' or improvisational videomakers re-edit appropriated images derived from transnational corporations and those of prominent political figures into politically astute parodic tapes which subvert the original meanings encoded in the images.

The radical recoding of source footage pioneered by Shub is extended and maintained in works which self-consciously recode appropriated images and sounds to create hybrid documentary/ avant-garde counterhistories. In another way, the practices of sound and image piracy continually evoke issues of availability of and access to source footage. In a direct and challenging approach, the work of media pirates problematizes the notion of 'found' footage and points to what is, in the era of extensive copyright provisions, its archaic connotation of an image domain which freely offers up recyclable images. Compilation film in the future will no doubt continue to confront issues of availability and accessibility in the production of new histories of experience.

## CHAPTER 8

# The Fact/Fiction Divide: Drama-Documentary and Documentary Drama

Television schedules reflect the increasing prominence of productions which meld the conventions of drama and documentary. Historical dramas, 'biopics' (filmed accounts of the lives of famous and infamous people), dramas constructed around incidents from news headlines, dramatic plays which replicate the visual styles of documentary and journalistic inquiries which include dramatic re-enactments, are all a part of this popular global televisual practice. The film industry also continues to produce work in this field, most notably filmed biographies and historical dramas including *JFK* (1991), *Malcolm X* (1992), *Braveheart* (1995), *Michael Collins* (1996), *Hurricane* (1999), *Pearl Harbor* (2000), *Iris* (2001), *Ali* (2001) and *Pollock* (2002). Works of this type raise a number of questions regarding the documentary form, and the legitimacy of its relationship to dramatic treatment of historical events. Depending on which interpreters are read, the meeting of fact and fiction results in either the subversion of documentary claims to authenticity and veracity, or, innovative and productive approaches to documentary representation. While the movement or dispersal (again, depending on which interpretations are followed) of the documentary impetus within dramatic forms occurs across both film and television, the presence of documentary/dramatic programmes on television has at times resulted in a number of issues and controversies which focus and inform discussion of such works. Within the context of such controversies, and the regulatory restraints imposed on the form by broadcasters often in response to controversy, this chapter examines Peter Watkins' *The War Game*, a representation of nuclear holocaust in Britain made for the BBC in 1965 but banned and unscreened for 20 years.[1] The analysis includes definitions of forms on the fact/fiction divide, and the history and functions of these forms. The future of such productions and emergent works within the field are also considered.

The meeting of 'documentary' and 'dramatization' has produced numerous variants. In defining these works it is important, as Corner (1996: 32) points out, to note the difference between the term 'drama', used to indicate an exciting, suspenseful event (as in the journalistic turn of phrase, 'the situation took a dramatic turn') and as a reference to enactment, a restaging of an event, often using professional actors. Though the forms discussed here negotiate both usages of the term, the emphasis is on drama and dramatization as related to restaging, reconstruction or the reenactment of events. Among these terms, 'reconstruction' has popularly been applied within the context of current affairs programming and investigatory journalistic documentaries where it is used to recreate certain details of an event. A more extensive use of dramatization – full-scale reconstruction, the focus of this chapter – occurs in the subgenre of documentary that includes the forms variously referred to as dramatized documentary, drama-documentary, documentary drama, docudrama, dramadoc and faction.

Paget (1998) refers to what he calls 'dramadoc/docudrama' as a genre, a form in its own right and devotes two chapters of his study of the form to definitions, while Goodwin and Kerr (1983: 1), in contrast, reject the notion of a homogenous category that can be conveniently defined or classified. The multiplicity of drama/documentary works and the problems associated with characterization have led certain commentators to favour descriptions which refer to a range of forms within a general field of conventions. In opposition to a strict categorization, Leslie Woodhead (1999: 103) theorizes fact/fiction forms within a spectrum running from journalistic reconstruction, on one end, to dramatic enactment, on the other. Goodwin and Kerr (1983) also refer to a range or continuum of works involving drama and documentary features, and Hoffer and Nelson (1978), in their study of US examples, posit nine formal variants in the field ranging from a so-called pure form of re-enactment based on investigatory and trial records, to programmes or films which include varying degrees of fictionalization.

Despite their increasing complexity, the interpretative value of such taxonomies is complicated by the continual emergence of new hybrid fact/fiction forms.

A useful and productive approach to the complexities of defining the forms on the fact/fiction divide has been provided by John Caughie in his important essay 'Progressive Television and Documentary Drama' (1980).[2] Caughie's essay provides succinct definitions capable of accommodating the majority of established and emergent works in this area. Within a discussion of the ideological implications of realist styles of television production, Caughie identifies two dominant forms within the fact/fiction representational divide: 'dramatized documentary' and 'documentary drama'. According to Caughie, dramatized documentary is an approach based on facts derived from investigation and research. Such practices are commonly signalled in a programme's opening titles, or within television scheduling guides through a statement to the effect that the content is 'based on fact'. In this form factual material, such as that contained in court transcripts, or the biographical details of a well-known historical figure, for example, is communicated through the conventions of drama. An example here is the work *Police State* (1989), a dramatized documentary from the Australian Broadcasting Corporation which uses professional actors to re-create the findings of a government commission of inquiry and journalistic investigations into police corruption in Queensland during the 1980s under the premiership of Joh Bjelke-Petersen.

A documentary drama, on the other hand, is a work which relies on dramatic codes and conventions for the basis of a fictional narrative that makes reference to factual or possible situations, people and events. Documentary drama draws heavily on what Caughie calls a 'documentary look', a style which creates the impression of facticity within a fiction by replicating the visual language of documentary film through techniques such as shaky camera shots and a reliance on natural lighting (Caughie, 1980: 27). A notable example of a documentary drama is *Cathy Come Home* (BBC, 1966), a programme dealing with the plight of a fictitious homeless family in the Britain of the 1960s. Though the characters were invented, the details of homelessness and its effects were informed by a range of factual sources. While he draws on a range of examples to establish the distinctions between the two forms, it can be noted that Caughie's distinctions are not comprehensive; certain examples, notably *The War Game*, tend to confound the categories. (*The War Game* can be considered a documentary drama, but one which deals with a non-existent event, unlike *Cathy Come Home* which derives its documentary effect from historically verifiable social conditions.) Nevertheless, the general distinctions between documentary drama and what Caughie calls dramatized documentary, or what is here called drama-documentary,[3] has a basic interpretative and definitional value which is drawn on in this chapter as a way of characterizing the varying historical and contemporary approaches to the intersection of documentary and dramatized material.

The recent high profile in television schedules and in cinemas of forms from the fact/fiction divide may tend to suggest that such forms are a new development on the production scene. However, the histories of cinema and television contain numerous examples of works which negotiate aspects of fact and fiction. Among the examples that can be pointed to in this regard is the work of George Méliès who, in the late nineteenth century, together with making the fantasy and trick films for which he is best known, produced a number of short films in which he used dramatic reconstruction to re-create real incidents. Similarly, D.W. Griffith's *Birth of a Nation* (1915) constructs a dramatic narrative, albeit one inscribed with the racial attitudes of its era, from scenes based on detailed historical research. Eisenstein's *Battleship Potemkin* (1925) drew on the historical details of a mutiny on board a pre-Revolutionary Russian warship as the basis of a work which mixes fact and fiction in an expressive way. The Inuit 'family' in Flaherty's 1922 key work of documentary cinema *Nanook of the North* was composed of unrelated Inuit individuals who re-enacted often anachronistic aspects of Inuit life for Flaherty's camera. In Britain, the documentary film movement of the 1930s and 1940s, following Grierson's definition of documentary as 'the creative treatment of actuality', established an inventive or 'creative' approach to documentary material which embodied an acceptance of the place of dramatization in the documentary text. Paul Rotha's comment (quoted in Winston, 1988b: 21) that 'Documentary's essence lies in dramatizations of actual material' made explicit the practices of many works from the documentary film movement, among them Harry Watt's *North Sea* (1938) and his *Target for Tonight* (1941) and Humphrey Jennings's *Fires Were Started* (1943). These films adopted a 'story-documentary' format which melded factual details to a heavy reliance on characterization and narrativization borrowed from fictional forms.[4]

The number of examples of work on the fact/fiction divide produced outside television tends to qualify the assertion, made by one commentator in 1956, that 'The dramatized story documentary is one of the few forms pioneered by television' (Doncaster, 1983: 8). Nevertheless, the demand of television to produce new and appealing forms in its search for wider audiences has provided a certain impetus for the production of works in the fact/fiction category. Corner (1996: 38) has noted the ways in which television producers in the 1960s developed the story documentary within realist plays which were based on intensive research and grounded in authentic social settings. A prominent broadcast environment for work of this kind was provided by the BBC's *The Wednesday Play*. Notable programmes produced for this slot in the 1960s included *Cathy Come Home* and *The War Game*, both of which created controversy, a characteristic that has consistently attended various documentary drama and drama-documentary practices.

## Unleashing the beast: controversy and functions of the forms

As the production of documentary drama and drama-documentaries increased with the expansion of television in the late 1950s, criticisms of the forms also increased. Typical of the growing criticisms was a review published in 1960 in *The Listener* of a drama-documentary series about the British police force produced by the BBC Documentary Department:

> Drama or documentary? – the 'Scotland Yard' programmes fall uneasily between. Basically these are documentaries, each dealing with some different aspect of the extremely complex activities of Scotland Yard. Unfortunately, it seems to have been felt, quite wrongly, that this would be insufficiently interesting in itself, so little shots of drama are injected and these give the impression that the police are incompetent or venal or both. (quoted in Caughie, 2000: 102)

The reviewer's unease over the melding of dramatic and documentary moments was echoed in the reception of the breakthrough documentary drama *Cathy Come Home*. In a review of the programme in the *Sunday Telegraph* in 1967 the reviewer complained that a description of the play in the *Radio Times* as a 'semi-documentary' created confusion and 'deliberately blurs the distinction between fact and fiction. Viewers have the right to know whether what they are being offered is real or invented' (in Petley, 1996: 15–16).

In 1980, Associated Television's *Death of a Princess*, a drama-documentary of the execution for adultery of two members of the Saudi Arabian elite, threatened diplomatic relations between Britain and Saudi Arabia and led to criticisms of the programme in Parliament. Speaking in the House of Commons, The Lord Privy Seal, Sir Ian Gilmour, insisted that 'the so-called dramatizations or fictionalizing of alleged facts or history is extremely dangerous and misleading' (quoted in Woodhead, 1999: 101), and Lord Wigoder argued in the House of Lords that 'television companies ... present programmes deliberately designed to give the impression of being documentary based on fact whereas the reality is that in substance they are no more than fictional reconstructions' (quoted in Petley, 1996: 11). Reviews of the programme in the British press fuelled the controversy. A reviewer for *The Sunday Times* (13 April 1980) argued that the programme distorted the 'known facts' through 'elaboration and embroidery'. A review in *The Guardian* (6 August 1980) asked of the form, 'Well, what is it? Fact or fiction? History or current affairs ... Significant episodes in [the] lives [of historical figures] are ... presented in fictitious form ("artificial, counterfeit, sham"), or, rather, in a mishmash of fact and fiction and producer's whim. It is a profoundly unsatisfactory development in the use of television' (quoted in Edgar, 1982: 15).

The substance of the various criticisms – essentially, that the dramatization of fact is misleading – has continued to impact on debates concerning drama-documentary and documentary drama. Interestingly, the criticisms reveal the persistence of a basic assumption concerning the nature of documentary representation. The claim that dramatizations are misleading carries with it the implication that a more accurate representation is available through 'traditional' documentary techniques which, supposedly, refuse dramatic re-enactment. As has been pointed out earlier in this book, Grierson's definition of documentary as the creative treatment of actuality admitted dramatic reconstruction as a legitimate component of 'creative' representation, and the practices of reconstruction have continued as a structuring component of much documentary work. The allusion to the existence of a documentary mode entirely devoid of 'dramatic' techniques or moments of dramatization posits the existence of a 'pure' documentary form which is difficult to locate in the documentary tradition.

An acknowledgement that conventional documentary contains reconstructive and dramatized elements does not, however, release drama-documentary and documentary drama from the requirements of meeting standards of accuracy which it is expected to uphold as a documentary form. All-too-often, though, it is clear that the emphasis on factual accuracy in criticisms of dramatization have functioned ideologically to mask concerns and anxieties generated by the politically or morally problematic nature of the content of these documentaries. The controversy surrounding *Death of a Princess* can be interpreted in these terms. Comments in Parliament on the programme's form only partially served to displace the fact that the real cause of the critical attack was the programme's politically sensitive subject and the threat it posed to relations between Britain and Saudi Arabia. In another example, much of the adverse critical reception of *Cathy Come Home* stemmed in part from the play's depiction of quite intimate scenes of marital life and not any confusion over distinctions between fact and fiction. The extended controversy surrounding Peter Watkins' *The War Game* and its subsequent banning is a significant example of the reactions of broadcasters to 'difficult' content. The reason given by the BBC for this action was that the programme was 'too horrifying' and likely to incite panic, even suicide, within an audience. However, research has revealed that the ban was in large part a result of official concerns over the effects of the programme on Britain's nuclear defence policy (Tracey, 1982). According to the research findings, the charge that the programme was 'too horrifying' takes on different resonance, one which suggests that the programme was censored for being 'too close' to the truth.

In addressing questions of accuracy and credibility, producers and broadcast regulators have implemented procedures and approaches which emphasize the distinction between factual and fictive elements in the drama-documentary and documentary drama. Promotional announcements for a programme often stress the factual basis of the content and, as Kilborn (1994b: 65) notes, the production of historically based drama/documentary forms is grounded in detailed research and the verification of factual sources similar to that operating in news and current affairs programming. Producers are aware of the move toward litigation arising from slander and defamation and are, as a consequence, careful to check their facts. The threat in the United States of such litigation may well account for the popularity of 'docudramas' based on transcripts of court proceedings which are by their nature verified as accurate records of evidence.

Broadcast regulators have implemented codes of practice which contain details concerning the production and scheduling of drama-documentaries and documentary drama. Both the BBC Producers' Guidelines and the Independent Television Commission's Programme Code, for example, include directives in this area. The latter code states that:

> a clear distinction should be drawn between plays based on fact and dramatized documentaries which seek to reconstruct actual events. Much confusion may be avoided if plays based on current or very recent events are carefully labelled as such, so that fictional elements are not misleadingly presented as fact…Care should be taken in scheduling drama and drama-documentary programmes portraying controversial matters…Impartiality may need to be secured by providing an opportunity for opposing viewpoints to be expressed. (quoted in Petley, 1996: 20)[5]

Leslie Woodhead, the founder of Granada's Drama Documentary Unit, acknowledged many of the concerns that such a code seeks to address – the potential for viewer confusion and deviations from historical accuracy – and pointed to other issues associated with the production of work on the fact/fiction divide, in particular that such work is 'uniquely time-consuming and alarmingly expensive' (1999: 102). In the presence of the many issues surrounding the forms, Woodhead asks why producers continue to invest in their production. 'Why unleash such an unruly beast at all?', asks Woodhead.

As if in answer to this question, the playwright and script writer David Edgar (1982: 23) insists that the power of the drama-documentary 'lies in its capacity to show us not that certain events occurred (the headlines can do that) or even, perhaps, why they occurred…but *how* they occurred: how recognizable human beings rule, fight, judge, meet, negotiate, suppress and overthrow'. In Edgar's assessment, a drama-documentary or documentary drama provides a way of invoking psychological or emotional motivations capable of rendering human action intelligible. Returning to his question, Woodhead argues that certain situations demand the use of reconstructions and justify the difficulties of unleashing the beast. Such situations include those events which occurred before the invention of the film camera, legal restrictions on cameras in courtrooms, subjects who are willing to provide information 'for the record' but who, for various reasons, are unable or unwilling to appear on camera, and incidents which governments declare 'off limits' to cameras. The media scholar Derek Paget (1998) summarizes what he interprets as the essential function of drama-documentary and documentary drama forms when he argues that such forms provide an effective means of representation when there is no other way to narrate the facts of an event.[6]

This capacity is especially relevant in the case of *The War Game*, a programme which deals with a hypothetical event, namely, nuclear attack on Britain. In the absence of documentary footage or eyewitness testimony, Watkins relies on dramatization to construct a fact-based account of the devastating effects of such an attack. Watkins recognized that the extent to which his critique of British nuclear policies accorded with the known facts of nuclear war was crucially important in a political environment supportive of nuclear weapons proliferation. Thus, within the boundaries of what is clearly a fiction, Watkins provides a range of information on thermonuclear war and its aftermath, while at the same time he uses the documentary drama form to comment on the factual validity of the information. The film performs this complex task through the construction of a hierarchy of knowledge in which varying modes of address, and the information delivered by the modes, is simultaneously criticized and informed by being placed against and superseded by other layers of articulation. The result is an ascending order of modes of address, and an accompanying presentation of varying knowledge concerning the effects of nuclear war.

## *The War Game*: addressing the information gap

*The War Game* deals with the time before, during and after a nuclear attack on Britain. The film, made in 1965, is set in the near future but draws on contemporary events such as the war in Vietnam and Cold War hostilities between the West and the Soviet Union as the basis of its narrative. Though it follows a chronological structure, overlapping levels of address and action replace a single narrative strand. The first part of the film describes the

lead-up to nuclear attack on Britain. The war in Vietnam precipi-
tates a Soviet invasion of West Berlin which, in turn, provokes
a decision by Western nations to retaliate by firing an 'Honest
John' nuclear missile. In response, the Soviets use intermediate
range thermonuclear missiles to attack NATO targets across
Europe. As this sequence of events unfolds, officials in Britain
begin to evacuate the women and children of London, and many
evacuees arrive in Kent to be billeted in local households. Citizens
are interviewed in the street about the effects of radiation as a
policeman delivers pamphlets containing rudimentary information on nuclear attack. Those citizens who can afford to purchase
expensive building materials begin to construct bomb shelters.

The narrative of disaster is fully realized when a Soviet thermonuclear missile falls short of its military target and explodes in
Canterbury, unleashing a firestorm which engulfs many people
and asphyxiates others. Intercut with scenes depicting the bomb's
physical effects, various authorities, among them a representative
of the Vatican Council, a bishop, and a nuclear strategist, speculate
on the moral and military implications of nuclear attack. In the
immediate aftermath of the strike, medical supplies and medical
personnel are in short supply, and corpses pile up in the street
awaiting burial. Two weeks after the blast law and order break
down and civilians arm themselves to battle the police. Food is
scarce and hunger and disease follow as firing squads are used in
an attempt to quell the social chaos. People lose any sense of
motivation and live in squalor, much as they did after the atomic
bombings of Hiroshima and Nagasaki. Three months after the attack
children interviewed in a refugee camp in Dover are apathetic and
anxious about the future.

Watkins used this chilling scenario to address what he saw as the
lack of widely available information on the possibility of nuclear
war and its effects. According to Watkins, this 'information gap'
was the result of a situation in which the British government
refused to release necessary information on nuclear build-up and
thermonuclear war (in Blue and Gill, 1965: 14). The film seeks to
ameliorate this situation by providing well-researched factual information to fill the information gap. Indeed, as Watkins pointed out,
overcoming the information gap demanded extensive research:
'With *The War Game*, I had to do a great deal of original research
because nobody had ever collated all the information into an easily
accessible published form. Quite a lot of books have been written

on the effects of thermonuclear bombs, but very few of these had ever been seen by the public' (quoted in Rosenthal, 1988: 595). As part of this research, Watkins met with biologists, radiologists, physicians and academics and studied the medical effects of exposure to nuclear radiation. Among the written sources he consulted were reports on the destruction of Hiroshima, Nagasaki and Dresden and the nuclear tests conducted by the US government in the Nevada desert in 1954. In order to gauge the nation's level of preparedness for nuclear attack Watkins wrote to the Home Office for information concerning plans for civil defence in case of nuclear war. (He received no reply, though the Home Office contacted the BBC regarding his inquiry, with the result that the BBC warned Watkins not to pursue that line of research.)

*The War Game* represents the information gathered from its array of sources within what can be identified as five major modes of address. Though other, lesser forms of address occur in the film (the megaphone-like voice derived from newsreels used to announce certain segments is a case in point), the principal hierarchically organized voices, or forms of representation, are those comments derived from interviews with people in the street; the opinions of authoritative figures; the voice-over narration which provides technical information on nuclear war; the voice-over of a second narrator which narrates the action in the present; and the visual image.

Whereas the majority of the action in *The War Game* is based on carefully scripted comments, some segments include unrehearsed spontaneous comments. One such segment includes a series of to-camera replies to an off-screen interviewer asking questions on the effects of the radioactive substance carbon 14. The respondents had volunteered to participate in the making of the film, though they had no prior knowledge of this scene. According to Watkins (in Rosenthal, 1988: 600) the ill-informed responses 'are perhaps the biggest single indictment in the entire film of the way we are conducting our society and of the lack of common public knowledge of the things that affect humanity'. It is this lack of knowledge of a crucial topic – nuclear armament and the potential for nuclear war – that the film works to overcome through the relentless delivery of information.

One level of information is represented in the form of statements on thermonuclear war made by real-life authorities, including a nuclear strategist who insists that in a nuclear war 'both sides could stop before the ultimate destruction of cities, so that both sides could retire for a period of ten years or so of post-attack recuperation, in which world wars four to seven could be prepared'. The words (drawn from statements made by Herman Kahn, a strategist of nuclear war), together with other 'authoritative' or so-called expert statements made by a bishop and a psychologist are, within the context of the ascending order of knowledge, presented as dangerous fictions. The presentation of information is extended through the use of two narrators. The dual narrators produce separate modes of commentary in a way which revises standard forms of exposition. One narrator uses the conditional tense to speak of what could happen, as in the voice-overs: 'Should Britain ever thus attempt the evacuation of nearly 20 percent of her entire population, such scenes as these would be almost inevitable'; 'What you are seeing now is another possible part of nuclear war'; 'It is more than possible that what you have seen happen in this film would have taken place before the year 1980.' Against this position a second narrator sets forth action in the present. This is the voice that introduces the evacuees on the bus and similarly introduces the physician Dr David Thornley as he makes house calls in Canterbury immediately after the nuclear attack. This narration, imbued with a sense of immediacy, cuts through the dry narrational evocation of what could happen as it provides dramatic descriptions of unfolding events.

These voices interact with and complement the final level of address, that of spectacle and the visual image. It is at the level of the visual image that the 'unthinkable' becomes horrifyingly real. Images of nuclear holocaust supersede both the 'expert' opinions on the utility of nuclear war and voice-over statements on the hypothetical effects of such a war. More particularly, the realistic and graphic imagery has its own rhetorical valence that undercuts the arguments and assessments made in support of the use of nuclear weapons. The cogency of Watkins' visual 'critique' is heightened through the deployment of conventions of direct cinema and its stylistic claim on reality, including a reliance on natural lighting, a soundtrack that captures muffled often indistinguishable dialogue, and filming with a hand-held camera that tilts and pans as it documents the action. The wedding of direct cinema conventions and dramatic enactment makes a powerful appeal to the emotions which ratifies the film's informational content; viewers 'feel' or register emotionally the ideas and information presented within the interviews and voice-overs. Through the use of dramatic conventions Watkins is able to represent the unrepresentable – nuclear apocalypse. It is only through dramatic enactment that a camera operator can survive a nuclear blast described as 'melting the up-turned eyeball' and 'thirty times brighter than the noonday sun'. Dramatization fulfils what Paget (1998: 89) calls the 'promise of complete seeing' that informs the film's mix of information and emotion. In documentary drama 'the camera's ability to go any-where and see anything is both borrowed from documentary on the part of the drama and extended by the drama on behalf of documentary'. Drama and documentary 'go together to increase the camera's truth claim by denying its actual deficiency (it was not there in fact but we can pretend it was in fiction)' (Paget, 1998: 89).

Paget argues that the resulting form, what he calls the 'dramadoc/docudrama', is principally indebted to the television drama, and that the 'direct influence of documentary has been less marked' (1998: 89). *The War Game* qualifies this assertion. In its 'preconstruction' of a hypothetical event *The War Game* draws on the imaginative potential of drama in such a way that it links with the informational and agitational focus of documentary. The hier-archy of knowledge operative in *The War Game* produces knowl-edge, which in a progressively propagandistic way, is an exhortation to protest the dangers of nuclear weapons. The purpose of the film was, as Watkins stated (in Gomez, 1979: 53), 'to break the silence on the subject [of nuclear threat]' and 'to evoke sufficient public discussion to enlarge the whole issue … and to try and provoke people … to political or social or media means of confrontation'. It is in this provocation, as much as the degree to which it is based in fact, that the film returns to the field of documentary as espoused by Grierson. According to Grierson, documentary represents real-ity using creative methods, among them the use of dramatic tech-niques, with the aim of imparting knowledge that will mobilize viewers to act in the world as responsible citizens.

## From the end of the world as we know it to the beginnings of the known world: from *The War Game* to *Walking with Dinosaurs*

In the three decades since the banning of *The War Game* the drama-documentary and documentary drama have featured prominently within various national broadcast environments. In the United States, the lives of infamous people have provided a staple of content for a new generation of drama-documentary/docudrama.[7] Such programmes often draw on salacious headlines to emphasize the 'human drama' aspect of stories in ways which extend the basic form of the so-called trauma drama, domestic melodramas focused on family problems (Feuer, 1995: 31). The proliferation on US television of the 'headline' docudrama (Carveth, 1993) or 'instant histories' (Nimmo and Combs, 1983) is evidence of the commercial viability of a form which is able to draw on a certain level of audience familiarity with stories which have circulated widely in the news media.

The productive arrangements and scheduling practices of Australian television during the 1980s were structured to accommodate a heavy reliance on drama-documentaries on historical subjects, often with nationalist themes, presented in a 'mini-series' format. The success of a number of such programmes (among them *The Dismissal,* 1983, *Bodyline,* 1984 and *Vietnam,* 1987) established the mini-series as a prominent format on Australian television during the decade. In these programmes, and in an array of fiction films of the 1970s and 1980s, dramatization was deployed to rework historical and political subject matter within recognizable frames. In the case of the mini-series *Vietnam,* for example, the homefront effects of Australia's involvement in the Vietnam War were reflected in a narrative of inter-generational conflict (the 'generation gap') which grounded the historical within the familial and the personal.

In Britain in the 1990s the drama-documentary was used as the basis of investigations into various politically sensitive topics, provoking the kind of controversy that attended earlier productions such as *Death of a Princess.* Among the programmes to meet with controversy were *Who Bombed Birmingham?* (Granada, 1989), an account of the 'Birmingham 6', *Why Lockerbie?* (Granada, 1990), a programme dealing with the bombing of a Pan Am flight over Lockerbie in Scotland, and *Hostages* (Granada, 1992), a reconstruction of the Beirut hostage crisis.[8] The prevalence of 'reality-based stories taken from topical journalism' on US and UK television in the early 1990s led one commentator to claim that such works 'are the most popular drama genre on U.S. and British television today' (Rosenthal, 1999: xiii).

While drama-documentary and documentary drama continued to be produced throughout the 1990s, the use of dramatized reconstructions during this time was largely displaced on to varieties of popular factual programming, chiefly programmes within the 'emergency services genre' in which high levels of dramatization are interspersed with observational and expositional sequences. In such works the evidentiary potential of dramatization – its capacity to reveal information that was not captured by cameras – is reinforced in sequences that concentrate on moments of intense 'human drama' (motor vehicle accidents, violent crimes and so on). More recently, the investigative functions and broadcast appeal of the drama-documentary and documentary drama forms have been extended through the application of new film technologies in the production of work on the fact/fiction divide. The recent television co-production *Walking with Dinosaurs* (BBC/Discovery, 1999[9]) exemplifies this trend.

Digitally constructed dinosaurs put flesh on the bones of scientific theories which postulate the existence of such creatures. The resultant dramatization of aspects of what is at times anthropomorphized dinosaur behaviour occurs in a form that combines elements of the nature documentary and dramatic reconstruction. The work conforms to drama-documentary practice whereby dramatization is routinely employed to imaginatively fill gaps in otherwise complete documentary evidence (Kilborn and Izod, 1997: 142). As such the practice continues to anchor drama-documentary and documentary drama within the field of non-fiction which, as Michel Renov (1993b: 2) has argued, 'contains any number of "fictive" elements, moments at which a presumably objective representation of the world encounters the necessity of creative interpretation'. *Walking with Dinosaurs* satisfies our desire to know by visually recreating extinct animals and in this way it fulfils what has been called 'an explicit "documentary desire"', that is, 'the desire for the evidence of our own eyes' (in Paget, 1998: 200). Digital dinosaurs represent a new mode of drama-documentary which has proved its ability to hold its own on crowded television schedules in which various 'traditional' and 'hybrid' forms compete for share of an audience, thereby pointing to a renewed future for work on the fact/fiction divide.

## CHAPTER 9

# The Evening Report: Television Documentary Journalism

The journalistic reporting of newsworthy issues is an essential feature of television programming. Two of the primary televisual modes deployed to report current events and notable personalities are news bulletins and current affairs programmes. Television news reports typically feature one or more news presenters or readers in a studio whose scripted to-camera comments are complemented by video footage of selected news items. Current affairs programming resembles new bulletins in those examples that include multiple studio-based items of interview and discussion. Alternatively, current affairs programming moves away from the format of the news bulletin in those cases where a programme is composed of short, filmed reports on a single topic. In such cases, current affairs programming intersects with a related, though distinct, form of television news reporting, that of the long-form television news documentary, the subject of this chapter.

In contrast to the routinized presentation of multiple items in television news bulletins, and the studio-based interviews and short filmed reports of current affairs, television news documentaries – also referred to as special or feature reports – are longer filmed investigations of a single issue or event. The television news documentary is formally similar to the extended investigative reports of print journalism, and in this it approximates the lead report in a newspaper. Schlesinger *et al.* (1983: 166) draw a useful distinction between television news and television news documentaries by focusing on their different journalistic approaches. According to the authors, television news reporting can be characterized as either 'closed' or 'open'. The reporting in television news, which the authors characterize as closed programmes, generally reflects official perspectives on events with little room for alternative or dissenting voices or positions. Open programmes such as television news documentaries permit investigations into the causes and effects of an issue and provide space for the expression of positions critical of prevailing political and social conditions. Not surprisingly, perhaps, such critiques point to the propensity of the form to confront and, in turn, be embroiled in, controversy and debate. The history of television news documentaries contains various examples of this effect.

News documentaries on American television have included the controversial reports *Harvest of Shame* (1960), a powerful exposé of the harsh experiences of migrant workers in the US, and *Hunger in America* (1968), an in-depth study of the prevalence of hunger and malnourishment in the richest country in the world, both of which were produced by the US network Columbia Broadcasting Service (CBS) under the banner *CBS Reports*. In 1971, at the height of the Vietnam War, *The Selling of the Pentagon*, from the same series, exposed the costly public relations campaigns conducted by the Department of Defense with taxpayers' money. A political uproar surrounded the allegations, leading to Congressional hearings into the programme's allegations ( Jowett, 1985). *Guns of Autumn* (CBS, 1975) investigated the human toll of the proliferation of weapons ownership in the US, angering the nation's powerful pro-gun lobby, the National Rifle Association. In 1970 the Public Broadcasting Service (PBS) screened *Banks and the Poor*, which accused the banking industry of actively contributing to impoverishment in urban areas. During the 1980s and early 1990s controversy surrounded the production and broadcast of a number of PBS programmes including *Dark Circle* (1985), a provocative report on the nuclear weapons industry, *Days of Rage: The Young Palestinians* (1989), and *Stop the Church* (1991), a polemical account of the Catholic Church's attitudes to AIDS and safe-sex education (see Bullert, 1997). A forerunner of the investigative report on American television was the CBS series *See it Now*, first broadcast in 1951. Produced by Fred Friendly with Edward R. Morrow as the researcher/presenter, *See it Now* programmes frequently confronted controversial topics, among them, the bullying tactics used by Senator Joseph McCarthy in his anti-Communist witch hunts. The rising costs of television programming and the network's jittery reaction to the backlash directed at many of the allegations made in *See it Now* programmes led to the cancellation of the series in mid-1958.

Inspired by the investigative zeal of *See it Now* the BBC series *Special Enquiry* (1952–57) reported on various public affairs topics, including education, housing and services to the disabled and the aged. The series departed from existing television documentaries which tended to focus on comments provided by experts or authorities in studio settings and examined the daily lives of people on location in schools, homes and hospitals. An investigative approach was maintained in the early 1960s in Granada Television's weekly series *World in Action*. The first executive producer of the series, Tim Hewat, interpreted television's potential in terms of 'modern journalism, journalism with an audience of millions. It is what every journalist should be doing' (quoted in Goddard *et al.*, 2001: 77). The tradition of investigative television journalism in the UK continued with the controversial programme *The Question of Ulster* (BBC, 1972), which the British home Secretary sought to ban, and the Thames Television investigative report *Death on the Rock* (1988), a programme involving reconstructions which suggested that members of the British Special Air Service had assassinated three unarmed suspected members of the IRA. In Australia, *Chequerboard*, a series from the Australian Broadcasting Company (now Corporation) [ABC], produced 26 feature reports a year throughout 1970–72 on current events topics. The pre-eminent Australian current affairs programme *Four Corners* (ABC, 1961) has screened a number of feature reports during its four decades of broadcasting. Among its many influential investigative reports, *The Moonlight State* (1987), a programme dealing with the Queensland police force, contributed to the establishment of a government commission of inquiry into police corruption in the state.

Not all special reports confront controversial or contentious topics, of course. However, in cases where the basis of the report is investigative journalism, with its emphasis on advocacy and exposing suppressed facts which contest official positions or expose political or bureaucratic malfeasance, the news documentary is constantly pushed toward controversy. In this way, too, the practices of a 'crusading' and 'committed' journalism often sit uneasily with the demands of broadcasters and regulators for the maintenance of impartiality in the journalistic representation of events. The two practices identified here – investigation and impartiality – together constitute a broad context affecting television news documentaries. This chapter examines the operation of both practices through reference to the formal approaches adopted in the long-form television news documentaries of John Pilger. Working within both British and Australian television, Pilger has produced a number of remarkable and often controversial feature news reports. In collaboration with a director, most notably David Munro (who died in 1999), Pilger researches, writes and presents each programme. Pilger's first documentaries were 30 minute programmes produced for the ITV series *The Pilger Report* (1974–77). In 1970 he began to produce hour-long reports for independent television, the first of which, *The Quiet Mutiny* (Granada, screened as part of the *World in Action* series), examined the breakdown of morale among US troops in Vietnam toward the end of the war. His subsequent work includes a prominent series of investigations of the legacies of repressive regimes in Cambodia, Burma and East Timor. Pilger's television news documentaries, produced over a period of 30 years, constitute a significant contribution to the genre. This chapter examines his investigative news report *Cambodia: The Betrayal* (1990), a programme which, while impassioned, confronts the matter of impartiality by constructing itself as an authoritative and factual account of events.

## Investigative journalism

Journalism, like documentary, is a discourse of fact. Over its 200–400 year history journalism has developed a set of guidelines, protocols, routines and practices that function in support of its claim to factually represent important and pressing events and issues. According to certain interpretations, this basic informational role performs an important task in liberal pluralist societies, contributing to the democratic process by supplying citizens with information required to make rational and measured decisions on matters of political and economic importance. In this way, it is argued, journalism bolsters democracy by extending a citizen's democratic right to information necessary for exercising informed choice in the public domain. In undertaking to provide factual information a journalist may adopt a neutral and observational role, or a more active and engaged stance. Dennis McQuail (1987: 146) summarizes the two positions by stating that the role of the 'neutral reporter' contributes to 'the press as informer, interpreter and instrument of government (lending itself as channel or mirror)'. In contrast, what he calls the journalist as 'participant' acts as a 'representative of the public, critic of government, advocate of policy'. According to McQuail, the 'weight of evidence ... is that the neutral, informative role is most preferred by journalists and it goes with the importance of objectivity as a core value and an element in the new professionalism'.

In the presence of a general preference for the 'neutral' position, however, certain journalists continue the tradition in which journalism is conceived as the 'Fourth Estate': a press which performs a watchdog role, scrutinizing and criticizing the activities of the three other estates – the government, the civil service and the judiciary – on behalf of the public. In such conceptions, journalism is a strong advocate for the public interest, engaged and committed in its critique of officialdom. The adversary role underpins the aims of an investigative journalism with its implicit or explicit appeal to social reform. A reformist impulse is different to a partisan position that stresses a particular point of view and, indeed, commentators have pointed to investigative journalism's dedication to a ' "scientific" model of news gathering' which emphasizes the meticulous collection and evaluation of evidence and the minimization of personal opinion and assumption (Ehrlich, 1996: 14). Reformism highlights social and political issues and conditions in need of ameliorative attention. In these terms, the reformist impulse may be expressed in outraged tones, especially pronounced in certain areas of print journalism in the US, and, more particularly, the impulse positions the journalist as a crusader on behalf of the public's right to know (Protess *et al.*, 1991; de Burgh, 2000). The image of the crusading investigative journalist, prominent in the film *All the President's Men* (1976), for example, emphasizes the actions of individuals as the basis of journalism's effectiveness.

Such an emphasis, however, tends to overlook the reality that journalism is an institution composed of a diversity of occupations, activities and skills. These features highlight the fact that an engaged and 'crusading' form of investigative reportage operates within the context of the institutional boundaries of journalism and broadcasting, both of which are dependent on a certain level of financial resources (Street, 2001: 151). The decline in recent years of broadcast investigative journalism has in part been attributed to a reduction in production budgets (Doig, 1997), which in turn has, it is claimed, contributed to the emergence of cheaply produced popular factual entertainment.[1] According to such interpretations, the dominance of market forces and the waning of the public service ethic have resulted in the rise of an unreflective, 'dumbed down' tabloidism at the expense of a committed journalism capable of exposing social injustice.

Whether or not there has been a widespread 'dumbing down' via the 'tabloidization' of the news is a matter of debate. The assertion of the recent rise in tabloidism overlooks the fact that the existence of a journalism that is at once informative and reflective and sensational and entertaining is not new. The so-called penny dreadful press is a case in point here. Following this line of argument, John Hartley argues that 'In communicating public truths (and virtue) … contemporary commercial journalism mixes seduction with reason, pop with politics, commerce with communication, as it has done since 1789, in the very service of public-sphere virtues' (1996: 201). In another way it has been argued that what has been criticized as the 'dumbing down' of journalism and the media generally is, in effect, a realignment of a journalism and media capable of addressing and communicating issues once marginalized as trivial, overly personal and apolitical. In this view 'tabloid' journalism expresses a demotic – rigorously 'public' – form of knowledge denied in the 'educated discourse' of traditional quality media (Lumby, 1999: xii).

The critics of contemporary tabloidism, however, dispute the form's ability to provide meaningful public information, pointing to tabloid television's lack of journalistic investigation in this regard (Caldwell, 1994: 224). Not surprisingly, broadcast journalists have been among the most strident critics of television tabloidism and the trend to replace news documentary with docusoaps and various forms of 'reality TV'. David Munro wrote in 1994 of reality TV: 'I personally don't think the ambulance-chasing, crime reconstruction programmes have any place at all on television; they are voyeuristic and don't achieve anything … I believe that every documentary filmmaker in this country, every filmmaker, every current affairs person, should stand up and say the public deserves better than this' (1994: 19). Pilger has referred to docusoaps as pestilential works, 'the cane toad of documentary', which are 'deeply offensive, patronizing programmes that don't take us anywhere' (quoted in Smith, 1999: 28). Against the trend toward tabloid forms, Pilger insists on the need to maintain a rigorous print and broadcast investigative journalism that is, he argues, capable of serving as an advocate for the public interest and custodian of the public conscience. According to Pilger 'all journalists should be investigative', and characterizes investigative journalists as 'people who should lift rocks, look behind screens, never accept the official point of view' (de Burgh, 2000: 13, 314). Within this focus, Pilger (1982: 4) argues that journalists can or should be committed and impassioned, qualities he rightfully points out that should not contradict an emphasis on truthfulness in reporting. For many people within and outside the profession of journalism, however, Pilger's insistence that journalists adopt the investigative role of unabashed crusaders on behalf of the public runs contrary to the professed need to maintain impartiality and balance in journalism. Indeed, Pilger's commitment to the practices of critique and advocacy has resulted in accusations of bias being levelled against a number of his programmes.

## Impartiality and bias

Television news documentaries, together with television news services in general, have been the focus of a debate in many national contexts concerning the function of an 'impartial' broadcast journalism. In Britain, broadcasters are enjoined to demonstrate 'due impartiality', a phrase that strongly alludes to the need for television journalists, editors and news readers to be 'fair' in the reporting and presentation of political, economic and social information. The concept of 'fairness' holds that one body of information should not be privileged over others, nor should personal viewpoints be presented in reports. The emphasis on impartiality in television journalism differs from the selective procedures of print journalism where a certain partisanship is acceptable, if not expected. The principal of fairness central to impartiality does not mean, as the BBC puts it, 'absolute neutrality, nor detachment from basic moral and constitutional beliefs. For example, the BBC does not feel obliged to be neutral as between truth and untruth, justice and injustice, compassion and cruelty, tolerance and intolerance' (quoted in McNair, 1999: 34). As Brian McNair (1998: 70) notes, 'due impartiality' refers to 'a degree of impartiality appropriate to the issue in question; for example, one would not expect a broadcast journalist to be impartial as between ... Pol Pot and his Cambodian pro-democratic opponents'.

The place of impartiality in British broadcast journalism has its roots in the origins of the BBC in the 1920s. Established as a public utility to serve the public interest, the BBC, under the directorship of its founder, John Reith, pursued its approach of informing public opinion as part of the process of contributing to the development of an active citizenship.[2] Print and radio journalism, and later television news reportage, were valued as modernizing forces capable of informing the political processes of a mass democratic society. In this role radio and television were understood to be central to the task of constructing a cohesive and unified national culture from a diversity of political, social and regional elements. In order to negotiate these differences the BBC was charged with being an 'impartial arbiter', unaligned to commercial, political or cultural interests (McNair, 1999: 34). The principal of impartiality was extended to commercial television broadcasting in Britain at the time of its establishment in 1954, and has since been adopted within the news programming of British satellite broadcasting systems.

John Corner has usefully noted that impartiality needs to be distinguished from three other notions that are frequently implicated and often confused in discussions of journalism's mode of representation: 'accuracy', 'objectivity' and 'balance'. Corner interprets 'accuracy' to mean the correctness of basic ingredients of a news account – dates, names, places, the number of people involved, legal verdicts and so on. Corner argues that though aspects of such basic features can be contested and debated from one news item to the next, it is possible for a journalist to correctly record most of the basic facts most of the time as agreed to by a wide range of opinion on the topic (Corner, 1995: 65). The issue of *accuracy* is, however, distinguishable from a *diversity* of fact; the accurate reporting of facts is part of the process of gathering various facts, a process that aligns factual claims and impartiality. Claims that impartiality has been contravened frequently rest on charges that a programme ignored certain facts or did not represent a diversity of fact and hence failed to present a 'full' account of a topic. While such charges overlook the obvious theoretical problem associated with providing a 'full' account – it would be impossible to include *all* the facts in any report, even if it were possible to know all the facts – they nevertheless continue to be directed at television news reports and news documentaries.

'Objectivity', which the Concise Oxford Dictionary defines as 'that which is external to the mind' and 'that which is unaffected by subjective mental operations', is, as Corner notes, virtually impossible for journalists or anyone else to achieve in practice. While the idea that journalists should aspire to reporting that exceeds subjective opinion and personal experience is a commonly held one, an objective position implies a clear and unarguable representation of events devoid of the very decisions concerning selection, frames of reference and modes of depiction involved in the representational process itself. The emphasis in journalistic codes of practice and elsewhere on objectivity points to its place as an ideal around which other notions such as 'balance' revolve.[3]

In journalistic practice, 'balance' is manifested as a 'fair-minded' approach and a proportional presentation of 'both sides' of an argument (Corner, 1999: 66). 'Balance' has also involved a 'stop watch' practice in which exactly equal time is dedicated to both sides of a debate. In another way, 'balance' has been reduced to the notion of a 'middle ground' between two opposing points of view. 'Balance' is a central requirement of broadcast journalism in the United States, enforceable by the Federal Communications Commission which administers the so-called Fairness Doctrine (see Corner and Harvey, 1996: 260–2). The policy stipulates that a station is obligated to present contrasting and balancing points of view, which can be addressed within its *overall* programming, as opposed to the need to provide balanced arguments within *each* programme.

Corner notes that the crucial term associated with accuracy, objectivity and balance, that of 'impartiality', is frequently and most elaborately defined in the negative sense against that which is not – 'not partial, not prejudiced' (Corner, 1999: 66). Bias, the inverse of impartiality, is an equally problematic term. Corner points out that 'bias' has been used to refer to an absence of objectivity and a 'significant departure from fairness' (Corner, 1999: 67). Claims of deviations from fairness frequently rest, as noted, on assertions that a report has failed to provide a 'full account' of the facts. Similarly, a definition of bias as that which is partial and prejudiced implies an account which is not factually accurate and complete. Corner points out that bias – a failure to maintain impartiality – is commonly interpreted as a form of 'skewing' produced by the activities and constraints of the news gathering process, reflecting a broader predisposition toward certain outcomes evident in the capitalist economy. Rarely do academic studies of broadcast journalism interpret bias in terms of an individual journalist's intention to distort a report (Corner, 1999: 68). However, contrary to the interpretive and critical focus of academic surveys, accusations of broadcast bias made in public and those brought before broadcast tribunals frequently focus on the reporting of individual television journalists. Pilger's work presents a case in point.

Pilger has been the recipient of numerous British and international awards for factual and committed reporting, though his work has also been subject to charges of bias.[4] Pilger's experiences in this regard cut across theoretical definitions of impartiality and bias and offer a useful study of the operation and regulatory enforcement of the notions in practice. For Pilger, 'impartiality' is itself a type of skewing which results in a non-contentious form of reporting devoid of critique. Speaking in 1982 Pilger wondered,

> how many journalists are prepared these days to stand up for a story which they believe the public has the right to know about, but which management or a host of unseen pressures decree should not be published, or published in a safe, measured, watered down, even distorted form – a form acceptable to what I would call the Prevailing Established Viewpoint, a kind of acceptable Bias. (Pilger, 1982: 5)

Pilger extended his criticisms of prevailing journalistic practice when, in his essay 'A Question of Balance' (in 1989: 502), he argued that British television news broadcasters claim a certain authority based on a consensus view of the world which operates through the practices of objectivity, balance and impartiality. For Pilger, 'There is no such thing as a genuine consensus view. Britain is not one nation with one perspective on events and with everyone sharing roughly the same power over their lives. "Consensus view" is often a euphemism for the authorised wisdom of established authority in Britain.' The writer Stuart Hood, once employed by the BBC in the area of news and current affairs, made a similar comment on the relationship between 'impartiality' and the politics of social consensus:

> In practice [impartiality] is the expression of a middle-class consensus politics, which continues that tradition of impartiality on the side of the establishment so clearly defined by Reith. Impartiality is impartiality within bounds and is applied to those parties and organisations which occupy the middle ground of politics; where impartiality breaks down

is when the news deals with political activities or industrial action which is seen as being a breach of the conventions of consensus. (Hood, 1972: 418)

The criticisms made by Pilger and Hood echo the conclusions of certain studies of impartiality and balance in news, current affairs and news documentaries. One such study examined the operation of 'impartiality' in the long-running BBC current affairs programme *Panorama*. The authors judged the programme to be impartial in the sense of giving equal attention to Conservative and Labour party viewpoints and proportional coverage of other parties (such as the Liberals, for example) operating within the boundaries of consensus politics. However, certain views deemed beyond the limits of consensus politics (Communist, anarchist or nationalist parties, for example) were not included in the news coverage. Thus, 'impartiality' was implemented within the framework of an assumed consensus in ways which the authors argue reproduced the impression of 'the unity of the Parliamentary political system as a whole', reinforcing an ideology of national cohesion and common purpose that overwrites conflicting class or party interests (Hall, Connell, Curti, 1985).

Pilger's experience of the operation of 'due impartiality' and 'balance' in British broadcasting began with his first news documentary, *The Quiet Mutiny* (1970). The documentary provoked a complaint by Walter Annenberg, the US Ambassador to Britain at the time, to Sir Robert Fraser, the Director-General of the Independent Television Authority (ITA), the regulatory body for commercial television (later the Independent Broadcasting Authority (IBA) and subsequently the Independent Television Commission, ITC[5]). Fraser, who admitted that he hadn't seen Pilger's report, described it as 'grossly unbalanced', 'anti-American' and 'in serious breach of the code of impartiality'. The ITA demanded that in order for the producer of the programme, Granada Television, to comply with the impartiality clause of the Broadcasting Act it would have to produce a programme to balance the Pilger report. The result was a *World in Action* programme dealing with Prime Minister Edward Heath's hobby of sailing. To Pilger, the rules were nonsensical and he facetiously concluded of the incident that 'the subject of Ted Heath's yacht was considered to contain enough ideological ballast to correct "listing" caused by a film critical of the American war in Asia' (Pilger, 1989: 510).

On another occasion the IBA refused to allow a broadcast of Pilger's documentary *The Truth Game* (Central Television, 1983), an investigation openly critical of the nuclear weapons policies of successive British governments, until a 'complementary' or 'balancing' programme was produced (Pilger, 1989: 529–32). In 1977 the Annan Report on the future of broadcasting services in the United Kingdom had recommended that the legal requirement of 'due impartiality' in news broadcasting 'should not preclude committed public affairs programmes from having a recognised place on the broadcasting outlets' (quoted in Holland, 2000: 150).[6] Broadcasting authorities had enacted such a recommendation by distinguishing between those programmes deemed to be impartial news and current affairs journalism and the newly created category of 'personal view reports' in which a reporter could express personal opinions. Placed within this latter category, Pilger's documentaries should, presumably, have been free of the 'balancing' requirement.

Pilger interpreted the IBA's insistence on a second programme to be 'insidious censorship' in the sense that any future broadcaster would be wary of producing a report on a controversial topic knowing that it would be required to pay the cost of producing a second, 'complementary' programme. Pilger also resented the 'personal view' tag as a form of intellectual ghettoization that suggested that a report so labelled was politically wayward. In an address to a gathering of journalists at the Melbourne Press Club in 1982, Pilger likened the personal view label to a government health warning on a cigarette packet. According to Pilger the label, in effect, alerts the viewer to be aware that the information in the report 'deviates from the prevailing wisdom – and may damage your preconceptions'. In the same address Pilger argued that the effect of labels which imply that a report is 'radical', 'emotional', 'committed' or 'controversial' 'is to conclude that a journalist has gone "too far" ... Whatever the adjective, the aim of the label is the same – to make the journalist appear different from his colleagues and therefore dangerous. The next step is easy – his or her work can be discredited' (Pilger, 1982: 4).

Questions of impartiality were refocused in Britain in 1990 during public discussions surrounding the introduction of a new broadcast bill. The bill required that due impartiality be achieved within 'a series of programmes considered as a whole' (not within a single programme) and the ITC would determine '(a) what due impartiality either does or does not require, either generally or in relation to particular circumstances; (b) the ways in which due impartiality may be achieved in connection with programmes of particular descriptions; (c) the period in which a programme should be included in a licensed service if its inclusion is intended to secure that due impartiality is achieved' (quoted in McNair, 1999: 96). Responses to the amendments were varied, though many sources were critical of the proposed changes. Broadcasters suggested that under the amendments they would be required to produce a series of programmes to satisfy impartiality requirements, as opposed to a single 'balancing' programme. Others feared a potential for litigation from those who perceived 'bias' in news or current affairs programmes (McNair, 1999: 96). Pilger argued that 'control is the real aim' and insisted that 'the amended bill will tame, and where possible, prevent the type of current affairs and documentary programmes that have exposed the secret pressures and corruption of establishment vested interests, the lies and duplicity of government ministers and officials' (quoted in McNair, 1999: 96). Pilger referred to *Death on the Rock* as a programme which revealed important events but which, nevertheless, would be subject to attack under the new act for its strident point of view. The need to maintain impartiality over a series of programmes would, Pilger predicted, result in a situation in which 'charlatans and child abusers, Saddam Hussein and Pol Pot, all will have the legal right to airtime should they be the objects of "one-sided" journalistic scrutiny' (Pilger [1990] quoted in Franklin, 2001: 191).

A new Broadcasting Act was introduced in Britain in late 1990 and came into effect on 1 January 1991.[7] The ITC, charged with implementing the Act, published its revised Programme Code in February 1991.[8] The Code allayed certain fears by confirming that due impartiality did not have to be achieved in a single programme and that it should be interpreted as meaning 'adequate or appropriate to the nature of the subject and the type of programme ... It does *not* mean that "balance" is required in any simple mathematical sense or that equal time must be given to each opposing point of view' (quoted in McNair, 1999: 98). The Code maintained the 'personal view' label, which was to be clearly attached to programmes deemed to contain subjective positions on controversial topics. Surveying the first four years of the Code's operation, Brian McNair (1999: 99) stated that 'Broadcasting journalists have not been embroiled in time-consuming and expensive legal battles on

the question of impartiality, nor have they been required to produce artificial "balancing" exercises. To this extent, the fears of
Pilger...and others of the similarly pessimistic disposition have
not been realised.'

Produced the same year that the new broadcasting act was
drafted (1990), Pilger's *Cambodia: The Betrayal* is a committed and
impassioned piece of television journalism, the kind of programme that, arguably, conservative supporters of the Broadcasting
Act felt the new act should address. Importantly, within its impassioned stance, the programme's representational strategies
operate to pull its rhetorical claims away from 'unfairness' or bias
or partiality by constructing a sense of legitimacy and believability,
what Brian McNair (1999: 34) calls a ' "truth" quotient', that functions to position the programme as an authoritative, complete and
factual account of events.

## Cambodia: the betrayal

Over the course of his career Pilger has reported extensively on
south-east Asia. He reported the war in Vietnam for the *Daily Mirror*
newspaper in Britain and wrote of the end of the war in his book *The
Last Day* (1975). His coverage of post-war Vietnam and Cambodia
has appeared in a variety of sources, among them the *New Statesman*
and *The Guardian* and in his books *Aftermath* (1982) and *Heroes*
(1986; rev. edn 1989). His broadcast journalism for British independent television has included reports on Vietnam (*The Quiet Mutiny*,
1970, *Do You Remember Vietnam?*, 1978, *Vietnam: The Last Battle*, 1995),
East Timor (*Death of a Nation*, 1994, and *The Timor Conspiracy*, 1999)
and Cambodia (*Cambodia: Year Zero*, 1980, *Cambodia: Year Ten*, 1989,
*Cambodia: The Betrayal*, 1990 and *Return to Year Zero*, 1993).
In *Cambodia: The Betrayal* Pilger and his team return to Cambodia a
decade after Pol Pot's infamous 'Year Zero' to investigate shipments
of arms and munitions to Cambodia's outlawed Khmer Rouge.
Pilger provides a broad framework for the investigation in his
opening on-camera comments to the programme:

> One year ago in a film broadcast around the world we showed that
> this uniquely tragic country was once again in danger of falling to the
> greatest mass murderers since Hitler, the Khmer Rouge of Pol Pot, and
> that Western governments and the United Nations were allowing this
> to happen for reasons of Cold War politics. The response from the

public was unprecedented: tens of thousands of people wrote to their governments seeking for Cambodia not charity, but action. Unfortunately, this film is not a celebration of a Cambodia now free from the threat of another holocaust. It's about betrayal, a betrayal of those who asked for help for Cambodia, regardless of whether that help meant offending the United States and China which give direct and indirect support to the Khmer Rouge. Above all, it's a betrayal of a people who have struggled virtually alone to rebuild their stricken country. For tonight's film will show that Western governments are among those secretly providing the means for Pol Pot's return to power.

The opening exposition situates *Cambodia: The Betrayal* as a 'follow-up report' on an earlier programme (*Cambodia: Year Ten*). In outlining the need for the current programme the exposition draws attention to the fact that the original report was 'broadcast around the world' and led to an 'unprecedented' response from the public. In these terms, the opening exposition suggests that the current report will also provide previously unknown information capable of inspiring a reaction by the public and governments. Notably, Pilger is not only claiming the significance of the events he reports, he is arrogating significance to his reportage.

Pilger delivers his opening commentary to-camera in a medium shot in which he is framed standing before the Cambodian countryside. The countryside is evoked as the scene of operations of the Khmer Rouge, and as such is presented as a dangerous and forbidding place, though there is no visual evidence of the Khmer Rouge. In this case, to quote John Corner on the operation of location reporting, the 'reporter is on the "stage"; the spaces and places of news occurrence can be viewed and can generate their interest and significance' though, in the absence of any sign of the Khmer Rouge, 'the *evidential* qualities of the visualisation itself … are negligible' (1995: 59).[9] A certain form of 'evidence' of Pol Pot's continuing war against civilians is provided in subsequent scenes in the form of maimed bodies in overcrowded hospitals. While the hospital scenes are dramatic and disturbing, the information they present is limited in its capacity as evidence of Khmer Rouge atrocities – few people admit that the Khmer Rouge were responsible for their injuries.

In the absence of visual images of their subject the filmmakers fall back upon methods commonly used to compensate for evidential inadequacies. As Corner notes, a lack of visual evidence may be partly overcome 'by news teams resorting to a variety of ruses.

Reconstructions, "stagings" (the asking of people to perform actions before the camera), the use of previously shot material, including library film, and the mixing-in of visuals from related but different stories can all be deployed in an attempt to make up for the deficit in actuality footage' (1995: 59). The limitation stemming from the absence of an effective visualization of Khmer Rouge activity is addressed in the opening of *Cambodia: The Betrayal* in a form of reconstruction achieved through visual association. The programme begins with a startling montage. Black and white photographs flash on the screen – images of land mines and other weapons are interspersed with images of limbless people. The connection between weapons and death and maiming is extended in footage of a young girl treading through the mud of a rice field, followed by a simulated explosion which frighteningly suggests the deadly effects of land mines. The sequence performs an evidentiary function, confirming the existence of land mines laid in the fields of Cambodia by the Khmer Rouge, through a method that does not rely on the presentation of verifiable evidence of the visual claim.

In keeping with a growing practice in television reporting, the images here function symbolically, evoking conditions in a secondary, particularistic way, as opposed to direct, iconic, depictions of events (a comparison with the use of 'generic' shots, discussed in Chapter 7, is useful here). A detailed case study of the visualizations included in Canadian news reports of a political assassination has pointed to the ways in which many images used in television news are essentially 'symbolic' and not iconic. The authors of the study argued that:

> In television news, in fact, a relatively small proportion of the total number of shots is iconic or directly representative of the people, places and events which are the subjects of the news text. A far greater proportion of shots has an oblique relationship to the text; they 'stand for' the subject matter ... symbolically. (quoted in Corner, 1995: 60)

In this way, *Cambodia: The Betrayal* contains other examples of images deployed symbolically or metaphorically. The foreboding concerning the fate of Cambodia that infuses Pilger's opening comments is enhanced in the fact that Pilger presents his comments against a background in which storm clouds are clearly evident on the horizon. Elsewhere in the programme Pilger comments in voice-over, 'Fear is like a presence here … the night belongs to the prospect of a second holocaust.' The accompanying image is that of motorcycle headlights piercing the early evening to form a scene in which the otherwise innocent arrival of night is burdened with menace. It is important to note that the shift from iconic images to the use of images functioning symbolically has been a focus of debates about bias in television news coverage (Corner, 1995: 60). Within the shift, particular meanings are constructed from images which in other contexts denote a different, less rhetorical, set of meanings. Clearly, the early evening scene of motorcycles on a quiet street of a Cambodian village could easily be reframed expositionally as evidence of the peace that reigns in the countryside. It is easy to see how charges of bias are levelled at the symbolic, metaphoric or generic use of images. Countering the potential for such a charge, *Cambodia: The Betrayal* deploys a number of strategies which construct the representation as authoritative, fair and correct.

The authority of the representation derives in part from an emphasis on Pilger's professionalism, a yardstick of acceptable journalistic behaviour. The notion of professionalism carries with it a sense of expertise and authority, and the professional draws on a wealth of experience to support and reinforce her/his rhetorical positions, in contrast to the amateur, who is inexperienced and hence lacking in credibility. Pilger's professionalism is reinforced through his on-screen attire, a variation of which he wears in all of his documentaries: beige slacks and a khaki or blue shirt with button-down pockets and epaulettes. It is the outfit of the professional hunter, or contemporary explorer or committed roving reporter. Dan Rather, the long-serving 'anchor' person of CBS evening news forged an identity for himself by wearing a v-neck pullover as he read the evening news. In the words of *Washington Post* critic Tom Shales, the pullover gave Rather a 'trust-me, you've-got-a-friend, hello-out-there-in-television-land sense' (Himmelstein, 1987: 269). Pilger's outfit, in contrast, evokes an impression of 'I'm a professional and committed globe-trotting journalist seeking out the facts in the manner of a hunter tracking prey.'

The appeal to professionalism is extended in on-screen comments, as when Pilger, having been refused any contact with the US Department of State, declares 'In all my years as a journalist I have not met such reluctance on the part of the State Department to answer questions.' The reference to a long and successful career in

investigative journalism – 'In all my years ...' – overtly defers to and
encodes notions of professionalism, authority and trustworthiness.
Such conceptions are complemented within the modes of presentation relied on in the programme. Standing before the State
Department building in Washington, DC, speaking directly to
camera, Pilger is 'on location'. Of the two, internationally established conventions available to news reports – the formal studio
setting in which information is read or presented, and the on-site
location in which information is reported – *Cambodia: The Betrayal*
consistently relies on location settings. In an analysis of both studio
and location conventions, Corner (1995: 56) outlines nine basic
location modes:

- Reporter's to-camera speech in 'stand-up' exposition (with
  varying framing, composition and shot types).
- Reporter's speech and actuality sound in ongoing participant-
  action sequences (e.g. report in flood relief boat; with emergency convoy; trapped in ambush; attempting to gain access to
  premises).
- Reporter's voice-over filmed sequences in which reporter is not
  shown.
- Filmed sequence, actuality sound, no speech. Such sequences
  may involve visual effects of a non-naturalistic kind, for instance
  rapid, associative editing and various forms of 'symbolic' shot.
- Reporter's voice over still image (telephoned report; the convention here is reporter's face superimposed in the corner of a
  shot of the report's location).
- Reporter interview with both speakers in shot.
- Reporter interview with only interviewee in shot and reporter's
  questions edited out.
- Interviewee voice-over used with film.
- Interviewee seen as social actor, carrying out activities with relevant dialogue and/or interviewee voice-over.

As Corner notes, 'Each mode offers up a different "way of knowing" about the subject of the news report' (1995: 56). In *Cambodia:
The Betrayal* ways of knowing are chiefly mediated by the first
two modes outlined above (other modes are used though not as
intensively as the first two operations). Both modes focus directly
on Pilger as reporter. In these two modes especially, the reporter is
on screen, foregrounded as the source of information (in the case
of the State Department scene, replete with Pilger attempting to
gain access to the premises). The intensive focus of the modes

draws attention to the credibility of the reporter (reinforced within Pilger's reference to 'all my years as a journalist') which functions in this instance to validate and legitimate the pronouncements and positions of the programme as a whole.

While Pilger's comment on his journalistic career endorses the information he presents, the location mode licenses the subjective, first person, remark. Corner notes that speech of studio-presented news 'is still most often projected in a strongly public address mode, the newsdesk acting as a marker of its "official" character. The speech of reporters on location is also direct address (both to-camera and voice-over) but a wider range of ... registers becomes available to location reporters.' This latitude 'is a result both of the more extensive possibilities available for self-visualisation in location settings and the shift in the basic talk form from "reading" to "reporting", with [as Pilger's case demonstrates] the valida-tion for what he said now being grounded in the personal experiences ... of the speaker' (1995: 62). Corner also suggests that the speech of reporters on location is open to a wider range of vocal turns than that of the presenter in the studio. Michael Buerk is one presenter who uses various tonal qualities in his location voice-overs.[10] Unlike his contemporaries, the tone of Pilger's presentation remains calm, measured and uniform – the voice of rationality – carrying with it an emphasis on professionalism in the face of the dreadful situation.

Professionalism and its attendant authority connect with and reinforce an appeal to fact implicit in the structure of the narrative as it begins to resemble a detective mystery. Within these terms, Pilger's role becomes that of the lone detective seeking clues and revealing facts. He inaugurates such a narrative when he states, 'Of all the mysteries surrounding support for Pol Pot two questions are outstanding: how and why Western arms are getting to the Khmer Rouge.' To unravel these questions his investigations lead him on a journey beginning in Bonn and from there to Brussels. A brief ani-mated sequence depicting a map, complete with an arrow pointing across Europe is used to link Germany to Belgium. An arrow stretching across a map of Europe evokes a similar convention in Capra's *Why We Fight* (1943–45) series of the Second World War documentaries which routinely used animated arrows to depict movements of Allied and enemy armies back and forth across Europe and the Pacific. In both *Why We Fight* and *Cambodia: The Betrayal* the animated arrow helps to reinforce narrative drive by providing a purposive line of spatial and rhetorical direction. In the case of *Cambodia: The Betrayal* the arrow also figuratively encodes the concept of the 'roving reporter' and the tradition of so-called passport journalism in which a globe-trotting journalist tracks events worldwide.

Pilger and his production team head south from Belgium to Singapore, and from there to rural Thailand. At each location Pilger searches for clues that will assist his investigation. The clues gathered during the journey, and the journey's end at a Khmer Rouge weapon store in Thailand, resolve the 'mystery' by demonstrating that the weapons are supplied by European and Singaporean arms manufacturers with the knowledge, if not the active assistance, of the US government. The 'mystery' is resolved in a way which not only reveals the facts but also demonstrates the extended processes and investigative prowess whereby the facts were exposed.

The pattern of resolution exemplifies what Corner has described as television's important capacity to 'present the viewer with an imaging of *the process of reporting itself*'. Corner notes that:

> This is simultaneously a spatial, social and personal imaging (who, where, talking to whom?), linking the viewer to a seen source of information and allowing the personalised investment of a trust in the visible processes of inquiry, of the search for truth. This trust is not available in the same way for other kinds of journalism ....(1995: 60)

The capacity of the visual medium of television to provide insights and identifications not available to other types of journalism is central to the effectiveness and appeal of broadcast journalism. This 'imaging' is, however, a subtle process which does not immediately draw attention to itself. The visualizations of a documentary news report are rallied in indirect ways to provide information on a nominated topic, which is the overt focus and object of the report. A director quoted by Bill Nichols (1991: x) underlines this point when he comments that 'A good documentary stimulates discussion of its subject, not itself.' *Cambodia: The Betrayal* effectively foregrounds the plight of Cambodia, drawing attention to the ongoing threat posed by a re-armed Khmer Rouge, within and through a subtle deployment of various depictive strategies. Together, these strategies function to reinforce the programme's evidentiary claims and journalistic authority to position the work as a 'fair', unbiased and factually correct representation of events.

## The long-form news documentary and contemporary 'news' forms

Traditionally, the filmed news report on a single topic such as those produced by Pilger constituted part of what Corner (1995: 75) has called the 'loose genre of television documentary'. Recent demands of television programming have, however, reconfigured the place of 'news' on television, thereby reworking and expanding the loose boundaries of the television documentary genre. 'News' has become a component of various formats, no longer necessarily a discrete category identifiable in terms of the multiple items of a news bulletin, or the single filmed report of current affairs programming and the long-form special news report. Forms of US-led versions of the so-called news magazine, for example, mix journalism, features and studio-based 'chat' (Corner, 1995: 75). Such formats have proved popular, and as a result they have been central to scheduler's strategies of attracting audiences, especially in the mid- to late-evening slots. Variants of the news magazine include the informal presentation of 'news' in 'breakfast TV' (where 'chat' tends to prevail over news items) and the tenuous connection to journalism found in 'infotainment'. In such works, the role of investigation and the issues of impartiality and bias which attend it in the long-form news documentary have been displaced by questions of entertainment within an 'informational' mode. As Chapter 10 points out, the place of entertainment within varieties of factual depictions is also at the centre of discussions of popular factual programming.

# CHAPTER 10

# Up Close and Personal: Popular Factual Entertainment

A string of recent Hollywood and independently produced feature films have drawn on popular factual media trends for their plots. *The Truman Show* (1998), *EdTV* (1999), *Series 7* (2000) and *15 Minutes* (2001) have all mocked the voyeuristic and competitive bases of proliferating forms of factual television programming. The ironies and inversions involved in the fact that these fictional films re-create the premise of television programmes which presume to present unscripted reality point in one way to the manner in which the 'truth' of reality television is stranger than fiction. *Series 7*, a black comedy about a reality show in which contestants stalk and murder one another, might appear to take the game show format of recent reality television to an ultimate satirical conclusion, nonetheless, its premise has, sadly, been accepted in the world of 'talk television', a precursor of reality television. As the executive producer of the *Jerry Springer* talk show has said, with an apparent lack of irony, 'There is no line to draw. If I could kill someone on television ... I would execute them on television.' (quoted in Maddox, 2000: 200).[1]

The producer's comment raises serious questions concerning the ethics of what increasingly is known as popular factual entertainment, whether it be crime-based 'reality TV' programmes, so-called docusoap serials, video footage in the *Funniest Home Video* format, or reality programmes based on competition (such as *Survivor* and *Big Brother*).[2] Certain commentators have begun to address specific ethical dilemmas raised by newer forms of television programming, including the fate of privacy within the voyeuristic focus of many of these programmes, though this area is in need of further consideration as part of a broader process of reappraising the ethical dimensions of documentary practices.[3] For a number of observers, forms of popular factual entertainment constitute a debasement of the documentary tradition and of television programming in general. This position is adequately, and bluntly, summarized in the assessment that variants of reality television comprise 'the trashiest and most manipulative televisual forms yet invented' (Goodwin, 1997). Such a statement, with its implicit appeal to conceptions of 'cultural value', falls within a long-standing debate in television studies concerning the place of quality in programming. Studies in this area have pointed out that far from being an immutable characteristic of the television programme, 'quality' reflects, and is constructed through, what are often class-based distinctions between forms of culture deemed to be inherently valuable and aesthetically pleasing (so-called high culture) and those which are assumed to be inherently inferior (so-called low culture). Frequently such distinctions are drawn without reference to the ways in which programmes are received by an audience. In this relation, one viewer's masterpiece is another viewer's trash, and the inverse is also true.[4]

The public debate over popular factual entertainment has, in other ways, implicated the division between public experience and the domain of private life. For some commentators, reality television crosses an assumed boundary between the two spheres of public and private life and in doing so contributes to the erosion of private space and the refuge it offers from a society increasingly dedicated to a voyeuristic surveillance of personal life (Calvert, 2000). This position is reflected in arguments that such works evoke Orwell's notion of Big Brother scrutinizing every action of the modern citizen, thereby contributing to a broader political and social process which constitutes an attack on civil liberties. (Orwell's warning in his novel *1984* about the potential of the surveillance function of the State, which he encapsulated in the figure of 'Big Brother', is evacuated of any political resonance in the programme of the same name which uses the concept of Big Brother as a metaphor for watching and observing.)

In place of the many arguments against forms of factual television, a species of 'popular culturalist' argument endorses the forms as popular and populist programming which invites viewers 'to rethink and possibly revalue' their attitudes to ethical, social and political issues (Blumler, 1999: 246). Other observers argue that reality television, and popular factual entertainment in general, provides opportunities for citizens to gain access to television broadcasting through methods such as the submission of videotape footage, as in the case of *Video Diaries* or the *Funniest Home Videos* format, or physical participation in reality game shows such as *Survivor* and *Big Brother*, or the online and telephone viewer voting associated with *Big Brother*. Such methods, it is claimed, empower the viewer, transforming him or her from a slumberous 'couch potato' into an active participant in the broadcasting process and through it wider participation in the public life of society.[5]

While notions of quality in television programming and the assessment of the social effects of the new forms of programming have provided the basis for various analyses of popular factual entertainment, this chapter focuses on a different set of concerns. Specifically, this chapter considers formal and stylistic features of the forms, in particular, narrative patterns, editing styles, the use of testimony and modes of observation and performance in popular factual television programming, and the ways in which such features force a reconsideration of 'entertainment' and its vexed relationship with documentary. The analysis draws on a range of programmes in the broad category of popular factual entertainment, with particular reference to crime-based reality television (specifically the influential example *Cops*, Fox, 1989), so-called docusoaps (among them MTVs *The Real World*, 1992) and 'reality game shows', with particular reference to the global televisual phenomenon *Big Brother* (UK: Channel 4, 2000; US: CBS, 2000; Australia: Channel Ten, 2001).[6] Bracketing together a range of examples from the increasingly diversified field of popular factual programming is not meant to suggest that programmes within the field can be reduced to a set of common formal features. The analysis here recognizes the differences between the formal techniques of varieties of popular factual entertainment, and notes variations within these programmes in different national contexts (particularly Britain, the United States and Australia) within a history of phases in the development of factual programming. The focus on central, formal and stylistic components derived from a range of popular factual television programming indicates the ways in which aspects of separate formats constitute an expansion of the techniques, approaches and styles of documentary. The analysis of these processes is contextualized through reference to a number of factors which have contributed to the rise of factual forms, principally the crucial issue of production economics, in particular the cost of producing popular factual entertainment and the advertising revenues generated by programmes that openly appeal to younger audiences.

## The rise of popular factual entertainment

Over the past two decades, forms of reality programming have mutated and multiplied to the point where actuality-based programming is now a central component of free-to-air television broadcasting in a variety of countries. Not insignificantly, the majority of the reasons which have contributed to this growth are associated with the demands of deregulated television broadcast environments. A commercialized context has seen an increase in the number of television channels and a decrease in budgets available for television production. These factors have led to a situation in which costly drama and comedy programmes have increasingly been replaced in the schedules by experiments with formats which are cheaper to produce and hold the potential to attract large audiences. These forces are clearly evident in the case of the Fox Broadcasting Company in the United States which, under the ownership of Rupert Murdoch, has expanded to become what is effectively America's fourth terrestrial television network (alongside ABC, NBC and CBS). Fox's strategy for growth has been to appeal to an audience not adequately captured by the other networks, in particular young, lower-income and minority viewers, while at the same time minimizing programme production costs. Actuality-based programming has performed both of these tasks (Fishman, 1998: 66). Fox's growth strategy has included investment in expensive drama and comedy programmes aimed at the younger market, the hit comedy series *Friends* being one such example. In many ways, however, such programmes were made possible through the savings on the production costs of the company's proliferating low-budget reality-based formats, among them *America's Most Wanted* and *Cops*.[7]

The relatively inexpensive production costs of certain forms of reality-based programming are exemplified in comparison with the production budgets of other formats. For example, the series *Star Trek: The Next Generation* produced by Paramount cost in excess of US$1.5 million for a one-hour episode while Fox's *America's Most Wanted* was produced in 1989 for a cost of US$140 000–$170 000 for a half-hour episode. More tellingly, perhaps, than contrasts between the production costs of reality television and expensive dramas is the fact that in the United States reality television costs a network less to produce than buying 'low end' programmes such as game shows. In the early 1990s the fee paid by a network to license a reality programme was, typically, US$500 000 an episode, only half of the amount paid for a one-hour dramatic series (Dempsey, 1991: 34). Reflecting these trends, docusoaps produced in Britain during 2000 cost less than a third of situation comedies and other forms of light entertainment (Bruzzi, 2000: 77). In contrast to the historical documentary miniseries, for example, reality programming does not require lengthy and hence costly research and scripting. Similarly, there are no costs associated with employing professional actors, and in certain cases, such as the popular 'funniest home video' format of reality programming, the producers construct a programme at minimal cost from footage that is provided to them by viewers. The major expense associated with the 'funniest home video' format is the salary paid to the resident host who introduces and narrates the programme.

Not only is popular factual entertainment relatively cheap to produce, it is economically attractive to broadcasters in terms of its resale potential. The programme *Cops*, for example, is constructed from segments that situate the action geographically ('Dallas', 'Boston' and so on) yet which are devoid of any temporal references. The 'timelessness' of episodes extends their shelf, or screen life thus contributing to the ability to recycle the programme to independent networks and cable stations. Practices have shown that certain formats developed for one national television market can be readily packaged or remade ('copycatted') to meet the requirements of international television markets (Moran, 1998). The process of franchising a programme format is now a lucrative component of television economics, and one which has contributed to the international proliferation of reality programming. The most obvious example of this process is *Big Brother*, a format devised in 1999 by the transnational Endemol Entertainment group that has since been sold to numerous television stations throughout the world, among them Australia's Channel Ten network which paid nearly A$20 million for the rights to the format

(Leech, 2001: 3).[8] The purchase price paid by Ten was a substantial outlay for a channel attempting to meet the challenges of multi-channel competition with reduced budgets; however *Big Brother*'s proven capacity to attract high revenues from advertisers justified the purchase price and helped defray production costs (the series had generated an estimated A\$16 million in advertising and sponsorship part way through its first season[9]).

As with the majority of reality programming, *Big Brother* openly appeals to younger audiences, in particular the lucrative market of 16–34-year-olds.[10] This cohort has a high disposable income and as such, it is heavily targeted by advertisers. Indeed, the demands of advertisers to place their products before this audience have led to the increasingly prevalent practice of product placement. The practice structures what are, effectively, advertisements for products *within* a programme in ways which extend the bracketing of advertisements in frequent breaks *between* segments of a programme. An example of product placement occurred in the US version of the series *Survivor* (CBS) when the winning contestant was presented with a motor vehicle as part of his prize. The camera's gaze emphasized the vehicle's brand, and the winner's emotive reactions to the prize ('How wild is this thing!') served as a spontaneous and heartfelt personal endorsement of the product. The contestants in the first series of Australian *Big Brother* were frequently seen eating a sponsor's brand of pizza in a way that redefined the phrase 'conspicuous consumption' and its reference to open displays of consumerism.

Economic factors such as cost of production and revenue from advertisers have gone hand-in-hand with other factors, among them, alterations to programming schedules, in the development of popular factual entertainment. A general shift toward popular 'light' entertainment programming in the television schedules of Britain, Australia and elsewhere has created a number of opportunities for the scheduling of the species of light entertainment referred to here as popular factual entertainment. Whereas once documentaries on television were typically screened in late-night slots, often after 11 p.m., popular factual entertainment has moved into the 'prime time' early- and mid-evening slots. (In Britain the watershed marking prime evening from late evening is 9 p.m.) Crime-based reality television led the way for such a move, though it was the docusoap format which fully established factual entertainment in evening prime time. The scheduling strategies of hammocking, moving an established series to a later slot to make room for a new series, and tent-poling, featuring a proven programme or format at mid-evening on week nights as a way of anchoring the programmes before and after it, have contributed to the recent rise of a range of light entertainment programming, including factual forms. Even a cursory glance at the early and mid-evening television schedules reveals the extent of the spread of popular factual entertainment such as docusoaps and reality game shows, and varieties of related light factual entertainment, among them, cookery, do-it-yourself and gardening programmes.[11]

## Phases in the development of factual programming

The media theorist John Corner (2000b) provides background to recent changes in the television environment by tracing various stages in the development of factual programming. Corner's schema was devised with reference to broadcasting in the United Kingdom though aspects of the outline are applicable to trends in other broadcasting environments. Running parallel to the phases Corner identifies – reality television, docusoap, presenter-led series and what can be called reality game shows – is a trend in factual programming which includes the *Video Nation* series and hidden camera formats. These various stages, which for the sake of analysis are divided here into separate categories (although in practice they contain a number of overlapping features), form the basis of a history of popular factual entertainment over the past 20 years.

The opening phase of popular factual entertainment, that of reality television, began in the late 1980s in the United States, with a number of commentators pointing to NBC's *Unsolved Mysteries*, launched in 1987, as one of the first programmes in this format (Kilborn, 1994a: 426). Fox's *America's Most Wanted* (1989) and CBS's *Real Life Heroes* (1989) and its *Rescue 911* (1989) soon followed, contributing to what became a major broadcasting trend in which the work of police and emergency service workers was depicted in actuality footage and dramatic re-enactments of crime and accident scenes. Kilborn (1994a: 423) describes as reality TV programmes which involve '(a) the recording, "on the wing", and frequently with the help of lightweight video equipment, of events in the lives of individuals and groups, (b) the attempt to simulate real-life events through various forms of dramatized reconstruction and (c) the incorporation of this material, in suitably edited form, into an attractively packaged television programme.' In reference to (a) above, Fetveit (1999: 792) notes that reality TV commonly relies on visual evidence composed of 'authentic footage from camera crews observing arrests or rescue operations; footage from surveillance videos; recordings (often by amateurs) of dramatic accidents and dangerous situations'. Buscombe (2000: 17) outlines the principal features of the format when he notes that reality programmes 'operate on a dual axis with regard to the "reality effect"': 'On one hand, they seek to heighten audience involvement by deploying the full range of techniques traditionally associated with news and documentary: hand-held cameras, direct sound, location shooting and so forth .... On the other hand, the programmes borrow from fiction the techniques of dramatic construction: actors, scripted dialogue, studio lighting.' These techniques were popularized on British television in the BBC1 series *999 Lifesavers* (1992) within its mix of reconstructions and sequences of dramatic actuality footage shot on hand-held cameras by emergency service workers or amateurs. The dramatic potential of shaky, grainy and hence 'authentic' footage was intensified through the use of a mood-enhancing music soundtrack, and the comments made over each segment by the narrator. The programme was presented by respected broadcaster and journalist Michael Buerk and was framed as a public service providing instructions to viewers on ways to avoid or react to situations similar to those depicted.

Subsequent developments in reality television continued to draw on representations of crime and emergencies. The US series *Cops* typifies the trend and, through its influence internationally on other programmes, came to epitomize the content and conventions of reality television. In the United States the *Cops* format was duplicated in *Top Cops* (CBS, 1990), *American Detective* (ABC, 1992) and *Real Stories of the Highway Patrol* (CBS, 1992), and in the UK programmes such *Blues and Twos* (Carlton, 1993) and *Coppers* (Sky One, 1994) emulated the format. Footage for *Cops* was taped by camera crews accompanying police on their duties in urban areas throughout the United States. The focus in *Cops* on murder and accident scenes, domestic and other brawls, and dangerous car chases, in many ways parallels the content of tabloid journalism. Indeed, John Langer (1998) extends the links between the two forms by arguing that reality television originated with tabloid television's sensationalist reporting of what he calls the 'other news' of violence and personal tragedy.[12]

Beginning in the mid-1990s and continuing throughout the decade, the docusoap, the second phase of popular factual entertainment in Britain and elsewhere, has featured regularly in mid-evening slots within the television schedules. The success of the factual programme *Animal Hospital* established the potential of such programmes to hold their own in prime time. *Animal Hospital* commenced in January 1995 as a weekly half-hour programme screened on the BBC in the prime 8 p.m. slot. Its competitor in the schedules was the extremely popular crime drama *The Bill.* The fact that *Animal Hospital* secured a sizable audience share in the presence of an established and popular drama series convinced programmers of docusoap's ability to occupy prime time slots successfully on British television. The series followed individuals who offered personal or professional comment on the fate of sick animals and frequently relied on the 'cliff-hanger' – 'will Fluffy get better?' – to drive the narrative and maintain viewer interest from week to week (Ellis, 2000).

Docusoaps are character-centred works which develop multiple storylines based on factual material in ways which, as the term itself suggests, are comparable to fictional soap operas. A precursor of the format, and an informing influence on its mixture of observation, characterization and narrativization is *An American Family* (PBS, 1973), Craig Gilbert's landmark series of observational programming on US television. For seven months during 1971 Gilbert's camera crew observed the Loud family of Santa Barbara, California.[13] The final edited series of 12 parts followed Pat and Bill Loud and their five children through various changes, including the breakdown of Pat and Bill's marriage and their subsequent divorce. The unravelling story of the family, and the resemblance to a domestic soap opera in the story of a family unravelling, proved immensely popular with audiences when screened on US television in 1973. Gilbert's observational experiment with the Loud family was replicated in the United Kingdom in Paul Watson's *The Family* (BBC, 1974) and repeated by Watson in Australia in the series *Sylvania Waters* (BBC/ABC, 1992) in which formal elements of the docusoap (multiple narratives and an emphasis on characterization) were pronounced.

The emphasis in each of these examples on close observation of a familial unit informs the contemporary docusoap, many of which replace observation of a family with an intense focus on pseudo-families composed of young people sharing a house. The structuring device of what can be called the 'group house' formula was devised by the US cable station MTV for its reality programme *The Real World*. The inaugural series of *The Real World* (1992) featured a carefully selected group of young people brought together for six weeks to live in a loft in Manhattan. The series proved immensely popular with MTV's youthful audience and the format has been repeated in towns across the United States (Los Angeles, Seattle, San Francisco, Boston) and elsewhere (London). The success of *The Real World* launched a number of copycat programmes based on the lives of people who live together for weeks or months in front of the cameras. The BBC copied *The Real World* format with *The Living Soap* (BBC2, 1993), which follows the experiences of a group of students sharing a house in Manchester, and Channel 4 used the formula as the basis of its programme *Flatmates* (Channel 4, 1999). The historical experiment *1900 House* (Channel 4/PBS, 2000), in which a contemporary family adopts the lifestyle of people living at the turn of the twentieth century, is another version of the formula.

Recent forms of docusoap depart from pure observation by using voice-over narration to link and integrate a series of short scenes within each programme. The addition of a voice which narrates action in a familiar even conversational manner contributes to a style of textual address intended to appeal to an audience in ways reminiscent of other forms of light entertainment. The conversational approach is extended in the space which the docusoap provides for its subjects to express themselves on, and occasionally to, camera. Drawing on the appeal of television talk shows, the docusoap provides opportunities for people to express their points of view and describe their experiences in the public forum of television. The frequent inclusion of personal reflections in the docusoap, one aspect of its character-centred approach, lends the format to varieties of conversation and confession. As in the fictional soap opera, the lives of various social actors dominate narratives which are constructed from the experiences of people who are typically depicted at work in hotels, airports, hospitals, veterinary clinics, driving schools, the armed forces and other occupations. While everyday actions form the basis of most docusoaps, the programmes build tension through a focus on conflict and misadventures and generate suspense through cliffhanger endings.

The third and most recent phase of popular factual entertainment includes two major developments. The first involves what

John Corner (2000b) calls the 'docushow', those programmes which rely on a presenter (often a television celebrity recycled from another format) to introduce the factual and informational content. The antecedents of the docushow are so-called infotainment programmes such as fitness, cookery and travel programmes and recent 'lifestyle' programmes, among them personal and home 'makeover' shows. The second major development in the latest phase in factual programming is the reality game show or 'gamedoc', a format that combines elements of various factual approaches. Dovey (2001: 136) notes this aspect in his description of the gamedoc series *Big Brother*:

> Firstly, it took the 'ordinary people' aspect of 'reality TV', exploiting the appeal of watching ordinary people interacting, with the permanent possibility of intimacy revealed. Secondly, it used CCTV techniques: the subjects were under constant camera observation, producing the impression of an indexical representation of reality with a chaser of voyeuristic pleasure. These two pre-existing elements were combined with three genuine innovations: firstly, the game show format. This was indeed a piece of factual television, though very few 'facts' of information were imparted: this was pure entertainment, a game, a competition. Secondly, it was a game with a peculiar psychological twist in that participants were called upon to act as a team: the idea of the team was constantly invoked by the participants themselves, yet they were simultaneously called upon to 'betray the team' by voting out some if its members. [Thirdly] ... the producers added elements of interactivity... [which included] the telephone voting system that the public used to make the weekly eviction decisions ... [and a reliance on the Internet], in so far as the user could log on to video streamed camera feeds from the house, plus audio, at any time ...

The emphasis on physical endurance and competition in such programmes recalls an earlier generation of television game structured around physical performance. The games and tasks set for contestants in the popular series *Survivor*, for example, occasionally resemble the activities performed in the television series *American Gladiators* (TNN, 1989), and its international variants, and *It's a Knockout* (BBC1, 1969–82; Channel 5, 1999). In another way, the element of physical endurance and 'staying power' in programmes such as *Survivor* is reminiscent of the physically demanding dance marathons held in the United States in the 1930s.

Other trends have contributed to the expansion of popular factual entertainment. Corner (1996: 55) notes the place of new sound and image technologies, particularly the camcorder and micro-cameras, in the development of reality formats. Hidden camera footage forms the basis of programmes such as *Disguises* (Granada, 1993), *Undercover Britain* (Channel 4, 1994) and *Taxicab Confessions* (HBO, 1995). The format and practices of such programmes reflect the increasing use of hidden micro-cameras in tabloid news and current affairs programmes to record illegal or salacious activities. Camcorders have lent themselves to 'do-it-yourself' documentaries such as those featured in the BBC series *Video Diaries* and the filming of footage for 'funniest home video' formats.

The recent trends in popular factual entertainment outlined here have led to a rigorous debate concerning the place of entertainment in documentary. Documentary has not always set out to be entertaining in the way of fiction, yet the documentary canon does contain examples of works which use reality as the basis of entertainment (e.g. Flaherty's real-life dramas). Similarly, a number of television documentaries have sought to entertain and inform (the programme *Drinking for England* [BBC2, 1998] is a satisfying example of this mix). However, as Corner (2002) notes, when documentary is designed specifically as entertainment its forms of representation are radically altered. In this way the emphasis on entertainment in reality programming produces a fundamental shift in documentary – away from argumentation, analysis and exposition toward the pleasures of entertainment, what Corner (2002) calls 'documentary as diversion'. With this recognition in mind, the features of formal and stylistic experimentation and innovation analysed in the following sections can be understood to function in ways which maximize the entertainment appeal of factual programming, thereby constituting a revision of the traditional so-called sober informational basis of documentary (Nichols, 1991).

## Narrative

As pointed out in Chapter 1, fictional narrative is constructed around a causal agent – such as a wedding, a death or four weddings and a funeral – and the unfolding of a sequence of effects stemming from the causal event(s) or situation(s). The structuring of sequences reveals various aspects of each character, often positioning them in generic terms as hero or villain, and the ending provides closure, or the successful resolution of all strands of the story. In contrast to fiction film, documentary places less emphasis on story and is often structured in ways intended to advance an argument. Increasingly, though, distinctions between fictional and non-fictional narratives are blurring in film and television practice. It is now commonplace to represent factuality through a certain reliance on fictional techniques, a situation which is especially marked in popular factual entertainment programmes. Each episode of *The Real World*, for example, relies on three writers to construct a plot for each week's episode from hours of videotaped footage. One of the producers of the series, Mary-Ellis Bunim, outlines the similarity of the process to the production of fictional television when she comments, 'We storyboard each scene, just like in a prime-time [fictional] series' (quoted in Bellafante, 1995: 38).

The popular US television series *Cops* is another example of programming that borrows heavily from fictional narrative structures in its representation of non-fictional material. Episodes of *Cops* resemble the plots of prime time dramas in which a villain commits a crime that is uncovered and resolved when a hero, typically a member of the police force or a private detective, identifies and arrests, or kills, the villain. The police, the 'cops' of the series title, are represented as clear-headed and brave heroes involved in a continual round of questioning suspects and apprehending dangerous criminals. The reference to forms of police drama is extended in certain stylistic devices employed in the programme. For example, the patterns of light cast by the flashing lights of a police car, and the frequent inclusion of scenes shot at night, evoke the play of light and shadow which was a prominent feature of *film noir* of the 1940s and early 1950s.

Similarly, viewers of docusoaps are not asked to agree or disagree with propositions about the world – 'this is life in a theme park, supermarket, a department store' – but to enjoy the spectacle of action for its own sake (Dovey, 2000: 151). As with fictional narrative, a problem or conflict faced by 'characters' serves as causal agent for a sequence of events to be worked through and solved in the course of the episode or series. Docusoaps employ and share a range of narrative techniques; typically, two or three plots are presented in parallel within each episode, with frequent intercutting between each narrative strand. The cumulative effect of the technique multiplies narrative interest and in part compensates for the low level of incident in each week's episode. Episodes frequently abandon strict observation within the fact that they open with a summary sequence which introduces that week's 'characters' and the events they will encounter.

Docusoaps rely on other devices, notably music, to perform narrative tasks. As in fictional melodramas (literally, dramas set to music) the docusoap uses music to enhance mood and reinforce specific aspects of the narrative. For example, one episode of *The Cruise* (BBC1, 1998), a depiction of life on board a luxury cruise ship, contains a scene in which Edwin, a steward on the ship, sits exhausted on his bunk at the end of a long day of work as Phil Collins' 'Another Day in Paradise' plays on a radio in the background. In this context, the song provides an ironic counterpoint to the difficult working lives of the ship's crew and contrasts the crew's experiences with the leisurely holiday being enjoyed by the ship's passengers. The same song is used nondiegetically in the first series of *The Real World* in scenes focused on Julie, one of the young people chosen to live in the New York loft apartment that is the setting for the inaugural series of the programme. The Phil Collins song is played on the soundtrack as Julie befriends Darlene, a homeless African American woman, and again when Darlene disappears two nights later. As in *The Cruise*, the song ironically underscores a particular situation and in both cases, music does not serve as evidence or function to support evidential claims. Instead, musical accompaniment sets a mood and comments on the action in ways reminiscent of the operations of musical soundtracks in fictional filmic and televisual forms.

Docusoaps extend narratives across a series of episodes, with a result that each episode is left relatively open in a way which encourages viewers to return to forthcoming instalments. Frequently the trailer at the end of each episode functions in this way by providing teasing glimpses of narrative developments – as in, for example, the line 'Next week, an ankle injury puts Kate's future in doubt!', from the docusoap *Guns and Roses* (BBC1, 2000). The problem of closure in the serial form has in certain cases been resolved through extratextual developments, as when subjects of docusoaps have been able to exploit their television exposure by gaining recording or acting contracts. The resultant celebrity status, fuelled by a print and broadcast press willing to report such developments, provides a successful and satisfying conclusion to the docusoap narrative.

The docusoap serial format of melodramatic moments is carried over into the reality game show *Big Brother*. Like *The Real World*, with which it shares the group house formula, *Big Brother* is predicated on domestic tensions and budding romantic relationships between housemates. The teasing suggestion of a developing romance or the initiation of sex between contestants provides the programme with what has been called its 'sexualized narrative', a focus reinforced by the voice-over commentary (and extratextually by the press's coverage of events and incidents within the *Big Brother* household) which works to focus the narrative and through which a form of closure is achieved in each episode (Tincknell and Raghuram, 2002: 206). The visual scrutiny of sexual, emotional and domestic issues prominent in *Big Brother* can be compared with the high profile of such issues in the talk shows popularized in the United States in the 1990s (Tincknell and Raghuram, 2002: 204). Like *Big Brother*, such programmes depended on the participation of 'ordinary people' as performers willing to discuss (and enact) interpersonal conflicts and relationships for the television viewer. In this way, '*Big Brother*… combine[s] the agenda of talk television with the style of the documentary and the format of the game show, and in so doing [is] able to speak to a wide and potentially diverse television audience' (Tincknell and Raghuram, 2002: 205).

*Big Brother* has also included an online component which extends and complements its 'sexualized narrative'. The intertextual connections between the television programme and the various *Big Brother* websites operate to produce a layering of the narrative through the fact that developments in the house are discussed online and expanded by the online webcam coverage. The use of the Web as an integral part of the *Big Brother* 'project' is a distinct innovation in television 'interactivity'. Scannell argues that '*Big Brother* online served as a support and extension of *Big Brother* on TV, and not the other way around' (2002: 281). Dovey (2001: 137) places a greater emphasis on the role of the Internet in the attractions of *Big Bother* when he writes that 'use of the Net by *Big Brother* created a core of user involvement with the programme, points of activity identification for the audience that in turn fed the most important marketing network of all – the word-of-mouth network'. The 'chicken and egg' argument suggested by Scannell's assessment is a difficult one to unravel, though Scannell's downplaying of the role of the Web overlooks the fact that the official *Big Brother* website and numerous unofficial sites are primary venues for audience discussions as to who will be voted off the programme. Through its chat room functions the online component of the programme, then, has a determining effect on the narrative developments documented by the television coverage.

## Editing: revising the documentary look

Editing – the interrelationship of shots in a scene, and the relationship of one scene to the next – functions to support the process of narrativization. In fictional modes, styles of editing assist the development of storylines by locating the action in time and place and by highlighting features of characterization. Continuity editing, the dominant system used in fictional representation, carries the narrative forward in an unobtrusive way. Indeed, a central feature of this form of editing is its invisibility, that is, the way in which sequences of shots are structured into a smooth and seamless continuous flow of images. Docusoaps, though grounded in factual material, rely heavily on the editing techniques of fiction. Docusoaps develop narratives through a careful process of post-production editing in which frequent intercutting between parallel stories creates the narrative effect that the real-life characters are unified in time and place and working toward a single occupational purpose. Intercutting thereby provides a way to develop the narrative through the integration of various plot strands and a continual cutting back and forth between short segments of parallel stories also produces an effect of increasing the pace of the action.

The programme *Cops* extends the technique and intensifies narrative pace and movement through the forms of editing characteristic of the visual style associated with rock video clips shown on MTV: montage sequences, jump cuts, and a heavy reliance on short segments produced through multiple editing cuts. An MTV aesthetic is reproduced in the introductory segment of each episode of *Cops*. The programme opens with a montage of 30 images of police pursuing and arresting criminals which flash by in the minute of screen time dedicated to the segment. Over the images of the soundtrack plays the programme's theme song, 'Bad Boy', a watered-down rap style vocal. The spectacle, intensity and excitement of the introductory segment cues the viewer to the quick-paced action to follow. The footage used in *Cops* is composed of shaking and unfocused hand-held camera shots heavily suggestive of the style of direct cinema and its claim to represent its subject authentically. In *Cops* the authentic meets the exciting; only the most exciting sequences, vouchsafed as authentic by the camera style, are edited together in a blur of actions and locations. The visual pace is increased within sequences by using various filming techniques, notably the quick zoom on a point of action, and tracking shots, a common method of simulating pursuit and chase. The traditional role of documentary as a source of information about the world is reworked in *Cops*, which tends to replace any information about or understanding of crime and its causes with the thrill of fast-paced action (Andersen, 1995: 175).

An emphasis on visual excitement is also apparent in *Big Brother*'s borrowings from the MTV aesthetic. The introductory episode of the first series of the Australian version of *Big Brother*, for example, represented the arrival of contestants at the studio/house in quick cuts, brief and frequently interrupted sound bite interviews with contestants, and a soundtrack composed of cheers of onlookers mixed with booming location music. Many of the episodes set within the house followed the style of docusoaps in using quick cuts between individuals in various locations within the house/studio to build a level of action and to maintain multiple plots. The example of *Big Brother*, as with each of the formats analysed here, demonstrates a move away from evidentiality and a 'documentary look' (Caughie, 1980: 26) toward a form of representation grounded in spectacle.

## Testimony and confession

Documentaries often rely on interviews to reinforce evidential claims. Interviews can take the form of questions posed of an expert or authority figure in a studio or, alternatively, interviews may be shot on location with citizens willing to respond on camera to an interviewer who, typically, remains out of frame. Whatever the style of the interview, talking heads constitute a rhetorical device which is employed by the documentarian to extend and inform the proposition and argument being developed in the documentary.

Popular factual entertainment commonly replaces the exposition of formal questioning contained in the interview procedure with seemingly spontaneous or structured moments of testimony and confession. Whereas the interview format is designed to provide content and contextual information pertaining to the topic under investigation, the testimonial and confessional forms of popular factual entertainment emphasize emotion and the display of subjective feelings. Corner comments on this effect in his analysis of an episode of the reality television series *999 Lifesavers*. The episode in question featured a report of an accident in which a young girl was trapped inside a car which had collided with a truck. As the girl's mother recounts the incident, her face is framed in an extreme close-up. The intense focus on the mother's face, allowing the viewer to read every nuanced expression of feeling, and the emotionally-charged language in which she and other witnesses recount the accident, produces what Corner (1995: 28–9) calls an 'intensive subjectivity (the feeling of being in the event)'. Crime, accidents and violence – the content of reality television – lends itself to emotional and excited responses by those who witness such experiences. In *Cops*, witnesses are rarely shown calmly recounting what they have seen. Most frequently witnesses are depicted in a state of agitation, often gesticulating in an animated way, pointing to the crime or accident scene, breathlessly attempting to narrate events. In many cases police on the scene serve the function of interviewer, asking a series of questions of witnesses that typically elicit further responses captured within a zooming close-up shot which frames the emotional condition of the witness.

Forms of exposition are further reworked in the docusoap which, drawing on the appeal of television talk shows, provides opportunities for people to express their points of view and describe their experiences in reflections which are presented without the mediation of a presenter or interviewer. In the docusoap, testimony is typically provided in terms of confession and its deeply personal revelations and admissions. The subjects of the docusoap find moments in their daily working lives to reflect on their intimate selves and personal experiences in ways which provide what is, in effect, an interior monologue in counterpoint to the more 'objective' voice-over narration of each episode. In a useful analysis of forms of popular factual entertainment such as talk shows, docusoaps and reality gameshows, Dovey (2000) discusses the ways in which the emphasis on personal revelation that frequently serves as the core of these formats reconfigures the traditional separation of 'public' and 'private' spheres. In the docusoap, as with the versions of first person media examined by Dovey, private reflections, gossip and confession replace public and 'official' knowledge as credible and authoritative interpretations of reality.

Such functions of the confessional mode are extended in *Big Brother*. The house/studio setting of the programme is specifically designed for eavesdropping on what would otherwise be personal and private conversations. Further, the *Big Brother* format includes a convention that has been adopted from other reality programmes: the diary room. The docusoap *The Real World* included a weekly segment in which members of the household entered a room alone and talked or confessed directly to the camera. In the series *The Living Soap* (BBC, 1993) the students who were the subjects of the programme entered a 'video room' to deliver direct-to-camera comments, and the series *Castaway 2000* (BBC, 2000) included a 'video box' in which participants addressed the camera. In *Big Brother*'s diary room, participants speak directly to camera in a confessional way about their situation and, in what are often unguarded comments, about other contestants. In the case of *Big Brother*, confession tends more to gossip than testimony thereby pushing confession further from any notion of an interview designed to complement or extend argumentation about the world.

## Observation and performance

Popular factual entertainment reconfigures observation and the observational mode in multiple ways. One example of this recon-figuration occurs in *Cops*, a series which radically reworks the sense of distance and presumptions of objectivity which inform observa-tional direct cinema and print and broadcast journalism. In *Cops*, the audience views the world from the point of view of the police. All actions depicted in the programme are captured by a 'cop cen-tric' camera that rides with the police, stands with the police, or tracks down a street or alley pursuing a criminal (Glynn, 2000: 52). Observation here becomes collaboration with one point of view.

*Big Brother* reinstates a certain objective distance lost in *Cops* within a form of observationalism which, through the use of multi-ple cameras, revises the fly-on-the-wall in a newer variant of fly, or flies, on the wall, ceiling, window and door. The method further exceeds classic observation by taking the viewer into the realms of the voyeuristic and the gratifications provided by access to per-sonal and private moments. The sense of watching or peeping in a voyeuristic way is reinforced in *Big Brother* through the common use of a camera angle which produces the perspective of looking down into the spaces of the house. This is the point of view of closed-circuit surveillance cameras, and a popular shot used on Web sites such as 'Jennicam', which is predicated on the voyeuristic pleasures of watching the private life of its subject. The observational position in the docusoap is distinguishable from *Big Brother*'s unseen fly-on-the-wall. Clearly, the subjects of the docusoap are aware of the camera, and at times, a subject will glance at the camera or talk to the camera, practices which were largely banished in direct cinema's emphasis on the appearance of unmediated observation.

The forms of observation in popular factual entertainment have, in addition to reconfiguring the traditional observational mode, reworked notions of performance and its relationship to observation. In classic observationalism the subject does not appear to be performing; there is an attempt by both subject and director to treat speech and behaviour as 'naturally' as possible.[14] In popular factual entertainment, observation becomes the impetus for the non-professional to perform. In *Cops*, and other variants of crime-based reality television in the United States, producers were known to advise the police on performance techniques, and were willing to direct police in the delivery of dialogue and how to 'act' for the camera (Andersen, 1995: 181).

Similarly, docusoaps are populated by people willing, or seeking, to appear before the camera and who, in their modes of personal presentation, often adopt histrionic styles and attitudes. However, this fact does not necessarily eliminate the possibility of depictions of 'real' or authentic behaviour. This understanding is implicated with the nature of self-revelation in performance:

> At times in life we meet people who we feel are acting. This does not mean that they are lying, dishonest, living in an unreal world, or necessarily giving a false impression of their character or personality. It means that they seem to be aware of an audience – to be 'on stage' – and that they relate to the situation by energetically projecting ideas, emotions, and elements of their personality, underlining and theatricalizing it for the sake of the audience. They are acting their own emotions and beliefs. (Kirkby, quoted in Roscoe, 2001: 14)

This quality impacts in a specific way on viewers' experience of the docusoap, notably in the fact that viewers derive gratification from the programme by locating the 'authentic' self within the performance. As the documentary theorist Jane Roscoe has appropriately noted, 'Audiences play the game of evaluating how well participants perform their role ... These moments of so-called authenticity – moments when we think we see the real person – take on key importance in these new factual hybrids. Such authenticity is both reassuring – linking us back to factual discourse and the "real" – and it is the prize in the audience game of performance, thus presenting us with a satisfying experience' (Roscoe, 2001: 14).

The 'game' of 'performing the real' (Corner, 2002) and locating the real within the performance is complicated within the gamedoc format of *Big Brother*. The viewer's search for moments of authenticity is increased in a programme that uses a non-natural setting, a house that is a studio (which, in the Australian version of the programme, was constructed in a theme park), which reinforces self-conscious and self-aware performance, not naturalism, as the prime focus of the programme. Finding the authentic moment in *Big Brother* is further complicated by the process of eviction which serves as the programme's premise. In the presence of the threat of eviction participants must remain appealing to their fellow contestants, 'they have to perform the role of team player and good house guest – while also remembering that, ultimately, they have to win over the viewers to stay in the game' (Roscoe, 2001: 17). The ways in which participants react to the various tests and contests posed to them, and interact with their fellow house guests, is a key element for the contestants and central to the viewing gratifications derivable from the programme. Annette Hill (2002: 336–7) offers a useful way to understand the process of identifying the 'authentic' person within the performative role by replacing the notion of performance with the practice of 'self-display':

> Although many viewers are aware of press reports questioning the truthfulness of popular factual [programmes], and my research illustrates their cynicism about the reality in factual entertainment, this does not mean audiences have rejected the *idea* of authenticity in factual TV. In fact, audiences have developed viewing strategies that foreground authenticity in a highly constructed TV environment. For the average TV viewer, judging authenticity in popular factual programmes such as BB [*Big Brother*] is related to judging the integrity of the self. When contestants in BB are faced with emotionally difficult situations, they often reveal their 'true' nature. Audience attraction to judging levels of authenticity in BB is primarily based on whether contestants stay true to themselves, rather than whether the programme is truthful in its depiction of contestants.

As Hill emphasizes, *Big Brother* and other variants of popular factual entertainment rework the search for evidence of the real within a focus on the presentation of the self.

The emphasis on performance within popular factual entertainment, coupled with the move to a broader range of visualizations and exposition within the formats, has resulted in a reworking of the notion of a 'divide' between information and entertainment. The forms and styles of popular factual entertainment demonstrate that 'documentary' is not a unified category but rather a continuum which involves both information and entertainment. The argument (Burton, 2000: 152) that there are degrees of documentary is an apposite reflection on the condition of documentary brought about mainly by hybrid forms such as popular factual entertainment. Just as the new hybrid forms force a reconsideration of what constitutes documentary, so too forms of popular factual entertainment revise assumptions concerning the nature of 'entertainment' and enlarge the concept to include factual material not traditionally associated with the category.

The revised relationship of documentary and entertainment suggested by the practices of popular factual entertainment is exemplified in the findings of studies of audience reception of popular factual programming. In one of the few large-scale studies of the audience of reality programmes, Annette Hill found that respondents enjoyed the hybrid qualities of the shows and derived both entertainment *and* information from the programmes (Hill, 2000). As this chapter has noted, the narratives, styles and approaches of popular factual entertainment shift documentary away from its traditional focus on argumentation and public education toward the pleasures and conventions of entertainment. Hill's survey highlights that this movement does not necessarily spell the end of documentary as a mode of public knowledge. In this connection, Nichols' (1994: 45) claim that crime-based reality TV destroyed an 'already suspect' documentary tradition committed to social purpose and 'civic-minded action' is premature. It is yet too soon to claim with any certainty the end of Reithian and Griersonian forms of public service documentary, though it is obvious that popular factual entertainment has reconfigured many of the formal and stylistic features of the expository and observational documentary traditions.

# CHAPTER 11

# The Burning Question: The Future of Documentary

In 1996 the editors of a collection of essays devoted to aspects of documentary film and television invited a selection of international documentary producers, directors and editors to answer a number of questions, among them, 'What is the future of the documentary?' The inquiry, undertaken in a chapter titled 'The Burning Question', provided a range of responses, including observations on documentary cinema, the fate of documentaries commissioned for television, the funding regimes ruling both environments, and occasionally, reference to the part new digital technologies will play in the future of documentary (Macdonald and Cousins, 1996). Perhaps the most striking aspect of the investigation was the number of participants who chose not to answer this particular question. Attempting to predict the future is a demanding and risky task which some filmmakers and commentators simply chose to ignore. Unfortunately, one result of such a silence is the suggestion that documentary does not have a future. One thing that can be stated with certainty is that documentary representations of the real will continue to be produced in the twenty-first century. This chapter speculates on the future of documentary forms and varieties of content available within film and cinema, television and new media by drawing on current and emerging documentary practices in Britain and the United States as the basis of the speculation. Both British and American examples are included as a way of indicating trends which transcend national boundaries and point to a nascent global dimension to documentary practices and institutions. These issues are analysed through reference to the economic contexts and considerations which increasingly impact on developments in documentary.

Throughout its history, documentary representation has been linked to changing technologies – the invention of colour and sound film, portable cameras, 16 mm and 8 mm film stocks, video and the camcorder have all impacted variously on documentary representation. In a similar way, the future of documentary is implicated with current and emergent digital technologies. Digital technology encodes information – images, sound, text – into a machine readable numeric code which is rapidly superseding analogue forms such as chemical-based photography and the magnetic particle emulsion of videotape. Digital media are more precise than analogue media in the sense that they can reproduce recorded information without loss of clarity or resolution. Digitalized language enables digital media to communicate with each other via digital telecommunications systems in a way which was not possible with the varying incompatible forms of analogue-based technology. Computers, the Internet, CD-ROMs, digital videodiscs and digital television are some of the newer products of the communications revolution, all of which present possibilities for documentary.

The notion of a digital 'revolution' itself suggests a radical change in media technology, which various commentators have interpreted as a 'paradigmatic shift', a phrase that refers to an epistemological rupture between existing ideas and patterns of thinking and the ways in which ideas will be conceptualized and conveyed in the future. Arguments such as these rest, however, on a species of technological determinism in which technology is interpreted as a force driving society toward a liberating and innovative future. The implication in the technological determinist argument is that technology impacts on society from some undefined position 'outside' or beyond social and cultural determinations (Kuhn, 1978: 75). The fallacy is challenged in the recognition that technology is not exterior to society but is a constitutive feature of society and culture. As such, technology is subject to and interacts with other aspects of society and culture, such as government policy and regulation (as expressed, for example, in plans by the United Kingdom, United States and Australian governments to phase out analogue broadcast before the end of the first decade of the new millennium). Significantly, the economics of production, delivery and exhibition and consumer demand will also continue to influence documentary output and documentary forms in the digital era. This is not to say that regulation or economic considerations will necessarily close off or deny the potential of documentary producers to apply the new media in innovatory ways. The observation does, however, factor considerations beyond technology, notably economic forces, into any account of the future of documentary.

## Documentary cinema

Writing in 1995, the theorist and historian of documentary film, Brian Winston, looked to the future of what he called the 'post-Griersonian documentary'. The form predicted by Winston, characterized by formal innovation and social commitment, would, he argued, supplant the heavy-hand of Griersonian forms. Winston's examples of the newer forms are the cinema-release documentaries *The Thin Blue Line* (1989), an innovative American film that mixes *film noir* conventions with investigative documentary, and *Cane Toads* (1987), a darkly humorous Australian film that rewrites the standard approaches of the nature documentary (Winston, 1995: 254–5). By referring to works which received commercial cinema release Winston implicitly marks film and the exhibitionary space of cinema as the arena for a post-Griersonian documentary practice. A number of recent cinema release documentaries have dealt with topics which contest the 'sobriety' of the Griersonian tradition, though such works have not always been formally or stylistically inventive or committed to social or political reform agendas in the ways suggested by Winston.

Such features are notable by their absence in documentations of music performances which are, and no doubt will continue to be, one of the few perennial forms of cinema-release documentary. While the styles of music featured in such works has changed recently (from rock to Latin jazz and world music[1]), the styles of visual representation adopted to depict the performances remain bound by what have become the generic features of the form. In a related way, the contemporary popularity of the filmed drama-documentary suggests a future for a form which increasingly reflects a cultural fascination with the intimate lives of the rich and (in)famous as opposed to any attempt to examine the social or political issues raised by the life of a celebrity subject.

The method of forecasting adopted here, in which possible future developments are extrapolated from current trends, can also be applied to patterns of exhibition. Current practice in both the United States and the United Kingdom suggests that mainstream commercial cinema will, generally, remain a difficult market for documentary sales. The mainstream cinema is dominated by fiction film and few developments in documentary form or content are likely to alter that century-long tradition. However, beyond the multiplex cinema, documentary has established a niche market in the smaller so-called art house venues which continue to screen innovative documentary work from the film festival circuit.

A very different venue, IMAX cinema, has opened a further market for documentary in the twenty-first century. Since the first public screening of an IMAX film in 1970, the large-format screen has flourished worldwide, attracting sizable audiences. According to one estimate, in 1996 alone, 16 million people worldwide watched an IMAX film (Hoffmann, 1998: 248). To date, the majority of IMAX films have been documentaries, a situation that is likely to continue in the foreseeable future given that the costs of producing drama for the format remain extremely high. However, the expansion of documentary in the IMAX realm does not, as yet, point to the development of a new documentary aesthetic. Beyond their large screen format, IMAX films are stylistically similar to other cinema documentaries and their content frequently reflects the preoccupation found in many cinema-release documentaries with topics based on natural history and popular music. The appeal of IMAX films for audiences is not, however, necessarily one that is linked to content or style, but stems, instead, from the unique quality of the large screen experience. As the media theorist Kay Hoffmann (1998: 248) has pointed out, the success of IMAX cinema demonstrates that a market exists for large-screen documentary films that are projected as a special event.

## Documentary on television

The documentary project launched in the 1930s in Britain and the United States was undertaken with the assistance of state sponsorship which, in effect, insulated documentary for much of its history from the demands of showing a commercial profit. This situation changed rapidly in the 1980s and 1990s in the wake of challenges posed by Thatcherism and Reaganism, economic deregulation and an associated waning of the public service ideal. Global trends toward deregulation of the media environment, and with them a weakening of notions of public service in television broadcasting will, in the absence of countervailing political and economic forces, continue to impact on the future of documentary. This is not to say that public service ideals have disappeared from the media scene. The BBC, the Public Broadcasting Service (PBS) of the United States and the ABC, among other broadcasters, continue to maintain a commitment, however attenuated, to notions of public service. However, a waning of the public service ethic and the impact of this situation on documentaries produced through publicly funded sources is likely to increasingly subject documentary to the market forces of supply and demand.[2]

Within this context, television in the United Kingdom in the twenty-first century enters a 'new broadcasting age' dominated by commercial imperatives (Kilborn, 1996: 142). Commercial demands are, as Chapter 10 noted, driving changes in programming and scheduling in both the publicly and privately funded sectors. The BBC, once committed to applying its public funding to providing a public service to viewers, has been restructured to contend with its commercial competitors, a move which has impacted on all forms of BBC programming, including forms of documentary (Kilborn, 1996). Indeed, in the presence of intense competition between broadcasters, certain types of documentary programming, in particular hybrid popular factual entertainments, have become central to the strategies used by broadcasters to raise ratings and attract audiences. The move within British television to the production of popular factual entertainment has attracted various criticisms and concerns, among them, as noted in Chapter 9, the objections by certain producers that these works will displace established forms of documentary based on investigation and research into subjects of historical and contemporary significance.

In the United States, the future of television documentary is most directly associated with changes to the PBS, one of the larger producers of documentary work. A loose network of non-commercial television stations, PBS was established in 1967 as an educative and informational alternative to commercial network television, which the chairman of the Federal Communications Commission, Newton Minow, only a few years earlier famously derided as a 'vast wasteland' of unredeemable programming (see Curtin, 1995: 32). Throughout the latter decades of the twentieth century PBS produced and commissioned a variety of documentaries, including the widely seen historical compilations of Ken Burns (among them *The Civil War*, 1990, *Baseball*, 1994 and *Jazz*, 2001) and his brother Ric (*The Way West*, 1994 and *New York*, 1999). In addition to such work, PBS has commissioned a number of politically committed investigative documentaries (see Bullert, 1997). However, the fate of documentary in general, and serious engaged documentary work in particular, is in doubt in the United States as PBS faces uncertain financial times. PBS has to date been supported by funding derived from a variety of sources including public subscription, corporate sponsorship and government grants. In 1972, President Nixon sought to veto funds to the fledgling public television network in America, arguing that it was adversely critical of his conduct of the Vietnam War. A more recent attack on public television in the United States has come in the form of increasing moves to privatize the system and government funding cuts which are pushing PBS to seek a larger share of its funding from corporate sponsors in a move which is impacting on the number and type of documentaries that can be produced (Hoynes, 1996). In an echo of certain reactions to the programming situation in the United Kingdom, critics in the United States argue that in the interests of meeting the demands and expectations of corporate underwriting PBS is abandoning committed and challenging investigative documentaries in favour of 'safer' forms of programming, including an increasing reliance on popular drama (Bullert, 1997; Ledbetter, 1997).

Beyond the established US networks, the numerous channels on cable television would seem to offer an array of opportunities for the exhibition of documentary. Pay-for-view cable television in the United States carries a number of channels dedicated to documentary, among them the Discovery Channel and the History Channel (both of which are screened under license in the United Kingdom on BSkyB). Cable television's trend toward specialist channels, so-called narrowcasting, results in small niche audiences for channels such as Discovery and History. The relatively modest revenue returns from small audiences is far from conducive to an expansion of documentary production, while the low operating costs of such channels is reflected in the content of many of the programmes. Much of the documentary work on the Discovery Channel, for example, tends toward what Corner (1996: 196) describes as 'extremely tacky, sensationalist and (occasionally) hilariously incompetent material' such as shark attack 'specials' and poorly produced programmes on aspects of the military and warfare (the latter is also a prominent feature of the History Channel).

The introduction of digital television, an event connected with the increasing deregulation of the broadcast environment and a demand for channels (Steemers, 1999: 236), implicates documentary production in various ways. The era of digital television commenced in Britain in 1998 with BSkyB, ONDigital, the BBC and ITV seeking customers for the new digital services.[3] The report *Extending Choice in the Digital Age* (1996), in which the BBC outlined its vision of a digital future, predicted that digital technology would transform broadcasting by providing numerous new television channels, and that within ten years over half of all households in the United Kingdom would be receiving multi-channel television delivered by digital terrestrial, satellite, cable telecommunications. The glossy future painted in the report is, however, being disputed in various ways. To date, there has been a relatively slow take up of digital television (Britain outstrips other countries, such as Australia in this regard, though the overall figures in the United Kingdom are not as encouraging as some pundits have predicted), a situation that may reflect a certain degree of scepticism toward the notion that an increased range of channels will necessarily result in greater viewer choice.

The debate over the potential of multi-channelling to revise programming and productive practices is of relevance to documentary in terms of whether or not the new multi-channel broadcast environment results in a demand for documentary 'content'. Commentators have argued that while the number of channels will increase, any increase in the production of new programmes, including documentaries, will be relatively small. Rather than a dramatic extension of choice the new channels will, it has been suggested, be filled by repeats of low cost productions, repeat programmes, high cost films and sporting events on premium channels (Steemers, 1999: 237; Corner, 1999: 123). The specialist channels on cable stations have demonstrated such a trend, one which is likely to continue, if not intensify, as cable television moves from its current pay-per-view subscription based services to video-on-demand digital services.

Another function of digital television, interactivity, is a further factor in the future of documentary in the newly emerging broadcast environment. Among its other capacities, interactive television offers ways to enhance programme content with on-screen complementary information and other features such as choice of camera angle and on-screen viewer polling, accessed through the television's remote control. Sporting events have proved popular in the enhanced format, though other genres have also been reworked through the new technology, among them documentary. The BBC's interactive series *Walking with Beasts* (2001) is a case in point. Following the success of *Walking with Dinosaurs*, the series relies on computer animation to reconstruct the lives and habitats of prehistoric creatures. *Walking with Beasts* was broadcast with a range of interactive components, including alternative voice-over track, and on-screen text. Other supplementary features included short documentaries on individual animals featured in the programme and 'behind the scenes' footage of the production of the special effects used in the programme. The BBC has created a portal for interactive television through the establishment of BBC Knowledge, a channel dedicated to cultural and educational content. Here as elsewhere, the demands of the market in terms of costs are ever present. Katharine Everett, of the new media division at the BBC, recognizes that 'Interactivity offers [producers] the opportunity to establish a one-to-one relationship with the television viewer, as long as one knows what one can supply and at what price' (quoted in Senges, 2000: 14).

Other current developments, notable among them, the intersection or 'convergence' of multiple media, will no doubt continue to impact on documentary production. Media convergence is exemplified in the popular television programme *Big Brother*, which supplements its television format through the capacities of the Internet and telephone. The feature is exemplified in the practice of online and telephone viewer voting on the eviction of residents from the *Big Brother* house. *Big Brother*'s incorporation of a website is a further enhancement of the programme; the website screens unedited footage from the house 24 hours a day and offers features such as online discussions with evicted players.[4] An extensive study of users of the website accompanying the Australian version of *Big Brother* indicates that so-called multi-platform delivery will expand in the future. Sixty per cent of the 23 000 respondents to the survey said they watched *Big Brother* because of the Web and 90 per cent of those surveyed said the website extended and informed their pleasure of the television programme. A majority of respondents said they were willing to pay for enhanced television content (see Harty, 2002). The findings attest to the durability of the emerging connections between specific television forms, content and various forms of supplementation, notably that provided by the Web. The conclusions indicate an expansion of content and formats, both fiction and non-fiction, designed to be 'enhanced' via the Web and other media. The findings also highlight the commercial considerations implicated in multi-platform delivery, particularly the cost to the viewer of enhanced content.

In a suggestive analysis of *Big Brother*, John Corner (2002) has argued that the radically altered economic context in which television broadcasting now operates is moving documentary into a 'postdocumentary' phase, marked by a decisive shift toward 'documentary as diversion', elements of which were discussed in Chapter 10. Corner uses 'diversion' to refer to a range of effects and outcomes, which he summarizes by focussing on three central points. First of all, an emphasis on diversionary or entertaining aspects has resulted in the dispersal of documentary features across a variety of programmes. The so-called documentary look is now widely adopted by various programmes and, inversely, documentary now relies heavily on the visual appeal of other genres, such as the rock music video, and the stylizations of advertising (2002: 263).[5] The effect of these changes, Corner argues, is a weakening of documentary's traditional status as a 'sober' representation of the socio-historical world. Second, diversion involves performative, playful components. The performative is apparent in *Big Brother* where the ever-present gaze of the cameras results in a simulation or feigning of natural behaviour by participants. Third, changes in documentary style and an increase in performance are likely to impact on patterns of reception and the ways in which people understand and experience documentaries. For Corner, the emergence of a 'postdocumentary culture' embodied in these features and effects does not spell the end of the documentary project. Rather, the features indicate the scale of the transformations to documentary forms and functions. Established forms of documentary will persist, argues Corner, though they will operate within a dramatically altered broadcast environment in which popular forms of documentary, heavily reliant on the technological and economic features outlined here, will dominate.

## CD-ROM/DVD/Internet

In addition to digital television, current digital forms of delivery and exhibition include CD-ROMs (compact disc read-only memory),

DVD (digital video disc) and the Internet. These technologies provide platforms for the exhibition of new forms of audiovisual textuality in which various media are combined in ways that hold the potential to extend the formal and communicative possibilities of the resultant work. This potential has, however, been accompanied by deep concerns regarding the digital manipulation of the image and the effects of this practice on documentary truth claims. Chemically based photographs can be manipulated to produce images that do not have a referent in the real world (examples here include photographs from the early history of photography of spirits and fairies, or a more recent example of Churchill, Roosevelt and Stalin seated at the Yalta conference with the actor Sylvester Stallone in character as John Rambo).[6] Despite the possibility of manipulation, the photograph has, through the technology that produces it and the dominant practices that circulate it, been widely accepted as a direct transcription of a pre-existing reality.

Digital images, in contrast to photographs, do not rely on light-affected negatives and the direct link they provide between physical appearances and their reproduction. As a result, digital images can be manipulated or altered in undetectable ways. For many interpreters, the potential of digitalization to erode the bond between image and referent jeopardizes notions of realism thereby disrupting the basis of the entire documentary tradition. According to such estimations one effect of the digital revolution in media is that seeing is no longer necessarily believing.[7]

Such assessments have, to a degree, been displaced by an emphasis on the ability of new media to rework established documentary forms through new combinations of print, sound, images, graphics and three-dimensional computer-generated modelling. The new media make it possible for viewers to arrange the order of material presented on screen in an interactive, non-linear process which enables a viewer to explore issues and perspectives at will, and hence to disrupt the unidirectional 'linear' rhetorical drive of established documentary forms. Online documentaries, in their capacity to be endlessly updated and expanded through the continual addition of new information and links to related websites, redefine the idea of documentary as a stable and fixed work which once complete and having been exhibited is retired to the archives. The practices of online forms can result in documentation as an open-ended process which spins off into other media such as CD-ROM or continues to expand online through the inclusion of discussion forums and the updating of informational content. Drawing on such practices, David Tiley, Project Coordinator for new media projects funded by the Australian Film Commission has painted an intriguing picture of the future of forms of interactive documentary in the online environment:

> Imagine the digital future of documentary. Production occurs on DVD, edited at home on a low-end non-linear system, with the complete project stored at broadcast quality. Icons and hotkeys take us to layers of material beneath the documentary experience, so we can find transcripts, additional information … the script, alternate edits … The program is accessed via the Web. Now go further. Imagine the interviews are shot online, using cameras linked to computers … imagine collaborators including their own images requested by e-mail … [together with] ongoing chatroom discussion about the images and the story … Imagine a Website which accretes material from various contributors online, which is hosted by filmmakers providing their material as a kind of spine. This never becomes a linear program, is never organized by choices and exclusions, is never authored in any traditional way at all. (quoted in 'Documentary Online', 1999: 2)

'How much is possible?' asks Tiley. The expansion of documentary works in such forms is, principally and unavoidably, dependent on basic issues of production, distribution and marketability. To date, most of the new media documentary work has been independently produced and distributed in a non-commercial way. Current trends suggest that developments in new media will, however, be constrained by the facts already raised here, chiefly, the market for any new documentary products. The Internet is a case in point. While certain documentary filmmakers are enthusiastic about the Internet as a distribution network (the direct cinema filmmaker Richard Leacock is one such advocate), the majority of commercial documentary producers, together with documentary distributors, are currently reluctant to pursue delivery by the Internet, citing the lack of revenue return from this form of distribution (O'Donovan, 2001: 12). So far the majority of websites carrying documentary work have not made money and documentary makers and distributors are unconvinced of the Web's financial potential, at least in the short term.[8]

## The question still burns

Spaces will remain for the production of documentary work not necessarily created for profit within the commercial media environment of the future. In fact, many commentators have hailed digital technology as the basis of forms of do-it-yourself film and video making which open opportunities for the non-professional documentary maker. Relatively low-cost digital video cameras and desktop computer editing suites are the tools which, according to some claims, will lead to an expansion of non-commercial documentary making in which everyone is a potential documentarian. This view was advanced by a number of respondents to a survey similar to that quoted in the introduction to this chapter. In a collection of essays and interviews devoted to film, selected international film makers were asked, in a section titled 'the burning question', their opinions on the future of cinema in the new millennium. One respondent, the film director Michael Verhoeven, argued that digital technology will encourage personal, individual forms of filmmaking. The American musician and filmmaker David Byrne recognized in George Holliday's camcorder footage of the beating of Rodney King a 'prototype of future "documentaries" ... made not by trained film-makers, but by witnesses, participants ... and innocent bystanders' (quoted in Boorman and Donohue, 1993: 37). Byrne's prediction is being realized in the practices of activist film and video makers who currently use media technology as a form of witnessing and documentation (see Harding, 2002).

While new media technologies present opportunities for the production of documentary they also 'enable the larger global media companies to become even more powerful', as media theorist Tom O'Regan (2001) has noted. Recent media history contains numerous examples of this latter effect. Satellite transmission in the United Kingdom is monopolized by BSkyB, and cable is dominated by a limited number of companies (chief among them the US consortia Nynex and Flextech). Commercial book publishers are looking to extend publishing opportunities through book/CD-ROM-based ventures. Sections of the Internet are being commercialized, not only by e-commerce but also by the companies that provide portal access points. The film studio and publishing company Time-Warner merged in 2000 with the online provider America Online to form what was at the time the largest media company in the world. The technologically retooled and financially realigned US film studios have recovered from the setbacks in the 1970s which saw a number of major studios on the verge of bankruptcy and are now economically more powerful than ever before in their history.

Within the conglomeration and corporatization of the future, a strong emphasis will be placed on the economic viability of documentary. Current trends suggest that increasingly documentary will be treated as a consumer product which is marketed to fill specific commercialized slots within nominated media, be it film, television, CD-ROM, DVD or the Internet. Under these circumstances, as John Corner (2002: 267) notes, an important factor in the survival of documentary as a form of public knowledge or popular entertainment is a commitment to the audience by producers which 'goes beyond profitability but that can nevertheless also generate profits'. The ability to perform such a demanding task, and its outcome for forms and styles of documentary, remains the burning question of the future.

# Conclusion

The analysis of documentary futures undertaken in the Chapter 11 emphasized that formal innovation will be circumscribed by commercial imperatives. We can note that it was always this way. As Chapter 1 pointed out, the tradition of documentary filmmaking inaugurated by Grierson was subject to financial restrictions imposed by sponsorship. Grierson acknowledged the effect of sponsorship on developing forms of documentary representation when he observed that documentary filmmakers were limited in their capacity to produce innovative poetic documentaries by the demands of the sponsor for formerly sober documentary works. In light of this history it is, then, ironic that the necessity to deliver audiences and maintain revenue returns from advertisers and sponsors in the era of increasingly commercialized television has resulted in forms of popular factual representation which have refigured documentary representation. While many observers lament the recent turn to popular factual entertainment in sociological terms – pointing to issues of surveillance and voyeurism prominent in the forms and their impact on the health of the public sphere – other commentators argue that such works extend the expressive range of documentary representation and move it away from what has often been its earnest, sober, sometimes bombastic, character. In this way, a specific outcome of the commercial desires and demands impacting on documentary work has been forms of non-fictional representation capable of attracting an identifiable type of viewer at nominated times in the broadcasting schedule (Kilborn and Izod, 1997: x).

Notably, the demands associated with trends in television implicate form and documentary production and output. As one insider in British broadcasting put it:

> [Documentaries] can be used to target strong drama or entertainment on rival channels, attracting a complementary audience. They are used to net specific social groups for the advertisers. In a regulated industry they are necessary ballast in the freightage of any station which also needs to carry, for example, a quantity of cheap American imports, vulgar game shows or tabloid-style news. (quoted in Kilborn and Izod, 1997: xi)

Holland (2000: 162) reinforces this observation when she notes that producers and commissioning editors are always interested in developing new forms of documentary, 'provided they are not so strange as to alienate their projected audience'. This latter provision points to the maintenance of 'core' documentary work (Corner, 2001b: 126) and recognizable subgenres of the type analysed in this book. However, this is not to suggest that core documentary work and current subgeneric classifications are immutable. Indeed, the development of new forms will continue to put pressure on foundational and existing work and the practical and critical boundaries of existing subgenres.

The emphasis here on commercial imperatives and context does not exclude the fact that other significant and pervasive contexts impact on, or inform documentary production. As the various chapters in this book have outlined, documentary is produced within a variety of material contexts or settings, each of which impact on the formal and expressive features of documentary film and television in specific ways. Changes to these settings – the academic discipline of ethnography, the political and historical features of colonialism, constructions of personal identity and policies concerning impartiality in broadcasting, for example – are likely to affect the form of documentary representation produced within each of the contexts. The inverse of the commonplace observation that documentary represents the socio-historical world is also true: the socio-historical world impacts on forms of documentary representation. Our understandings of documentary representation are informed and enlarged by the recognition within documentary studies that the epistemological and evidentiary functions of documentary representation are linked to the socio-historical world beyond the text.

As fiction film moves increasingly toward the special effects blockbuster, the 'quieter pleasures' (Corner, 2000a) associated with visual and aural documentary depictions of the socio-historical world continue to appeal to viewers. In another way, too, realistic documentary depictions maintain their referential and evidentiary appeal in the presence of a certain scepticism toward the traditional claims of the documentary to truthfully represent the world (see Carroll: 1996). Documentary appears on an increasing array of screens – television, cinema and computer – as it enters its second century. Tuning in to those screens – with an understanding of the histories, formal features and patterns of argument employed by the texts on the screens – offers, to paraphrase a remark here, a diversity of extended pleasures for the viewer.

# Appendix
## Screenings and Additional Resources

The analyses of various films and television programmes undertaken in this book are intended to function 'interactively' with screenings of the films and programmes. To this end, a complete list of works to accompany each chapter is provided below. Certain of these works are available from national and international distribution companies. Specific locations in the United States, the United Kingdom and Australia for each of the listed works are, nevertheless, provided below. The entries include running time and format (16 mm, VHS, or DVD) for each work. (Please note: In certain countries films require copyright clearance for public screening.) Also included below are further or additional screenings of works not analysed or referred to in each chapter. This information is supplemented by suggested further reading.

## 1 'Believe me, I'm of the world': documentary representation

### Further reading

Corner, J. 'Civic visions: forms of documentary' in J. Corner, *Television Form and Public Address* (London: Edward Arnold, 1995).

Corner, J. 'Television, documentary and the category of the aesthetic', *Screen*, 44, 1 (2003) 92–100.

Nichols, B. *Blurred Boundaries: Questions of Meaning in Contemporary Culture* (Bloomington: Indiana University Press, 1994).

Renov, M. 'Toward a poetics of documentary' in M. Renov (ed.), *Theorizing Documentary* (New York: Routledge, 1993).

## 2 Men with movie cameras: Flaherty and Grierson

*Nanook of the North*, Robert Flaherty, 1922. 55 min. (Alternative title: *Nanook of the North: A Story of Life and Love in the Actual Arctic*).

US: Facets Multimedia, Inc
1517 West Fullerton Ave
Chicago IL 60614
Telephone:             773 281 9075
Fax:                   773 929 5437
Email:                 sales@facets.org
Website:               www.facets.org
VHS and DVD

UK: British Film Institute
21 Stephen St
London W1T 1LN
Telephone:             20 7255 1444
Email:                 films@bfi.org.uk
Website:               bfi.org.uk
VHS

Australia: Australian Centre for the Moving Image (National Access Film
and Video Collection)
222 Park St
South Melbourne
Vic 3205
Telephone:             03 992 7040
Fax:                   03 9929 7027
Email:                 collections@acmi.net.au
Website:               www.acmi.net.au
16 mm and VHS

*Drifters*, John Grierson, 1929. 58 min.
US: Facets Multimedia, Inc.
1517 West Fullerton Ave
Chicago IL 60614
Telephone:             773 281 9075
Fax:                   773 929 5437
Email:                 sales@facets.org
Website:               www.facets.org
VHS

UK: Concord Video
Rosehill Centre
22 Hines Rd
Ipswich
Suffolk IP3 9BG
Telephone:             01473 726012
Fax:                   01473 274531
Email:                 concord video@btinternet.com
Website:               www.ConcordVideo.co.uk
16 mm

Australia: Australian Centre for the Moving Image (National Access Film
and Video Collection)
222 Park St
South Melbourne
Vic 3205
Telephone:         03 992 7040
Fax:               03 9929 7027
Email:             collections@acmi.net.au
Website:           www.acmi.net.au
16 mm and VHS

## Additional resources

Under Grierson's tutelage the so-called British documentary film movement produced a rich field of documentary films. Among the many works
made by filmmakers associated with the movement during the 1930s and
1940s are: *Cargo from Jamaica* (Basil Wright, 1933), *Song of Ceylon* (Basil
Wright, 1934), *BBC: The Voice of Britain* (Stuart Legg, 1934), *Workers and Jobs*
(Arthur Elton, 1935), *Housing Problems* (Arthur Elton and Edgar Anstey,
1935), *Night Mail* (Harry Watt and Basil Wright, 1936), *The Saving of Bill
Blewitt* (Harry Watt, 1936), *North Sea* (Harry Watt, 1938), *Spare Time*
(Humphrey Jennings, 1939), *London Can Take It* (Harry Watt and
Humphrey Jennings, 1940), *Target for Tonight* (Harry Watt, 1941), *Listen to
Britain* (Humphrey Jennings, 1942), *Fires Were Started* (Humphrey Jennings,
1943), *The Silent Village* (Humphrey Jennings, 1943), *Western Approaches*
(Pat Jackson, 1944) and *A Diary for Timothy* (Humphrey Jennings, 1946).

Robert Flaherty produced a variety of films during his life. Following
*Nanook of the North* he made, among other films, the collaborative work
*Industrial Britain* (John Grierson and Robert Flaherty, 1933), *Moana: A
Romance of the Golden Age* (1926), *Man of Aran* (1934) and *Louisiana Story*
(1948).

In 1942 Flaherty made *The Land* at the invitation of Pare Lorentz for
the US Agricultural Adjustment Administration, a federally funded New
Deal project. *The Land* was originally commissioned by the United States
Film Service (an organization created in 1938 with Lorentz as its head),
which was disbanded in 1940. During the brief period of its existence the
US Film Service used government sponsorship in the Griersonian manner
to produce films that, as with the British documentary film movement,
deployed documentary film as a form of civic education. Lorentz's own
films are exemplary in this regard: *The Plow that Broke the Plains* (1936), *The
River* (1937) and *The Fight for Life* (1940).

## Further reading

Aitken, I. (ed.) *The Documentary Film Movement: An Anthology* (Edinburgh:
Edinburgh University Press, 1998).

Flaherty, R. 'How I filmed *Nanook of the North*', in H. M. Geduld (ed.), *Film Makers on Film Making* (Bloomington: Indiana University Press, 1971).

Snyder, R. L. *Pare Lorentz and the Documentary Film* (Reno: University of Nevada Press, 1993).

Winston, B. *Claiming the Real: The Documentary Film Revisited* (London: British Film Institute, 1995).

## 3 Constructing and contesting otherness: ethnographic film

*The Ax Fight*, Timothy Asch and Napoleon Chagnon, 1971. 30 min.
US and UK: Facets Multimedia, Inc
1517 West Fullerton Ave
Chicago IL 60614
Telephone:          773 281 9075
Fax:                773 929 5437
Email:              sales@facets.org
Website:            www.facets.org
VHS

Australia: Australian Centre for the Moving Image (National Film and Video Lending Service)
222 Park St
South Melbourne
Vic 3205
Telephone:          03 992 7040
Fax:                03 9929 7027
Email:              collections@acmi.net.au
Website:            www.acmi.net.au
16 mm and VHS

'*Cannibal Tours*', Dennis O'Rourke, 1987. 70 min. (Alternative title: '*Cannibal Tours*': *Postmodern Encounters on the Upper Sepik*).
US: Direct Cinema Ltd
PO Box 10003
Santa Monica CA 90410 1003
Telephone:          310 636 8200
Email:              orders@directcinemalimited.com
Website:            www.directcinema.com
VHS

UK: Camerawork Pty Ltd
PO Box 199
Canberra Australia 2601
Email: mail@cameraworklimited.com
VHS

Australia: Australian Centre for the Moving Image (National Access Film
and Video Collection)
222 Park St
South Melbourne
Vic 3205
Telephone:              03 992 7040
Fax:                    03 9929 7027
Email:                  collections@acmi.net.au
Website:                www.acmi.net.au
VHS

## Additional resources

Films prominent within the ethnographic tradition include: *The Hunters*
(John Marshall, 1958), *Dead Birds* (Robert Gardner, 1964), *The Feast*
(Timothy Asch and Napoleon Chagnon, 1969), *Coniston Muster: Scenes
from a Stockman's Life* (Roger Sandall, 1972), *Rivers of Sand* (Robert
Gardner, 1974), *Trobriand Cricket* (Gary Kildea, Jerry Leach and the
Kabisawali Movement, 1975), *Goodbye, Old Man* (David MacDougall, 1977),
*The House Opening* (Judith MacDougall, 1980) *First Contact* (Bob Connolly
and Robin Anderson, 1982), *Celso and Cora* (Gary Kildea, 1983), *Forest of
Bliss* (Robert Gardner, 1985), *Joe Leahy's Neighbours* (Bob Connolly and
Robin Anderson, 1988) and *Black Harvest* (Bob Connolly and Robin
Anderson, 1992).

## Further reading

Biella, P. and G. Seaman. *Yanomamo Interactive: The Ax Fight* (book and CD
    ROM) (New York: Harcourt Brace, 1997).
Grimshaw, A. *The Ethnographer's Eye: Ways of Seeing in Modern Anthropology*
    (Cambridge: Cambridge University Press, 2001).
MacBean, J. R. 'Degrees of otherness: a close reading of *First Contact, Joe
    Leahy's Neighbors,* and *Black Harvest*', *Visual Anthropology Review,* 10, 2
    (1994) 55–70.
MacDougall, D. *Transcultural Cinema* (Princeton: Princeton University
    Press, 1998).
Ruby, J. *Picturing Culture: Explorations of Film and Anthropology* (Chicago:
    University of Chicago Press, 2000).

# 4   Decolonizing the image: Aboriginal documentary productions

*Two Laws,* Carolyn Strachan and Alessandro Cavadini, with the Borroloola
community, 1981. 130 min. (Alternative title: *Two Laws/Kanymarda Yuwa*).

US and UK Smart Street Films
PO Box 198
Sandringham
Vic Australia 3191
Telephone:             03 9521 8598
Fax:                   03 9521 8690
Email:                 smartst@ozemail.com.au
Website:               www.smartstreetfilms.com.au
VHS

Australia: Australian Centre for the Moving Image (National Access Film
and Video Collection)
222 Park St
South Melbourne
Vic 3205
Telephone:             03 992 7040
Fax:                   03 9929 7027
Email:                 collections@acmi.net.au
Website:               www.acmi.net.au
16 mm and VHS

*Quest for Country*, Michael Riley, 1993. 24 min. (Part of the series *Spirit to
Spirit*)
US and UK: Blackfella Films Pty Ltd
8 Hastings Parade
Bondi Beach
NSW Australia 2026
VHS

Australia: Australian Centre for the Moving Image (National Access Film
and Video Collection)
222 Park St
South Melbourne
Vic 3205
Telephone:             03 992 7040
Fax:                   03 9929 7027
Email:                 collections@acmi.net.au
Website:               www.acmi.net.au
VHS

*Bush Mechanics*, Francis Jupurrurla Kelly and David Batty, 2001. A televi-
sion series of four episodes (*Motorcar Ngutju, Payback, The Chase, The
Rainmakers*), each episode 26 min.
US: First Run Icarus Films
32 Court St, 21st floor
Brooklyn NY 11201

Telephone:            718 488 8900
Email:                mailbox@frif.com
Website:              www.frif.com
VHS

UK and Australia: Film Australia
PO Box 46
Lindfield
NSW Australia 2070
Telephone:            02 9413 8634
Fax:                  02 9416 9401
Email:                sales@filmaust.com.au
Website:              www.filmaust.com.au
VHS

## Additional resources

See Tracey Moffat, *Moodeitj Yorgas* (*Solid Women*, 1988), Wayne Barker, *Milli Milli* (ABC, 1993), Rachel Perkins, *Freedom Ride* (1993), *Broken English*, co-produced by Rachel Perkins, with director Ned Lander (SBS, 1993), Frances Peters-Little, *Tent Embassy* (ABC, 1997), Steven McGregor, *Apekathe* (Central Australian Aboriginal Media Association, 1998) and Darlene Johnson, *Stolen Generations* (SBS, 2000).

## Further reading

Janke, T. and Company, *Towards a Protocol for Filmmakers Working with Indigenous Content and Indigenous Communities* (Sydney: Australian Film Commission, 2003).

Langton, M. *'Well, I Heard it on the Radio and I saw it on the Television': An Essay for the Australian Film Commission on the Politics and Aesthetics of Filmmaking by and about Aboriginal People and Things* (Sydney: Australian Film Commission, 1993).

Molnar, H. and M. Meadows, *Songlines to Satellites: Indigenous Communication in Australia, the South Pacific and Canada* (Sydney: Pluto Press, 2001).

Singer, B. *Wiping the War Paint Off the Lens: Native American Film and Video* (Minneapolis: University of Minnesota Press, 2001).

# 5   The truth of the matter: cinéma vérité and direct cinema

*Chronicle of a Summer* (*Chronique d'un été*), Jean Rouch and Edgar Morin, 1960. 90 min.
US and UK: Facets Multimedia, Inc

1517 West Fullerton Ave
Chicago IL 60614
Telephone:        773 281 9075
Fax:              773 929 5437
Email:            sales@facets.org
Website:          www.facets.org
VHS

Australia: Australian Centre for the Moving Image (National Access Film
and Video Collection)
222 Park St
South Melbourne
Vic 3205
Telephone:        03 992 7040
Fax:              03 9929 7027
Email:            collections@acmi.net.au
Website:          www.acmi.net.au
VHS

*Don't Look Back*, D. A. Pennebaker, 1966. 96 min.
US and UK: Facets Multimedia, Inc
1517 West Fullerton Ave
Chicago IL 60614
Telephone:        773 281 9075
Fax:              773 929 5437
Email:            sales@facets.org
Website:          www.facets.org
VHS and DVD

Australia: Australian Centre for the Moving Image (National Access Film
and Video Collection)
222 Park St
South Melbourne
Vic 3205
Telephone:        03 992 7040
Fax:              03 9929 7027
Email:            collections@acmi.net.au
Website:          www.acmi.net.au
VHS

## Additional resources

Works of French cinéma vérité include Mario Ruspoli's *Regards sur la folie*
(1961), Jacques Rozier's *Adieu Philippine* (1963) and Chris Marker's *Le joli
mai* (1963). The notion of the camera as catalyst has been further
explored by Ross McElwhee in *Sherman's March* (see Chapter 6).

*Adventures on the New Frontier* (1961), a film dealing with John Kennedy's first year as President, brought together many of the directors commonly associated with direct cinema: Richard Leacock, D.A. Pennebaker Albert Maysles, with Kenneth Snelson. Leacock, Pennebaker and Albert and David Maysles have forged long careers in direct cinema. Leacock's work includes *Happy Mother's Day* (1963), co-directed with Joyce Chopra, *Chiefs* (1968) and *Dun and Miss Farfen* (1996). Before *Don't Look Back* and *Monterey Pop*, Pennebaker had made *Jane* (1962), a profile of the actress Jane Fonda, and he subsequently went on to direct, among other films: *Original Cast Album: Company* (1971), *Ziggy Stardust and the Spiders form Mars* (1973), *Randy Newman isn't Human* (1980) and *Black Dance America* (1983). In 1971 Pennebaker made *Town Bloody Hall*, a record of an energetic public discussion of women's liberation. Apart from *Salesman* and *Gimme Shelter*, Albert and David Maysles have directed, among other films, *Grey Gardens* (1976) and *Running Fence* (1978).

Standing apart from the directors originally associated with the Drew unit is the filmmaker Frederick Wiseman. Wiseman's films are significant contributions to the field of direct cinema and are chiefly composed of intricate, mosaic-like records of the exercise of power in various social institutions. His films include *High School* (1968), *Law and Order* (1969), *Hospital* (1970), *Juvenile Court* (1972), *Welfare* (1975) and *The Store* (1983). Wiseman's films can only be obtained under licence from his production and distribution company Zipporah Films <www.zipporah.com>.

Other works in the direct cinema vein include Allan King's *A Married Couple* (1969), Craig Gilbert's *An American Family* (1973), Barbara Kopple's *Harlan County, U.S.A* (1976) and Steve James' *Stevie* (2002). In the United Kingdom Roger Graeff pursued a form of direct cinema in, among other works, the BBC series *Police* (1982), co-directed with Charles Stewart, and the Granada series *Decision* (1976). Paul Watson adopted features of direct cinema in his television serials *The Family* (1974) and *Sylvania Waters* (1991). In Australia the legacies of direct cinema inform the work of, among other directors, Bob Connolly and Robin Anderson (*Rats in the Ranks* (1996) and *Facing the Music*, 2001), as mentioned in Chapter 5, Michael Cordell (*Year of the Dogs*, 1997), and Tom Zubrycki (*Kemira: Diary of a Strike*, 1984, *Friends and Enemies*, 1987 and *Molly and Mobarak*, 2003).

## Further reading

Graham, P. 'Cinéma-vérité in France', *Film Quarterly*, 17 (1964) 30–6.
Grant, B. K. *Voyages of Discovery: The Cinema of Frederick Wiseman* (Urbana: University of Illinois Press, 1992).
Ruoff, J. *An American Family: A Televised Life* (Minneapolis: University of Minnesota Press, 2001).
Stubbs, L. 'Albert Maysles: father of direct cinema' in L. Stubbs, *Documentary Filmmakers Speak* (New York: Allworth Press, 2002).

Vaughan, D. 'The space between shots' in D. Vaughan, *For Documentary: Twelve Essays* (Berkeley: University of California Press, 1999).

Winston, B. 'Direct cinema: the third decade' in A. Rosenthal (ed.), *New Challenges for Documentary* (Berkeley: University of California Press, 1988).

# 6  The camera I: autobiographical documentary

*Sherman's March*, Ross McElwee, 1985. 155 min. (Alternative titles: *Sherman's March: A Meditation on the Possibility of Romantic Love in the South during an Era of Nuclear Weapons Proliferation; Sherman's March: An Improbable Love Story*).
US and UK: First Run Features
153 Waverly Place
New York NY 10014
Telephone:           800 229 8575
Fax:                 212 989 7649
Email:               info@firstrunfeatures.com
Website:             www.firstrunfeatures.com
VHS

Australia: Australian Centre for the Moving Image (National Access Film and Video Collection)
222 Park St
South Melbourne
Vic 3205
Telephone:           03 992 7040
Fax:                 03 9929 7027
Email:               collections@acmi.net.au
Website:             www.acmi.net.au
VHS

*History and Memory*, Rea Tajiri, 1991. 33 min. (Alternative title: *History and Memory: For Akiko and Takashige*).
US and UK: Women Make Movies
462 Broadway, Suite 500WS
New York NY 10013
Telephone:           212 925 0606
Fax:                 212 925 2052
Email:               info@wmm.com
Website:             www.wmm.com
VHS

Australia: Australian Centre for the Moving Image (National Film and
Lending Service)
222 Park St
South Melbourne
Vic 3205
Telephone:        03 992 7040
Fax:              03 9929 7027
Email:            collections@acmi.net.au
Website:          www.acmi.net.au
VHS

**Additional resources**

Autobiographical films produced over the past three decades include
Martin Scorsese's *Italianamerican* (1974), Amali Rothschild's *Nana, Mom
and Me* (1977), Joel DeMott's *Demon Lover Diary* (1980), Su Friedrich's *The
Ties that Bind* (1987), *Finding Crista* (1992) by Camille Billops and James
Hatch, *In Search of Our Fathers* (1992) by Marco Williams, Ellen Spiro's
*Greetings from Out Here* (1993), *Grandfathers and Revolutions* (2000) by Peter
Hegedus, *Obsessive Becoming* (1995) by Daniel Reeves and *Regret to Inform*
(1998) by Barbara Sonneborn.

**Further reading**

Lane, J. *The Autobiographical Documentary in America* (Madison: University
    of Wisconsin Press, 2002).
Macdonald, S. 'Ross McElwee' in S. MacDonald, *A Critical Cinema 2:
    Interviews with Independent Filmmakers* (Berkeley: University of California
    Press, 1992).
O'Shaughnessy, M. 'Producing *First Person*: an interview with Alan Carter,
    Series Producer *First Person*', *Continuum: The Australian Journal of Media
    and Culture*, 11, 1 (1997) 100–15.
Stubbs, L. 'Ross McElwee: personal journeyman' in L. Stubbs, *Documentary
    Filmmakers Speak* (New York: Allworth Press, 2002).

# 7   Finding and keeping: compilation documentary

*In the Year of the Pig*, Emile de Antonio, 1969. 101 min. (Alternative title:
*Vietnam: In the Year of the Pig*).
US: Facets Multimedia, Inc
1517 West Fullerton Ave
Chicago IL 60614
Telephone:        773 281 9075

Fax:                773 929 5437
Email:              sales@facets.org
Website:            www.facets.org
VHS

UK: Amazon.com
PO Box 81226
Seattle 98108-1226
Website:            www.amazon.com
VHS

Australia: Australian Centre for the Moving Image (National Access Film
and Video Collection)
222 Park St
South Melbourne
Vic 3205
Telephone:          03 992 7040
Fax:                03 9929 7027
Email:              collections@acmi.net.au
Website:            www.acmi.net.au
VHS

*The Atomic Café*, Kevin Rafferty, Jayne Loader, Pierce Rafferty [The
Archives Project], 1982. 92 min.
US: Facets Multimedia, Inc
1517 West Fullerton Ave
Chicago IL 60614
Telephone:          773 281 9075
Fax:                773 929 5437
Email:              sales@facets.org
Website:            www.facets.org
VHS and DVD

UK: British Film Institute
21 Stephen St
London W1T 1LN
Telephone:          20 7255 1444
Email:              films@bfi.org.uk
Website:            bfi.org.uk
VHS

Australia: Australian Centre for the Moving Image (National Access Film
and Video Collection)
222 Park St
South Melbourne
Vic 3205
Telephone:          03 992 7040

Fax:                    03 9929 7027
Email:                  collections@acmi.net.au
Website:                www.acmi.net.au
VHS

## Additional resources

See Alan Berliner, *Myth in the Electronic Age* (1981), Fred Marx, *House of UnAmerican Activity* (1984), Isaac Julien, *Territories* (1984), John Akomfah, *Handsworth Songs* (1986), Yervant Gianikian and Angela Ricci Lucchi, *From the Pole to the Equator* (1986), Robert Stone, *Radio Bikini* (1987), Greta Snider, *Futility* (1989).

Use of interviews and archival footage is the central structuring device of Marcel Orphuls' impressive and chilling *The Sorrow and the Pity* (*Le chagrin et la pitié*, 1970), *The Trials of Alger Hiss* by John Lowenthal (1980), *Lousy Little Sixpence* by Alec Morgan (1982), *Vietnam: A Television History* (PBS, 1983), *Frontline* by David Bradbury (1983), *For Love or Money* by Megan McMurchy, Margot Nash, Margot Oliver and Jeni Thornley (1983), *Red Matildas* by Sharon Connolly and Trevor Graham (1985) and *Berkeley in the 60s* by Mark Kitchell (1990).

## Further reading

Crowdus, G. and D. Georgakas, 'History is the theme of all my films: an interview with Emile de Antonio' in A. Rosenthal (ed.), *New Challenges for Documentary* (Berkeley: University of California Press, 1988), reprinted in part in K. Macdonald and M. Cousins (eds), *Imagining Reality: The Faber Book of Documentary* (London: Faber and Faber, 1996).

Kellner, D. and D. Streible (eds), *Emile de Antonio: A Reader* (Minneapolis: University of Minnesota Press, 2000).

Zimmermann, P. 'Pirates of the New World Image Orders', Chapter 5 of P. Zimmermann, *States of Emergency: Documentaries, Wars, Democracies* (Minneapolis: University of Minnesota Press, 2000).

*Public Shelter* (1996), a CD-ROM sequel to *The Atomic Café*. The disc contains a collection of 'found' items on aspects of atomic culture: 1600 text files, 75 video clips, 400 photographs and 10 hours of audio extracts. See <www.publicshelter.com>.

# 8   The fact/fiction divide: drama-documentary and documentary drama

*The War Game*, Peter Watkins, 1966. 47 min.
US: Facets Multimedia, Inc

1517 West Fullerton Ave
Chicago IL 60614
Telephone:            773 281 9075
Fax:                  773 929 5437
Email:                sales@facets.org
Website:              www.facets.org
VHS

UK: British Film Institute
21 Stephen St
London W1T 1LN
Telephone:            20 7255 1444
Email:                films@bfi.org.uk
Website:              bfi.org.uk
VHS and DVD

Australia: Australian Centre for the Moving Image (National Access Film
and Video Collection)
222 Park St
South Melbourne
Vic 3205
Telephone:            03 992 7040
Fax:                  03 9929 7027
Email:                collections@acmi.net.au
Website:              www.acmi.net.au
16 mm

## Additional resources

For drama-documentary see the television series *Holocaust* by Marvin
Chomsky (NBC, 1978), *Tumbledown* by Charles Wood (BBC, 1987) and
*Hostages* by David Wheatley (Granada/HBO, 1992), and the Australian
television series *The Dismissal* by George Miller, Phillip Noyce, George
Ogilvie, Carl Schultz and John Power (Channel Ten, 1983). See also the
so-called biopics *My Brilliant Career* by Gillian Armstrong (1979), *Raging
Bull* by Martin Scorsese (1980), *Silkwood* by Mike Nichols (1984) and
*Gandhi* by Richard Attenborough (1982).

   For documentary drama see *Culloden* (BBC, 1964) by Peter Watkins, *Up
the Junction* (BBC, 1965) by Ken Loach and James McTaggart, *Boys from the
Blackstuff* (BBC, 1982) by Peter Saville, *Scales of Justice* by Michael Jenkins
(ABC, 1983), *Vietnam* (Channel Ten, 1987) by John Duigan and Chris
Noonan and *Blue Murder* by Michael Jenkins (1995; screened ABC, 2001).

## Further reading

Custen, G. *Bio/Pics: How Hollywood Constructed Public History* (New Brunswick:
   Rutgers University Press, 1992).

Feldman, S. 'Footnote to fact: the docudrama' in B. K. Grant (ed.), *Film Genre Reader II* (Austin: University of Texas Press, 1995).

Paget, D. *No Other Way to Tell It: Dramadoc/Docudrama on Television* (Manchester: Manchester University Press, 1998).

Rosenthal, A. '*The War Game:* An interview with Peter Watkins' in A. Rosenthal (ed.), *New Challenges for Documentary* (Berkeley: University of California Press, 1988).

Rosenthal, A. (ed.), *Why Docudrama? Fact-Fiction on Film and TV* (Carbondale: Southern Illinois University Press, 1999).

# 9   The evening report: television documentary journalism

*Cambodia: The Betrayal,* Produced and directed by David Munro, written and presented by John Pilger, 1990. 52 min.
US: American Friends Service Committee
Video and Film Lending Library
2161 Massachusetts Ave
Cambridge MA 02140

| | |
|---|---|
| Telephone: | 617 497 5273 |
| Fax: | 617 354 2832 |
| Email: | pshannon@afsc.org |
| Website: | www.afsc.org |
| VHS | |

UK and Australia: Carlton Television

| | |
|---|---|
| Telephone: | 0870 600 6766 |
| Fax: | 0121 634 4898 |
| Email: | dutyoffice@carltontv.co.uk |
| Website: | www2.carlton.com |
| VHS | |

### Additional resources

Pilger's television programmes include *The Pilger Report* (ITV, 1974–77), *The Secret Country* (Central Television, 1985), *The Last Dream* (Central Television, 1988), *Death of a Nation: The Timor Conspiracy* (Central Television, 1994), updated and re-edited as *The Timor Conspiracy* (ITV, 1999) and *Paying the Price: Killing the Children of Iraq* (Carlton, 2000).

### Further reading

Corner, J. 'See it happen', Chapter 3 of J. Corner, *Television Form and Public Address* (London: Edward Arnold, 1995).

Hayward, A. *In the Name of Justice: The Television Reporting of John Pilger* (London: Bloomsbury, 2001).

'Impartiality (ITC)', extracts from The Independent Television Commission programme code, London, ITC, 1995, reprinted in J. Corner and S. Harvey (eds), *Television Times: A Reader* (London: Arnold, 1996).

'The fairness doctrine and procedures to be used in filing fairness doctrine complaints (FCC)' from Federal Communications Commission, 1983, reprinted in J. Corner and S. Harvey (eds), *Television Times: A Reader* (London: Arnold, 1996).

## 10 Up close and personal: popular factual entertainment

*Cops*
*Cops: Caught in the Act* (1989), and *Cops: In Hot Pursuit* (1996), compilation tapes from the series *Cops*
US: Amazon.com
PO Box 81226
Seattle 98108-1226
Website:              www.amazon.com
VHS

UK and Australia: *The Best of Cops*
Medusa Communications and Marketing Ltd
Regal Chambers, 51 Bancroft St
Hitchin
Herts SG5 1LL
Telephone:          01462 421818
Fax:                   01462 420393
Email:                steve@medusacom.co.uk
VHS

*The Real World*
US, UK and Australia: *The Real World: New York – The Complete First Session*
Amazon.com
PO Box 81226
Seattle 98108-1226
Website:              www.amazon.com
VHS and DVD

*Big Brother*
US: CBS Television
Online video footage streamed at <www.cbs.com>. The site contains archives of a number of episodes.

UK: *Big Brother Uncut, Series 3 and 4*
Channel 4 Television

124 Horseferry Rd
London SW1P 2TX
Telephone:          0870 1234 344
Website:            www.channel4.com/bigbrother/shop
VHS and DVD

Australia: *The Best of Big Brother*, 2001. 115 min.
Australian Centre for the Moving Image (National Access Film and Video Collection)
222 Park St
South Melbourne
Vic 3205
Telephone:          03 992 7040
Fax:                03 9929 7027
Email:              collections@acmi.net.au
Website:            www.acmi.net.au
VHS

## Additional resources

Popular factual entertainment in its variant forms (reality TV, docusoaps, gamedocs etc.) show little sign of abating on television schedules. In addition to the programmes discussed in the chapter, examples of the formats include *Faking It* (Channel 4, which first aired in 2000), in which people adopt various identities; *Wife Swap* (Channel 4, 2003), a programme in which women swap houses and families; *Marry Me* (BBC1, 2000), which follows the lives of people about to be married; *Frontier House* (PBS, 2002), a version of the earlier *Edwardian House, The 1940s House* and the original, *1900 House; Spy TV* (NBC, 2001; BBC1, 2003), an updated version of *Candid Camera; Single Girls* (Channel 7, 2000), in which single women share a luxury house in Sydney as they seek romantic partners; numerous UK-produced programmes dealing with 'vets-and-pets', including *Animal Hospital* (BBC1, 1995), *Vets' School* (BBC1, 1996), *Vets in Practice* (BBC1, 1997), *Animal Rescuers* (ITV, 1998), *Pet Rescue* (Channel 4, 1998), *Wildlife SOS* (Channel 5, 1998) and *Animal Police* (BBC1, 1996); and a slew of docusoaps in which aspiring pop singers are moulded into a band – a format which, among other series, has been replicated under the name *Popstars* in New Zealand (TVNZ, 1999), Australia (Channel 7, 2000), the United States (WB, 2001), the United Kingdom (ITV, 2001) and in South Africa, France and Spain.

## Further reading

Brenton, S. and R. Cohen. *Shooting People: Adventures in Reality TV* (London: Verso, 2003).

Dovey, J. *Freakshow: First Person Media and Factual Television* (London: Pluto Press, 2000).

Hill, A. 'Crime and crisis: British reality TV' in E. Buscombe (ed.), *British Television: A Reader* (Oxford: Oxford University Press, 1999).

Hill, A. and G. Porter (eds), *Big Brother* issue of *Television and New Media*, 3, 3 (August 2002).

Fishman, M. and G. Cavender (eds), *Entertaining Crime: Television Reality Programs* (New York: Aldine de Gruyter, 1998).

Bagley, G. 'A mixed bag: negotiating claims in MTV's *The Real World*', *Journal of Film and Video*, 53, 2–3 (2001) 61–76.

## 11   The burning question: the future of documentary

### Additional resources

Examples of online documentary include the works mounted on the website of the Australian Broadcasting Corporation <www.abc.net.au/documentaryonline/> and <www.abc.net.au/ sharkfeed/>.

### Further reading:

Bunt, B. 'The texture of actuality: new media documentary', *Metro Magazine*, 135 (2003) 166–171.

Junko, T. and S. Teasley (eds), 'Documentary in the age of digital reproduction' in *Documentary Box*, at <www.city.yamagata.yamagata.jp/yidff/docbox/15/box15-2-1.html>.

Muhammad, E. 'Black high-tech documents' in P. R. Klotman and J. C. Cutler (eds), *Struggles for Representation: African American Documentary Film and Video* (Bloomington: Indiana University Press, 1999).

# Notes

## Introduction

1 A point made by Ellis (2000: 62).
2 The term is used by Renov (1999a: 321), whose description of the approach I have paraphrased here. Renov sketches a method similar to that adopted in this study when he writes 'we are now beginning to see documentary studies jettison its once single-minded focus on documentary history, aesthetics, and ideological criticism in favor of producing a kind of situated knowledge in which cultural representation is linked to larger social and historical forces'.
3 Derek Paget (1998) uses this phrase as the title of his book on drama-documentary/documentary drama.

## Chapter 1

1 Plantinga (1997) and Ponech (1999) address many of the epistemological issues embedded in these connections.
2 The production of digital images does not involve a photochemical process. A photographic negative (the 'evidence' of a connection between image and object) is absent under computer-generated imaging, a situation that has the potential to disrupt belief in the authenticity of the image.
3 There is an illusory basis to the indexical 'guarantee' which is revealed in the fact that an image of a thing is, of course, not the thing itself. The conclusion points to the fact that the prevailing investment in an indexical bond is the result of commonly accepted, culturally specific, approaches to photographic and filmic representation, circulating in association with characteristics of the image itself.
4 Corner (1995: 79–81) provides details of the transformations undertaken within the process of producing a documentary.
5 Winston is here specially referring to assessments of narrative made in various places by the influential film theorists Kristin Thompson and David Bordwell.
6 The term 'voice of God' was coined by Paul Rotha and is featured by Nichols (1985) in his analysis and taxonomy of documentary modes.

7 In recognition of the filmmaker's presence in this type of documentary practice, Nichols (2001) has recently recast the interactive engagement as a participatory mode.

## Chapter 2

1 The word documentary as a term used to refer to a specific type of non-fictional representation was coined by Grierson in a review for the New York *Sun* (published on 8 February 1926) of Flaherty's film *Moana*.

2 For most of its history, fictional filmmaking in the United Kingdom and the United States was a studio-based mode of production. Location shooting did not become prominent until the late 1960s.

3 Grierson made the distinction in an unpublished essay written shortly after he completed *Drifters*. See Aitken (1998: 40).

4 Aitken (1990: 60) explains that Grierson's ideas at the time were influenced by idealist sources, including Kant. In his reference to 'more real in the philosophic sense' Grierson was not referring to material or physical reality but to a complex of physical and abstract, including moral, forces.

5 Later in his career, Flaherty altered his position toward Hollywood. In later years, Flaherty famously compared working in Hollywood to 'going through a sewer in a glass bottomed boat' (Barsam, 1988: 5).

6 Recalling this screening some years later, Flaherty ([1950] 1996) mentions that staff at Paramount sat through the session without a word, and at the end of the film silently left the screening room. The reaction of the commercial distributors is contrasted in the same account to the responses of the Inuit subjects of the film who, according to Flaherty, were enthralled by the film and shouted excitedly during a screening of the film.

7 Brian Winston (1999: 163) theorizes reconstruction within terms of a continuum, with non-intervention of any kind – 'the filming of, say, natural disasters' – at one end, and total intervention – 'that is, the completely fictional representation of people, locations, and events' – at the other. Winston fills in the gradations on the continuum as: non-intervention; permissions (the filmmaker asks for a subject's permission to film); delays and repetitions ('specific unfilmed requests made without prior research to repeat or delay the action'); re-enactment of witnessed history; re-enactment of history; re-enactment of the typical; enactment of the possible; acting. Flaherty's reconstructions involve all of these features, to a varying degree. Most commonly, however, his reconstructions approximate the categories 're-enactment of history' and 're-enactment of the typical'.

8 Paul Rotha (in Winston, 1988: 21) recognized the synonymy of the terms 'treatment' and 'dramatisation' in his rephrasing of Grierson's definition as the 'creative dramatisation of actuality.'

9 On Vertov's *Man With a Movie Camera* see Michelson (1984) and Petrić (1987). On Ruttmann's *Berlin, Symphony of a City* see Bernstein (1984) and Natter (1994). On *Las Hurdes* see Conley (1987).

10 The tradition of 'agit/prop' and oppositional documentary in the United States, the United Kingdom and Australia is partly retrievable through works which include Alexander (1981), Ansara and Milner (1999), Boyle (1997), Dickinson (1999), Harding (2002), Hogenkamp (1986), Klotman and Cutler (1999), Macpherson (1980), Nichols (1980), Waugh (1984) and Zimmermann (2000).

## Chapter 3

1 In 1895, Regnault filmed the pottery-making techniques of a Wolof woman at the Exposition Ethnographie de l'Afrique Occidentale in Paris. In the same year, the Lumiere brothers held the world's first film screenings. As David MacDougall (1998: 179) notes: 'Ethnographic film is thus as old as the cinema.'

2 Quotation marks are placed around the word race to draw attention to the socially constructed nature of the referent. 'Race' and 'races' are not essential or biological conditions.

3 Ethnography has been defined as a branch of anthropology which describes cultures (Preloran, 1987: 464). As the quotation by Slomovics points out, ethnography also involves the textual practices of representing (other) cultures. In this way, ethnographic films have been described as those 'which represent and interpret people's attitudes and culture usually to people of another culture' (Preloran, 1987: 464).

4 'The Other' is a construction which has been analysed and applied in a variety of disciplinary contexts, including literary studies, psychology and psychoanalysis, philosophy, cultural history, ethnography and film and media studies. Interpretations of applications of the term in various contexts, particularly that of ethnography, are discussed in Hallam and Street (2000) and Ashcroft *et al.* (1998), who provide a list of further readings on the topic.

5 This chapter does not examine the implications of ethnography on television. For discussions of this topic, with reference to the *Disappearing World* series, see Banks (1994), Singer and Seidenberg (1992) and Turton (1992).

6 Grimshaw (2001: 191) notes that Heider is preoccupied with classificatory features 'as the means to assert [the] distinctiveness of ethnographic film from its rival forms and thereby to lay claim to academic respectability'.

7 Loizos (1993) offers an extended analysis of the MacDougalls' East African films.

8 Ruby (1991) addresses a number of the issues raised for the ethnographer by these speaking positions.

9 Allen (1977) provides further definitions of self-reflexivity in documentary.

10  Asch offered various comments on the making of *The Ax Fight*. See Asch (1979) and Asch in Ruby (2000).

11  Asch subsequently revised the form of ethnographic interpretation undertaken in *The Ax Fight*. In an interview first published in 1995 Asch says that he came to recognize the 'simplistic, straightjacket, one-sided explanation' offered in *The Ax Fight* (reprinted in Ruby, 2000: 128). In his essay 'The story we now want to hear is not ours to tell' (1992) Asch insists that the ethnographer's interpretations cannot be as cogent as those provided by the indigenous subject, and argues for Yanomamo self-representation as an ethical solution to questions of ethnographic authority.

Ethical issues have been raised in another way in relation to the ethnographic research undertaken by Napoleon Chagnon, Asch's collaborator on *The Ax Fight*. Chagnon's studies of the Yanomamo were partly funded by the US Atomic Energy Commission (AEC), which sought out the Yanomamo (as a population uncontaminated by nuclear radiation) for a comparative study involving survivors of Hiroshima and Nagasaki. According to allegations contained in Tierney (2000), Chagnon undertook ethically suspicious human genetic research among the Yanomamo with AEC funds.

12  In his analysis of the film, Brian Winston (1995: 178) accepts the validity of the film's conclusions though nevertheless poses a number of provocative possibilities intended to question the film's legitimating narrative. 'Perhaps the Yanomamo and Chagnon see the relationships differently. Perhaps Yanomamo women see them differently from Yanomamo men, or the old see them differently from the young. Perhaps they have kept their vision of how relationships work a secret.'

13  Interestingly, such a form of 'ethnography' is as much a reflection on the filmmaker's culture as it is of another culture. O'Rourke (in Beattie, 2001b) maintains that *Cunnamulla* (2001), his depiction of the town by that name in rural Queensland, is ethnographic in the sense of a representation of one's *own* culture.

14  Carl Plantinga (1997: 218) argues that 'Reflexive strategies do not guarantee honesty, integrity, or genuine self-revelation on the part of the filmmaker(s). A reflexive film can be as manipulative as any other.' In '*Cannibal Tours*', however, O'Rourke's willingness to openly *display* and *critique* his own positions is achieved through (self-) reflexive strategies.

15  The autobiographical *History and Memory*, discussed in Chapter 10, can be considered a work of domestic ethnography according to the outline of the form provided by Renov.

16  Rachel Moore (1994) provides an illuminating critique of the notion that indigenous media necessarily effectively address the positions of ethnographic film.

# Chapter 4

1 Indigenous media produced in various parts of the world (notably North America, New Zealand and Australia) are examined in Riggins (1992), Kuth (1995), Browne (1996), Molnar and Meadows (2001) and Singer (2001).

2 Representations of Aborigines in fiction and documentary film, in addition to those referred to in this chapter, include, among others, Moore and Muecke (1984), Bostock (1987), Leigh (1988), Maynard (1989), Jennings (1993) and O'Regan (1996).

3 The word 'Aborigine' is used here to refer to indigenous Australians. It is recognized that indigenous Australians also include Torres Strait Islanders.

4 Langton abandons the term 'postcolonial' (and with it any sense of a national formation after – or devoid – of the traces of colonialism) in favour of an *anti*colonial and *de*colonial critical position. The terms of Langton's analysis are adopted in this chapter. A broad description of the historical and political features of decolonization, and a list of further readings, is provided in Ashcroft *et al.* (1989).

5 The ABC and SBS are national broadcasters in the dual sense of broadcast range and public ownership.

6 The programme was first screened within the *Blackout* series of indigenous programmes on the ABC.

7 Peters-Little has also produced *Tent Embassy* (1991), the first documentary of the Aboriginal [now Indigenous] Programs Unit of the ABC. Using interviews and archival footage the programme documents a significant protest by Aboriginal Australians: the establishment of an Aboriginal embassy (in the form of a calico tent) on the lawns of Parliament House in Canberra and the declaration by the protesters of an Aboriginal sovereign nation.

8 The programme was commissioned by the Special Broadcasting Service within its commitment to Aboriginal programming.

9 A 'pilot' version of the programme was screened by the ABC in 1999. The four-part series was produced by Film Australia and screened on the ABC in 2001. When screened nationally on ABC television the programme was preceded by the following message: 'The ABC seeks to treat indigenous cultures and beliefs with respect. To many communities it is distressful and offensive to depict persons who have died. Indigenous communities which may be offended are warned that the following program may contain such scenes.' The same message is applicable to any screening of *Two Laws*.

10 Certain of the features of colonization intersect with and are continued in aspects of globalization. In this way, the negotiation of globalizing

forces by indigenous people is an extension of indigenous engagement with colonization. Hinkson (2002) analyses Warlpiri electronic media in terms of an 'accelerated globalization'.

11 These programmes and the 'Outback adventure' formula are discussed in Carter (1998).

12 The work of John Heyer (1916–2001) has been studied in various quarters. Gibson's essay 'Yarning', in Gibson (1992), is an informative reading of Heyer's *Back of Beyond*. Heyer's career is discussed in Moran (1991) and Williams (2001).

## Chapter 5

1 The terms direct cinema and cinéma vérité have been used interchangeably in writings on documentary. Marcorelles (1973), for example, refers to developments in both France and the United States as direct cinema, while Mamber refers to both forms as cinéma vérité. The tendency to refer to both forms as cinéma vérité, or merely vérité (or verite), is increasing. The separate terms are retained here as a way of pointing to their usage by practitioners in France and the United States in the late 1950s and for most of the 1960s.

2 Drew's career and the development of direct cinema are examined in O'Connell (1992). As Bluem (1965) points out, Drew was primarily a producer; he organized finance for the programmes and negotiated their transmission, while his colleagues acted as directors, camera operators, sound recordists and editors of the programmes.

3 As noted anthropologist Claude Levi-Strauss (1966: 126) declared, speaking for many anthropologists and ethnographers on this point, anthropology is an objective 'science of culture as seen from the outside'.

4 The transcription and translation comes from Loizos (1993) 61–2.

5 Rouch (1985: 32) claimed Flaherty's *Nanook of the North* and Vertov's *Man With a Movie Camera* as influences on *Chronicle*. Rouch admired Vertov's reflexive methods and praised Flaherty's method of screening unedited footage to his subjects, a practice he replicated in *Chronicle* in the scene in which the filmmakers screen a rough cut of the film to its subjects. Morin (1985: 5) acknowledged Lionel Rogosin's *On the Bowery* (1956) as an influence on his conceptions of filmmaking. Rogosin employed a number of destitute occupants of Bowery Street, then New York's 'skid row', to enact their lives for his camera. The process bears some resemblance to the way in which the participants in *Chronicle* 'perform' a role. In certain scenes Rogosin used a hidden camera in an attempt to capture behaviour unaffected by the camera's presence. This observational approach is echoed in the scenes in the Renault factory in *Chronicle*.

6 This chapter focuses on the work of direct cinema filmmakers associated with Robert Drew. The films of Frederick Wiseman, not an associate of

Robert Drew, also constitute a significant contribution to direct cinema. Wiseman's films are discussed in, among other sources, Atkins (1976), Nichols (1978) and Grant (1992).

7 Bruzzi (2000: 70–3) examines the multiple ways in which *Salesman* deviates from the direct cinema philosophy of a pure observationalism.

8 The image has been recently reprinted in Dixon, 2003, page 185.

9 Winston (1995: 205) argues that 'Direct cinema made the rock performance/tour movie into the most popular and commercially viable documentary form thus far.' The inverse may be closer to the point: the rockumentary turned direct cinema into a commercial and widely available form.

10 Among the limited writings on the form see Wootton (1988), Sarchett (1994), Bell (1999) and a brief assessment by the German film director Wim Wenders (1986).

11 Dylan's parody of his own stage persona is continued in his recent fictional film *Masked and Anonymous* (2003), in which Dylan plays an ageing rock star, Jack Fate. The title of the film is a reference to the impossibility of 'knowing' the Fate character and, by extension, to the elusiveness of the Dylan persona.

12 Graef's work is examined in Wyver (1982). British observational documentaries are discussed in Vaughan (1976) and Bruzzi (2000).

13 *An American Family* was filmed by Alan and Susan Raymond.

14 Made by Paul Watson, who some years earlier had produced *The Family*.

# Chapter 6

1 Although McElwee has made films on various subjects (the fall of the Berlin Wall, an Iranian exile in the United States, the local residents of Cape Canaveral, Florida), he is best known for his autobiographical work. McElwee's first film, *Charleen* (1978), features his relationship with his long-time friend Charleen Swansea, who subsequently appears in *Sherman's March*. In 1982 he made *Backyard* (1982), a film about his father, and after *Sherman's March* he continued his autobiographical documentations with *Time Indefinite* (1993), a moving reflection on his father's life and death, and *Six O'Clock News* (1996).

2 Elsewhere, Marks (2000) applies many of the features of hybrid cinema within an analysis of what she calls 'intercultural cinema'.

3 Lise Yasui's *A Family Gathering* (1988) and Janice Tanaka's *Memories from the Department of Amnesia* (1991) and *Who's Going to Pay for these Donuts Anyway?* (1992) resemble *History and Memory* in their attention to themes of family, memory and Americanism. Each work was made by a daughter of parents who experienced internment during the Second World War. These and other works dealing with the memory of

Japanese American internment are discussed in Van Buren (1997), Payne (1997) and Feng (2002).

4 The video diary has been a feature of the avant-garde tradition of film and video making. In the United States, George Kuchar and Sadie Benning (to cite two examples) have used the video camera to produce works which innovatively represent aspects of personal identity. See Russell (1999), chapter 10, 'Autoethnography: Journeys of the Self.'

5 The term access has also been used in relation to political broadcasting, in particular audience participation within broadcast debates. See, for example, McNair *et al.* (2002).

## Chapter 7

1 The tradition of politically engaged compilation filmmaking is also a prominent feature of Latin American cinema, as in, for example, *Hour of the Furnaces* (*La hora de los hornos*, 1968) by Agentinian directors Fernando Solanas and Octavio Getino, *The Battle of Chile* (*La battalla de Chile*, 1975–79) by Chilean filmmaker Patricio Guzman, and *Hanoi, Tuesday the 13th* (*Hanoi, martes trece*, 1967) and other films by the Cuban director Santiago Alvarez.

2 Bill Nichols (1985: 53) discusses such criticisms of observational documentary.

3 The method was not, however, without its critics. A debate ensued over the political effects of a representational focus on the individual in verbal testimony. In his analysis of the political documentaries *Harlan County, U.S.A.* (1976) and *Union Maids*, Noel King (1981) criticized the films for a reliance on realistic representation in place of any form of innovative self-reflection. According to King, biography and autobiography operate in *Union Maids* as a series of mini-narratives which serve as the basis of the film's construction of a teleological history. King argues that the mini-narratives are reinforced through archival images whose meanings are specified in the comments made by each of the film's witnesses. Aspects of King's criticism echoed in various sources. Writing in 1986, historian Jesse Lemisch criticized what he called the 'voice of the first person heroic' operative in a number of politically committed documentary films of the 1970s and 1980s based on oral testimony and archival footage, among them *Union Maids*, *The Good Fight* and *Seeing Red: Portraits of American Communists*. According to Lemisch, the documentaries contain an excess of talking by subjects and a relative absence of any direct questioning of interviewees (Lemisch, 1986: 96). An element of the criticisms by King and Lemisch resounds in Michael Renov's comment that such works reduce public history to a collection of private histories which, while valuable in themselves, fail in the absence of interrogation of the individual points of view to reveal

a broad history of contradiction and complexity (Renov, 1993a: 27). Bill Nichols (1991: 252), writing of many of the films addressed by King and Lemisch, argues that such documentaries endorse the partial and at times self-defensive views of individuals as the basis of history rather than contesting common notions of historical experience in working towards alternative forms of historical representation.

4 William Wees (in Russell, 1999: 255) describes *The Atomic Café* as a 'compilation film' that 'does not continually question the representational nature of the images it uses'.

5 Features of Conner's *Report* are discussed in Kelman (1975). Peterson (1986) has examined what he calls Conner's 'assemblage aesthetic', a topic also analysed briefly in O'Pray (1987).

6 Patricia Zimmermann (1989) refers to avant-gardist artists' compilations as works of 'new compilation' in her examination of the form. Catherine Russell (1999) also examines varieties of avant-garde compilations, including Conner's *A Movie*.

## Chapter 8

1 The programme was eventually shown in July 1985, during a series of special presentations to commemorate the fortieth anniversary of the atomic bombings of Hiroshima and Nagasaki. This detail comes from Pilger (1989: 532), who discusses the official response to the programme's production.

2 Caughie's essay, a contribution to a wider debate about the progressive or radical potential of dramatic realism and the representation of (working class) social and political experiences, was originally published in *Screen* magazine and collected in edited form in T. Bennett *et. al.* (1981). Caughie has revised the content of the essay and included it as part of his book *Television Drama* (2000).

3 Paget (1998: 113) argues that the terms dramatized documentary and drama-documentary are the 'commonest historical terms' used to refer to the forms. This chapter follows Paget in this usage, though it is recognized that the terms are by no means unchallenged. The contending terms docudrama and dramadoc are also used to refer to programmes that mainly follow the drama-documentary methodology (Paget, 1998: 83).

4 Works of this kind are discussed in Higson (1995).

5 Many of the details contained in the ITC Code were reissued in *Statements of Best Practice* covering factual drama issued by ITV in 1994. Extracts of the *Statement* are reprinted as 'Guidelines for Drama-Documentary (ITV Network Centre)' in Corner and Harvey, 1996.

6 Paget examines work from both the United Kingdom and the United States, with an emphasis on the former. Breitbart (1986) contains an analysis of US 'docudramas' and historical re-creations. Contrasting

with Paget's analysis of the utility of the forms is Kuehl's (1988) adversely critical assessment of the drama-documentary.

7 Murderous mistresses, for example, have proved to be a popular subject for docudrama coverage, as in the multiple productions of the story of Amy Fisher, the so-called Long Island Lolita.

8 Kilborn (1994b) and Paget (1998) examine these works.

9 *Walking With Dinosaurs* is a co-production of the BBC, the Discovery Channel, Television Asahi with Prosieben and France 3. An extended critical discussion of the series appears in Scott and White (2003).

## Chapter 9

1 The decline of 'serious' television documentary programming is an issue raised in documents reproduced in Franklin (2001) 117–22.

2 Reith encapsulated his philosophy of public service broadcasting in the maxim that broadcasting should seek to 'inform, educate and entertain'.

3 Phillips (1977), Schiller (1981) and Lichtenberg (1996) usefully consider the notion of objectivity in journalism and the theoretical issues surrounding the term.

4 Pilger has also been accused of altering an interview with the then Australian Prime Minister, Bob Hawke. It was argued by Hawke's press team that Pilger replaced the original questions he asked of the Prime Minister with variants in the final edit of the programme. Pilger (1987) insisted that his editorial emendations did not alter the substance of the questioning and argued that the charges against him were politically motivated and an affront to freedom of the press. Issues of impartiality in journalism continue to concern Pilger. The Carlton Television website pages dedicated to Pilger's work <www.pilger.carlton.com> feature a number of articles he has recently published on the topic.

5 The ITC is the regulatory body for all commercially funded television, whether available via terrestrial, cable or satellite transmission. The ITC also drafts and enforces programming codes, advertising codes and rules governing the provision of service.

6 Among its other findings, the Annan Committee recommended the establishment of a new television channel, leading to the launch in 1982 of Channel 4.

7 The Act has since been revised as the Broadcasting Act of 1996. The Broadcasting Act of 1996 established the Broadcasting Standards Commission, a regulatory body charged with drafting a code of practice for broadcasters and addressing complaints arising from the code.

8 Aspects of the Code relating to impartiality are reproduced in Franklin (2001). A complete version of the ITC Code on Impartiality is available at <www.itc.org.uk>.

9 Corner (1995) makes these comments in a useful chapter in which he examines the conventions of television news reporting (chapter 3,

'See It Happen'). Many of these conventions are relevant to the long-form news documentary and are applied here in this recognition.

10 Wilson (1993: 146–7) examines the various tonal qualities adopted by Michael Buerk in the voice-overs to his special report on South Africa, *No Easy Road* (BBC, 1986).

## Chapter 10

1 So-called reality TV has, in certain cases, focused on images of near-death; the Fox special presentation *Close Call: Cheating Death* exemplifies this trend. An analysis of the boundaries of 'taste and decency' in reality programmes is offered in Shaw (1999) and Brenton and Cohen (2003).

2 The terms 'popular factual entertainment' and its variants (factual programming; factual entertainment) are used in various sources (e.g. Brunsdon *et al.*, 2001 and Roscoe, 2001). The use of the term in this chapter derives from Corner (2000a,b and 2002).

3 Winston (2000) has contributed to the investigation of the ethical issues associated with documentary launched by Gross *et al.* (1988).

4 A number of useful documents relating to 'quality in [British] broadcasting' (and the effects of deregulation and commercialization on programme 'quality') are contained in Franklin (2001: 92–9). Debates concerning 'quality' programming are not a prominent component of discussions of the commercialized environment of the majority of US television.

5 This position is quoted and critiqued in Goodwin (1997).

6 All production dates refer to the inaugural series of a programme.

7 According to one commentator (Caldwell, 2002: 272), by the late 1990s the Fox network committed almost half of its programme development budget to reality series.

8 As an indication of the popularity of the format and the related increase in franchising expenses, the third series of Australian *Big Brother* is estimated to have cost the Channel Ten network more than A$25 million ('Son of Big Brother', 2002: 13).

9 The figure comes from 'Is Reality TV a Survivor?' in *Ad Age Global* (June 2001) 21.

10 This 'demographic' comes from figures available for the viewing audience of the first series of the British version of *Big Brother*. The programme reached 75 per cent of viewers in this cohort (Palmer, 2002: 303). Hill (2002) gives a detailed profile of the audience for this series. The audience targeted by the Channel 10 network for the Australian version *of Big Brother* was the age group of 19 to 39 year olds, and the programme reached 50 per cent of viewers in this age bracket (Hill, 2002: 326).

11 The rise and proliferation within English-speaking broadcasting of cookery, DIY, gardening and 'makeover' programmes is discussed at length in Bonner (2003).

12 Bondebjerg (1996) argues that programmes such as *Cops* merely rework footage into updated versions of so-called direct cinema.

13 Gilbert produced the series, with Alan and Susan Raymond as the camera and sound team.

14 The attempt is complicated when the subject is a professional performer who is constantly performing on and off the stage, as is the case with Bob Dylan in Pennebaker's *Don't Book Back* and, in a far less self-conscious way, Ozzy Osbourne in MTV's *The Osbournes*.

## Chapter 11

1 As in, for example, *Buena Vista Social Club* (1999), *Ghenghis Blues* (1999) and *Calle 54* (2001).

2 Garnham (1990) argues that the BBC abandoned the notion of public service as it adapted to market forces, and as such the BBC is not dissimilar to any other major media company. In an alternative interpretation, Connell (1983) argues that support by the political left in Britain of publicly funded media betrays a fear of commercialization which ignores the potential of commercial broadcasters to meet the popular concerns of audiences in the current broadcasting era.

3 The rise of digital television, and television services in general in Britain during the Tory era of 1979–97 are examined in Goodwin (1998).

4 Current developments in interactive forms have resulted in interactive fictional narratives that rely on television, websites, email, voicemail and SMS to enhance the story, and through which viewers can vote on plot alternatives and thereby contribute to the outcome of the narrative (see Harty, 2002). Similar developments are also being applied to non-fictional forms such as historical documentaries (see Peacock, 2002).

5 Caldwell (1994) has examined the influence of such styles on television documentary in the United States.

6 The image is reproduced in Mitchell (1992).

7 Such claims are addressed in Marchessault and Wasson (1998). Certain of the arguments concerning the potential of digital technology to manipulate images verge on a form of what can be called 'digital panic'. The potential to manipulate images does not automatically result in widespread digital fakery and forgery. Indeed, recent examples of fakery revolve around long-standing issues surrounding the practices of attribution and reconstruction (not digital image manipulation), as in the scandal surrounding Carlton Television's documentary *The Connection* (1996) in which scenes were fabricated using professional actors. See Winston (2000).

8 A variant of this practice is the use of the Web to promote documentaries screened or broadcast off-line. *The Gate of Heavenly Peace* (Carma Hinton and Richard Gordon, 1995), a documentary film that examines the 1989 protests in Beijing's Tiananmen Square is, for example, supported by a website that provides among other features in English and Chinese, a complete transcript of the film, an interactive tour of Tiananmen Square, a chronology of the protests and the repressive government response, and links to additional readings and related websites. See <www.nmis.org/Gate/>. The television production company Illuminations, producer of *The Net* for BBC2, used the Web to support the series by emailing programme-related information and mounting on-line discussions of the programme (Chapman, 1998: 182).

# Bibliography

Aitken, I. (ed.). 1988. *The Documentary Film Movement: An Anthology* (Edinburgh: Edinburgh University Press).

Aitken, I. 1990. *Film and Reform: John Grierson and the Documentary Film Movement* (London: Routledge).

Alexander, W. 1981. *Film on the Left: American Documentary Film from 1931 to 1942* (Princeton: Princeton University Press).

Allen, J. 1977. 'Self-reflexivity in documentary', *Cine-Tracts*, 1, 2, 37–43.

Allen, R. and D. Gomez. 1985. *Film History: Theory and Practice* (New York: Alfred Knopf).

Andersen, R. 1995. *Consumer Culture and TV Programming* (Boulder: Westview Press).

Ansara, M. and L. Milner. 1999. 'The Waterside Workers Federation Film Unit: the forgotten frontier of the fifties', *Metro Magazine*, 19, 28–39.

Armes, R. 1978. *A Critical History of the British Cinema* (London: Secker and Warburg).

Arthur, P. 1993. 'Jargons of authenticity (three American moments)' in M. Renov (ed.), *Theorizing Documentary* (New York : Routledge).

Arthur, P. 1999–2000. 'The status of found footage', *Spectator*, 20, 1, 57–69.

Asch, T. 1979. 'Making a film record of the Yanomamo Indians of southern Venezuela', *Perspectives on Film*, 2, 4–49.

Asch, T. 1992. 'The ethics of ethnographic film-making' in P. Crawford and D. Turton (eds), *Film as Ethnography* (Manchester: Manchester University Press).

Asch, T., J. I. Cardozo, H. Cabellero and J. Bortoli. 1992. 'The story we now want to hear is not ours to tell: relinquishing control over representation: toward sharing visual communication skills with the Yanomami', *Visual Anthropology Review*, 7, 2, 102–6.

Ashcroft, B., G. Griffiths and H. Tiffin. 1998. *Key Concepts in Post-Colonial Studies* (London: Routledge).

Atkins, T. (ed.). 1976. *Frederick Wiseman* (New York: Monarch Press).

Aufderheide, P. 2000. 'Camcorder confessions' in P. Aufderheide, *The Daily Planet: A Critic on the Capitalist Culture Beat* (Minneapolis: University of Minnesota Press).

Bachmann, G. 1961. 'The frontiers of realist cinema: the work of Ricky Leacock', *Film Culture*, 22–3, 12–23.

Bagley, G. 2001. 'A mixed bag: negotiating claims in MTV's *The Real World*', *Journal of Film and Video*, 53, 2–3, 61–76.

Banks, M. 1994. 'Television and anthropology: an unhappy marriage?', *Visual Anthropology*, 71, 1, 21–45.

Barclay, B. 1990. *Our Own Image* (Auckland: Longman Paul).

Barnouw, E. 1983. *Documentary: A History of the Non-Fiction Film*, rev. edn (Oxford: Oxford University Press).

Barsam, R. 1988. *The Vision of Robert Flaherty: The Artist as Myth and Filmmaker* (Bloomington: Indiana University Press).

Barsam, R. 1992. *Non-Fiction Film: A Critical History* (Bloomington: Indiana University Press).

Batty, P. 1993. 'Singing the electric: Aboriginal television in Australia' in T. Dowmunt (ed.), *Channels of Resistance: Global Television and Local Empowerment* (London: British Film Institute).

Beattie, K. 1996. 'First say and last cut: a conversation with Gaylene Preston', *New Zealand Journal of Media Studies*, 3, 1, 4–16.

Beattie, K. 2001a. 'Sick, filthy, and delirious: surf film and video and the documentary mode', *Continuum: Journal of Media and Cultural Studies*, 15, 3, 333–48.

Beattie, K. 2001b. Interview conducted with Dennis O'Rourke.

Bell, D. (ed.), 1999. *Woodstock: An Inside Look at the Movie That Shook Up the World and Defined a Generation* (Studio City: Michael Wise Productions).

Bellafante, G. 1995. 'Their so-called lives', *Time* (US edn), 146, 5 (31 July) 38–9.

Bennett, T. *et al.* (eds). 1981. *Popular Television and Film* (London: British Film Institute/Open University Press).

Bernstein, M. 1984. 'Visual style and spatial articulations in *Berlin, Symphony of a City* (1927)', *Journal of Film and Video*, 36, 5–12, 61.

Bhabha, H. 1994. *The Location of Culture* (London: Routledge).

Biella, P. and G. Seaman. 1997. *Yanomamo Interactive: The Ax Fight* (book and CD ROM) (New York: Harcourt Brace).

Blau, A. 1992. 'The promise of public access', *The Independent*, 15, 3, 22–6.

Blue, J. and M. Gill. 1965. 'Peter Watkins discusses his suppressed nuclear film *The War Game*', *Film Comment*, 3, 4, 14–19.

Bluem, W. 1965. *Documentary in American Television* (New York: Hastings House).

Blumler, J. G. 1999. 'Political communication systems all change: a response to Kees Brants', *European Journal of Communication*, 14, 2, 241–9.

Bondebjerg, I. 1996. 'Public discourse/private fascination: hybridization in "true-life-story" genres', *Media, Culture and Society*, 18, 1, 27–45.

Bonner, F. 2003. *Ordinary Television: Analyzing Popular TV* (London: Sage).

Boorman, J. and W. Donohue (eds). 1993. 'The burning question: cinema after the millennium?' in *Projections 2: A Forum for Film-Makers* (London: Faber and Faber).

Bostock, L. 1987. 'From "grunt" roles to creative control', *Filmnews* (November) 7.

Bostock, L. 1990. *The Greater Perspective: Guidelines for the Production of Film and Television on Aborigines and Torres Strait Islanders* (Sydney: Special Broadcasting Service).

Boyle, D. 1982. 'The Atomic Café', *Cineaste*, 12, 12, 39–40.

Boyle, D. 1997. *Subject to Change: Guerrilla Television Revisited* (New York: Oxford University Press).

Branigan, E. 1992. *Narrative Comprehension and Film* (London: Routledge).

Breitbart, E. 1986. 'The painted mirror: historical re-creation from the panorama to the docudrama' in S. Benson, S. Brier and R. Rosenzweig (eds), *Presenting the Past: Essays on History and the Public* (Philadelphia: Temple University Press).

Brenton, S. and R. Cohen. 2003. *Shooting People: Adventures in Reality TV* (London: Verso).

British Broadcasting Corporation. 1996. *Extending Choice in the Digital Age* (London: BBC).

Browne, D. 1996. *Electronic Media and Indigenous Peoples: A Voice of Our Own?* (Ames: Iowa State University Press).

Brunsdon, C., C. Johnson, R. Moseley and H. Wheatley. 2001. 'Factual television on British television: the Midlands TV Research Group's "8–9 project"', *European Journal of Cultural Studies*, 4, 1, 29–62.

Bruzzi, S. 2000. *New Documentary: A Critical Introduction* (London: Routledge).

Bullert, B. J. 1997. *Public Television: Politics and the Battle over Documentary Film* (New Brunswick: Rutgers University Press).

Bunt, B. 2003. 'The texture of actuality: new media documentary', *Metro Magazine*, 135, 166–71.

Burton, G. 2000. *Talking Television: An Introduction to the Study of Television* (London: Arnold).

Buscombe, E. 2000. 'Introduction' to E. Buscombe (ed.), *British Television: A Reader* (Oxford: Clarendon Press).

Calder-Marshall, A. 1966. *The Innocent Eye: The Life of Robert J. Flaherty* (New York: Harcourt Brace Jovanovich).

Caldwell, J. T. 1994. *Televisuality: Style, Crisis, and Authority in American Television* (New Brunswick: Rutgers University Press).

Caldwell, J. T. 2002. 'Prime-time fiction theorizes the docu-real' in J. Friedman (ed.), *Reality Squared: Televisual Discourse on the Real* (New Brunswick: Rutgers University Press).

Calvert, C. 2000. *Voyeur Nation: Media, Privacy, and Peering in Modern Culture* (Boulder: Westview Press).

Campbell, R. 1987. 'The discourse of documentary: narrational strategies in *Bastion Point Day 507, Wildcat, The Bridge,* and *Patu!*', *Illusions*, 4, 10–16.

Carroll, N. 1983. 'From real to reel: entangled in nonfiction film', *Philosophic Exchange*, 14, 5–45.

Carroll, N. 1996. 'Nonfiction film and postmodernist skepticism' in D. Bordwell and N. Carroll (eds), *Post-Theory: Reconstructing Film Studies* (Madison: University of Wisconsin Press).

Carroll, N. 1997. 'Fiction, non-fiction, and the film of presumptive assertion: a conceptual analysis' in R. Allen and M. Smith, *Film Theory and Philosophy* (Oxford: Clarendon Press).

Carter, D. 1998. 'The wide brown land on the small grey screen: the nature of landscape on Australian television', *Journal of Australian Studies*, 58, 116–26.

Carveth, R. 1993. 'Amy Fisher and the ethics of "headline" docudramas', *Journal of Popular Film and Television*, 21, 3, 327–52.

Caughie, J. 1980. 'Progressive television and documentary drama', *Screen*, 21, 3, 9–35.

Caughie, J. 2000. *Television Drama: Realism, Modernism, and British Culture* (Oxford: Oxford University Press).

Cavadini, A. and C. Strachan (with C. Merewether and L. Stern). 1981. 'Two Laws/Kanymarda Yuwa' in J. Allen *et al.* (eds), *Media Interventions* (Sydney: Intervention Publications).

Chapman, D. 1998. 'Downloading the documentary' in M. Wayne (ed.), *Dissident Voices: The Politics of Television and Cultural Change* (London: Pluto).

Clifford, J. 1986. 'On ethnographic allegory' in J. Clifford and G. Marcus (eds), *Writing Culture: The Poetics and Politics of Ethnography* (Berkeley: University of California Press).

Conley, T. 1987. 'Documentary surrealism: on *Land without Bread*' in R. Kuenzli (ed.), *Dada and Surrealist Film* (New York: Willis Locker and Owens).

Connell, I. 1983. 'Commercial broadcasting and the British left', *Screen*, 24, 6, 70–80.

Corner, J. 1995. *Television Form and Public Address* (London: Edward Arnold).

Corner, J. 1996. *The Art of Record: A Critical Introduction to Documentary* (Manchester: Manchester University Press).

Corner, J. 1998. 'Why study media form?' in J. Corner, *Studying Media: Problems of Theory and Method* (Edinburgh: Edinburgh University Press).

Corner, J. 1999. *Critical Ideas in Television Studies* (Oxford: Clarendon Press).

Corner, J. 2000a. 'Documentary in a post-documentary culture? A note on forms and their functions', http://info.lut.ac.uk/research/changing. media.

Corner, J. 2000b. 'What can we say about "documentary"?', *Media, Culture and Society*, 22, 5, 681–8.

Corner, J. 2001a. 'Documentary realism' in G. Creeber (ed.), *The Television Genre Book* (London: British Film Institute).

Corner, J. 2001b. 'Studying documentary' in G. Creeber (ed.), *The Television Genre Book* (London: British Film Institute).

Corner, J. 2002. 'Performing the real: documentary diversions', *Television and New Media*, 3, 3, 255–69.

Corner, J. 2003. 'Television, documentary and the category of the aesthetic', *Screen*, 44, 1, 92–100.

Corner, J. and S. Harvey (eds), 1996. *Television Times: A Reader* (London: Edward Arnold).

Corner, J. and K. Richardson. 1986. 'Documentary meanings and the discourse of interpretation' in J. Corner (ed.), *Documentary and the Mass Media* (London: Edward Arnold).

Court, D. 1995. 'Documenting the nation: a personal evaluation of Australia's documentary regime', *Metro Magazine*, 104, 58–60.

Crawford, P. I. 1995. 'Nature and advocacy in ethnographic film: the case of Kayapo imagery', *Intervention: Nordic Papers in Critical Anthropology*, 1, 7–22.

Crowdus, G. and D. Georgakas. 1988. 'History is the theme of all my films: an interview with Emile de Antonio' in A. Rosenthal (ed.), *New Challenges for Documentary* (Berkeley: University of California Press).

Curtin, M. 1995. *Redeeming the Wasteland: Television Documentary and Cold War Politics* (New Brunswick: Rutgers University Press).

Custen, B. 1992. *Bio/Pics: How Hollywood Constructed Public History* (New Brunswick: Rutgers University Press).

De Burgh, H. 2000. 'Introduction: a higher kind of loyalty?' and 'Endword' to H. de Burgh (ed.), *Investigative Journalism: Context and Practice* (London: Routledge).

Dempsey, J. 1991. 'Hot genre gluts TV market', *Variety* ( 3 June) 34, 75.

Dickinson, M. (ed.). 1999. *Rogue Reels: Oppositional Film in Britain, 1945–90* (London: British Film Institute).

Dixon, W. W. 2003. 'An interview with Albert Maysles', *Quarterly Review of Film and Video*, 20, 177–92.

'Documentary online'. 1999. *AFC* [Australian Film Commission] *News*, 190–1, 2.

Doig, A. 1997. 'The decline of investigatory journalism' in M. Bromley and T. O'Malley (eds), *A Journalism Reader* (London: Routledge).

Dominguez, V. 1987. 'Of other peoples: beyond the "salvage paradigm"' in H. Foster (ed.), *Discussions in Contemporary Culture* (Seattle: Bay Press).

Doncaster, C. 1983. 'The story documentary' [1956] in A. Goodwin and P. Kerr (eds), *BFI Dossier 19: Drama-Documentary* (London: British Film Institute).

Dovey, J. 1994. 'Old dogs and new tricks' in T. Dowmunt (ed.), *Channels of Resistance: Global Television and Local Empowerment* (London: British Film Institute).

Dovey, J. 2000. *Freakshow: First Person Media and Factual Television* (London: Pluto).

Dovey, J. 2001. 'Big Brother' in G. Creeber (ed.), *The Television Genre Book* (London: British Film Institute).

Eakin, P. 1992. *Touching the World: Reference in Autobiography* (Princeton: Princeton University Press).

Eaton, M. (ed.). 1979. *Anthropology/Reality/Cinema: The Films of Jean Rouch* (London: British Film Institute).

Edgar, D. 1982. 'On drama documentary' in F. Pike (ed.), *Ah! Mischief: The Writer and Television* (London: Faber and Faber).

Ehrlich, M. 1996. 'The journalism of outrageousness: tabloid television news vs. investigative news', *Journalism and Mass Communication Monographs*, 155 (complete issue).

Eitzen, D. 1995. ' "When is a documentary?": documentary as a mode of reception', *Cinema Journal*, 35, 1, 81–102.

Ellis, J. 2000. *Seeing Things: Television in the Age of Uncertainty* (London: I. B. Tauris).

Ellis, J. 2001. 'Television as working through' in J. Gripsrud (ed.), *Television and Common Knowledge* (London: Routledge).

Else, E. 1968. *The Back of Beyond* (London: Longmans).

Engelman, R. 1990. 'The origins of public access cable television, 1966–1972', *Journalism Monographs*, 123, 1–47.

'The fairness doctrine and procedures to be used in filing fairness doctrine complaints (FCC)' from Federal Communications Commission, 1983, reprinted in J. Corner and S. Harvey (eds), 1996. *Television Times: A Reader* (London: Arnold).

Feld, S. 1989. 'Themes in the cinema of Jean Rouch', *Visual Anthropology*, 2, 3–4, 223–47.

Feldman, S. 1995. 'Footnote to fact: the docudrama' in B. K. Grant (ed.), *Film Genre Reader II* (Austin: University of Texas Press).

Feng, P. X. 2002. *Identities in Motion: Asian American Film and Video* (Durham: Duke University Press).

Fetveit, A. 1999. 'Reality TV in the digital era: a paradox in visual culture?' *Media, Culture and Society*, 21, 6, 787–804.

Feuer, J. 1995. *Seeing Through the Eighties: Television and Reaganism* (London: British Film Institute).

Fischer, L. 1998. 'Documentary film and the discourse of hysterical/historical narrative: Ross McElwee's *Sherman's March*' in B. K. Grant and J. Sloniowski (eds.), *Documenting the Documentary: Close Readings of Documentary Film and Video* (Detroit: Wayne State University Press).

Fishman, M. 1988. 'Ratings and reality: the persistence of the reality crime genre' in M. Fishman and G. Cavender (eds), *Entertaining Crime: Television Reality Programs* (New York: Aldine de Gruyter).

Flaherty, R. 1971. 'How I filmed *Nanook of the North*', in H. M. Geduld (ed.), *Film Makers on Film Making* (Bloomington: Indiana University Press).

Flaherty, R. 1996. 'Robert Flaherty talking' [1950] in K. Macdonald and M. Cousins (eds), *Imagining Reality: The Faber Book of Documentary* (London: Faber and Faber).

Foucault, F. 1996. 'Film and popular memory' in S. Lotringer (ed.), *Foucault Live (Interviews, 1961–1984)* (New York: Semiotext(e)).

Franklin, B. 2001. *British Television Policy: A Reader* (London: Routledge).

Fusco, C. 1993. 'Passionate irrelevance: the cultural politics of identity' in *1993 Biennial* (New York: Whitney Museum of American Art).

Garnham, N. 1990. *Capitalism and Communication: Global Culture and the Economics of Information* (London: Sage).

Gibson, R. 1992. *South of the West: Postcolonialism and the Narrative Construction of Australia* (Bloomington: Indiana University Press).

Ginsburg, F. 1991. 'Indigenous media: Faustian contract or global village?', *Cultural Anthropology*, 6, 1, 92–112.

Ginsburg, F. 1993. 'Aboriginal media and the Australian imaginary', *Public Culture*, 5, 2, 557–78.

Glynn, K. 2000. *Tabloid Culture: Trash Taste, Popular Power, and the Transformation of American Television* (Durham: Duke University Press).

Goddard, P., J. Corner and K. Richardson. 2001. 'The formation of *World in Action*: a case study in the history of current affairs journalism', *Journalism*, 2, 1, 73–89.

Goffman, E. 1969. *The Presentation of Self in Everyday Life* (London: Allen Tate).

Gomez, J. 1979. *Peter Watkins* (Boston: Twayne).

Goodwin, A. 1997. 'Riding with ambulances: television and its uses' in T. O'Sullivan and Y. Jewkes (eds), *The Media Studies Reader* (London: Arnold).

Goodwin, A. and P. Kerr. 1983. 'Introduction' to A. Goodwin and P. Kerr (eds), *BFI Dossier 19: Drama-Documentary* (London: British Film Institute).

Goodwin, P. 1998. *Television Under the Tories: Broadcasting Policy, 1979–1997* (London: British Film Institute).

Graham, P. 1964. 'Cinéma-vérité in France', *Film Quarterly*, 17, 30–6.

Grant, B. K. 1992. *Voyages of Discovery: The Cinema of Frederick Wiseman* (Urbana: University of Illinois Press).

Grierson, J. 1998. 'Drifters (1929)' in I. Aitken (ed.), *The Documentary Film Movement: An Anthology* (Edinburgh: Edinburgh University Press).

Grierson, J. 1998. 'First principles of documentary (1932)' in I. Aitken (ed.), *The Documentary Film Movement: An Anthology* (Edinburgh: Edinburgh University Press).

Griffiths, G. 1995. 'The myth of authenticity' in B. Ashcroft, G. Griffiths and H. Tiffin (eds), *The Post-Colonial Studies Reader* (London: Routledge).

Grimshaw, A. 2001. *The Ethnographer's Eye: Ways of Seeing in Modern Anthropology* (Cambridge: Cambridge University Press).

Gross, L., J. Katz and J. Ruby (eds), 1988. *Image Ethics: The Moral Rights of Subjects in Photographs, Film, and Television* (New York: Oxford University Press).

Hall, J. 1991. 'Realism as a style in cinema vérité: a critical analysis of *Primary*', *Cinema Journal*, 30, 4, 24–50.

Hall, S., I. Connell and L. Curti. 1985. 'The "unity" of current affairs television' in T. Bennett, S. Boyd-Bowman, C. Mercer and J. Woollacott (eds),

*Popular Television and Film: A Reader* (London: British Film Institute Publishing).

Hallam, E. and B. Street. 2000. 'Introduction: cultural encounters – representing "otherness"' in E. Hallam and B. Street (eds), *Cultural Encounters: Representing 'Otherness'* (London: Routledge).

Harding, T. 2002. *The Video Activist Handbook*, 2nd edn (London: Pluto).

Hartley, J. 1996. *Popular Reality: Journalism, Modernity, Popular Culture* (London: Arnold).

Harty, J. 2002. 'Interactive television: the future of Geeksville?', *Encore*, 20, 9, 49–50.

Hayward, A. 2001. *In the Name of Justice: The Television Reporting of John Pilger* (London: Bloomsbury).

Heider, K. 1976. *Ethnographic Film* (Austin: University of Texas Press).

Heylin, C. 1991. *Dylan: Behind the Shades* (London: Penguin).

Higson, A. 1995. *Waving the Flag* (Oxford: Oxford University Press).

Hill, A. 1999. 'Crime and crisis: British reality TV' in E. Buscombe (ed.), *British Television: A Reader* (Oxford: Oxford University Press).

Hill, A. 2000. 'Fearful and safe: audience response to British reality programming', *Television and New Media*, 1, 2, 193–213.

Hill, A. 2002. '*Big Brother*: the real audience', *Television and New Media*, 3, 3, 323–40.

Hill, A. and G. Porter (eds), 2002. *Big Brother* issue of *Television and New Media*, 3, 3.

Himmelstein, H. 1987. 'Television news and the television documentary' in H. Newcomb (ed.), *Television: The Critical View* (New York: Oxford University Press).

Hinkson, M. 2002. 'New media projects at Yuendumu: inter-cultural engagement and self-determination in an era of accelerated globalization', *Continuum: Journal of Media and Cultural Studies*, 16, 2, 201–20.

Hoffer, T. W. and R. A. Nelson. 1978. 'Docudrama on American television', *Journal of the University Film Association*, 30, 2, 21–7.

Hoffmann, K. 1998. 'Electronic cinema: on the way to the digital' in T. Elsaesser and K. Hoffmann (eds), *Cinema Futures: Cain, Abel or Cable? The Screen Arts in the Digital Age* (Amsterdam: Amsterdam University Press).

Hogenkamp, B. 1986. *Deadly Parallels: Film and the Left in Britain, 1929–1939* (London: Lawrence and Wishart).

Holland, P. 2000. *The Television Handbook*, 2nd edn (London: Routledge).

Hood, S. 1972. 'The politics of television' in D. McQuail (ed.), *Sociology of Mass Communications* (London: Penguin).

Hoynes, W. 1996. 'Public television: the historical and political context' in J. Corner and S. Harvey (eds), *Television Times: A Reader* (London: Arnold).

Huhndorf, S. 2000. 'Nanook and his contemporaries: imaging Eskimos in American culture, 1897–1922', *Critical Inquiry*, 27, 7, 122–48.

'Impartiality (ITC)', extracts from The Independent Television Commission program code, London, ITC, 1995, reprinted in J. Corner and S. Harvey (eds), 1996. *Television Times: A Reader* (London: Arnold).

'Is Reality TV a survivor?'. 2001. *Ad Age Global*, 1, 10, 6.

James, D. 1989. *Allegories of Cinema: American Film in the Sixties* (Princeton: Princeton University Press).

Janke, T. and Company. 2003. *Towards a Protocol for Filmmakers Working with Indigenous Content and Indigenous Communities* (Sydney: Australian Film Commission).

Jarvie, I. C. 1983. 'The problem of the ethnographic real', *Current Anthropology*, 24, 3, 313–25.

Jennings, K. 1993. *Sites of Difference: Cinematic Representations of Aboriginality and Gender* (Melbourne: The Moving Image).

Johnson, D. 1999. 'Aboriginality and the politics of representation' in B. French (ed.), *Photo Files: An Australian Photography Reader* (Sydney: Power Publications/Australian Centre for Photography).

Jowett, G. 1985. '*The Selling of the Pentagon*: television confronts the first amendment' in J. O'Connor (ed.), *American History/American Television: Interpreting the Video Past* (New York: Ungar).

Juhasz, A. 1999. 'They said we were trying to show reality – all I want to show is my video: the politics of the realist feminist documentary' in J. Gaines and M. Renov (eds), *Collecting Visible Evidence* (Minneapolis: University of Minnesota Press).

Junko, T. and S. Teasley (eds) 1999. 'Documentary in the age of digital reproduction' in *Documentary Box*, <www.city.yamagata.yamagata.jp.yidff/docbox/15/box15-2-1.html>.

Keighron, P. 1993. 'Video diaries: what's up doc?', *Sight and Sound*, 3, 10, 24–5.

Kellner, D. 1992. 'Public-access television and struggle for democracy' in J. Wasko and V. Mosco (eds), *Democratic Communications in the Information Age* (New Jersey: Ablex).

Kellner, D. and D. Streible (eds), 2000. *Emile de Antonio: A Reader* (Minneapolis: University of Minnesota Press).

Kelman, K. 1975. 'The anti-information film: Conner's *Report*' in P. A. Sitney (ed.), *The Essential Cinema: Essays on Films in the Collection of Anthology Film Archives*, 1 (New York: Anthology Film Archives/New York University Press).

Kilborn, R. 1994a. '"How real can you get?": recent developments in "reality" television', *European Journal of Communication*, 9, 4, 412–39.

Kilborn, R. 1994b. '"Drama over Lockerbie": a new look at television drama-documentaries', *Historical Journal of Film, Radio and Television*, 14, 1 (1994) 59–76.

Kilborn, R. 1996. 'New contexts for documentary production in Britain', *Media, Culture and Society*, 18, 1, 141–50.

Kilborn, R. and J. Izod. 1997. *An Introduction to Television Documentary: Confronting Reality* (Manchester: Manchester University Press).

King, N. 1981. 'Recent "political" documentary: notes on "Union Maids" and "Harlan County USA"', *Screen*, 22, 2, 7–18.

Klotman, P. R. and J. K. Cutler (eds), 1999. *Struggles for Representation: African American Documentary Film and Video* (Bloomington: Indiana University Press).

Kriwaczek, P. 1997. *Documentary for the Small Screen* (Oxford: Focal Press).

Kuehl. J. 1988. 'Truth claims' in A. Rosenthal (ed.), *New Challenges for Documentary* (Berkeley: University of California Press).

Kuhn, A. 1978. 'The camera I: observations on documentary', *Screen*, 19, 2, 71–83.

Kuhn, A. 1980. 'British documentary in the 1930s and "independence": recontextualising a film movement' in D. Macpherson (ed.), *Traditions of Independence: British Cinema in the Thirties* (London: British Film Institute).

Kuhn, A. 1995. *Family Secrets: Acts of Memory and Imagination* (London: Verso).

Kuth, M. 1995. *Signal in the Air: Native Broadcasting in America* (Westport: Praeger).

Lane, J. 2002. *The Autobiographical Documentary in America* (Madison: University of Wisconsin Press).

Langer, J. 1998. *Tabloid Television: Popular Journalism and the 'Other' News* (London: Routledge).

Langton, M. 1993. *'Well, I Heard it on the Radio and I saw it on the Television': An Essay for the Australian Film Commission on the Politics and Aesthetics of Filmmaking by and about Aboriginal People and Things* (Sydney: Australian Film Commission).

Leacock, R. 1963. 'Interviews', *Movie*, 8, 16–18.

Leacock, R. 1996. 'Richard Leacock remembers the origins of "direct cinema"' in K. Macdonald and M. Cousins (eds), *Imagining Reality: The Faber Book of Documentary* (London: Faber and Faber).

Ledbetter, J. 1997. *Made Possible By... The Death of Public Broadcasting in the United States* (London: Verso).

Leech, G. 2001. 'Ten's big bucks beat Big Brother suitors', *The Australian* (August 22) 3.

Leigh, M. 1988. 'Curiouser and curiouser' in S. Murray (ed.), *Back of Beyond: Discovering Australian Film and Television* (Sydney: Australian Film Commission).

LeMahieu, D. L. 1988. *A Culture of Democracy: Mass Communication and the Cultivated Mind in Britain Between the Wars* (Oxford: Clarendon Press).

Lemisch, J. 1986. 'I dreamed I saw MTV last night', *The Nation* (18 October) 96–101.

Lesage, J. 1999. 'Women's fragmented consciousness in feminist experimental autobiographical video' in D. Waldman and J. Walker (eds),

*Feminism and Documentary* (Minneapolis: University of Minnesota Press).

Levi-Strauss, C. 1966. 'Anthropology: its achievements and future', *Current Anthropology*, 7, 120–8.

Lewis, R. 2000. *Emile de Antonio: Radical Filmmaker in Cold War America* (Madison: The University of Wisconsin Press).

Leyda, J. 1964. *Films Beget Films* (London: George Allen and Unwin).

Leyda, J. 1983. *Kino: A History of Russian and Soviet Film*, 3rd edn (Princeton: Princeton University Press).

Lichtenberg, J. 1996. 'In defence of objectivity revisited' in J. Curran and M. Gurevitch (eds), *Mass Media and Society*, 2nd edn (London: Arnold).

Loader, J. 1996a. 'Up close and personal', <www.publicshelter.com>.

Loader, J. 1996b. *Public Shelter* (CD-ROM), see <www.publicshelter.com>.

Loizos, P. 1993. *Innovation in Ethnographic Film: From Innocence to Self-Consciousness, 1955–1985* (Chicago: University of Chicago Press).

Loizos, P. 1997. 'First exits from observational realism: narrative experiments in recent ethnographic films' in M. Banks and H. Morphy (eds), *Rethinking Visual Anthropology* (New Haven: Yale University Press).

Lucia, C. 1993. 'When the personal becomes the political: an interview with Ross McElwee', *Cineaste*, 20, 2, 32–7.

Lumby, C. 1999. *Gotcha: Life in a Tabloid World* (Sydney: Allen and Unwin).

Lutkehaus, N. C. 1989. ' "Excuse me, everything is not all right": on ethnography, film, and representation: an interview with Dennis O'Rourke', *Cultural Anthropology*, 4, 4, 422–37.

Lutkehaus, N. and J. Cool. 1999. 'Paradigms lost and found: the "crisis of representation" and visual anthropology' in J. Gaines and M. Renov (eds), *Collecting Visible Evidence* (Minneapolis: University of Minnesota Press).

MacBean, J. R. 1988. ' "Two Laws" from Australia, one white, one black' in A. Rosenthal (ed.), *New Challenges for Documentary* (Berkeley: University of California Press).

MacBean, J. R. 1994. 'Degrees of otherness: a close reading of *First Contact, Joe Leahy's Neighbors*, and *Black Harvest*', *Visual Anthropology Review*, 10, 2, 55–70.

MacCannell, D. 1994. 'Cannibal tours' in L. Taylor (ed.), *Visualizing Theory: Selected Essays from V.A.R., 1990–1994* (New York: Routledge).

Macdonald, K. and M. Cousins (eds), 1996. 'The burning question' in *Imagining Reality: The Faber Book of Documentary* (London: Faber and Faber).

Macdonald, K. and M. Cousins (eds), 1996. *Imagining Reality: The Faber Book of Documentary* (London: Faber and Faber).

Macdonald, S. 1992. 'Ross McElwee' in S. MacDonald, *A Critical Cinema 2: Interviews with Independent Filmmakers* (Berkeley: University of California Press).

MacDougall, D. 1998. *Transcultural Cinema* (Princeton: Princeton University Press).

Mackinolty, C. and M. Duffy. 1987. *Guess Who's Coming to Dinner in Arnhem Land?* (Darwin: Northern Land Council).

Macpherson, D. (ed.). 1980. *Traditions of Independence* (London: British Film Institute).

Madden, K. 1982. 'Video and cultural identity: the Inuit Broadcasting Corporation experience' in F. Korzenny, S. Ting-Toomey and E. Schiff (eds), *Mass Media Effects Across Cultures* (Newbury Park: Sage).

Maddox, S. 2000. 'Never let the truth get in the way of a good story', *Metro Magazine*, 129–30, 197–201.

Malik, K. 1996. *The Meaning of Race: Race, History and Culture in Western Society* (Houndmills: Macmillan Press).

Maltby, R. 2003. *Hollywood Cinema*, 2nd edn (Oxford: Blackwell).

Mamber, S. 1973. *Cinema Verite in America: Studies in Uncontrolled Documentary* (Cambridge, MA: MIT Press).

Marchessault, J. and H. Wasson. 1998. 'Eyewitness history: new technologies and the production of visual evidence', *Convergence*, 4, 3, 17–23.

Marcorelles, L. 1973. *Living Cinema: New Directions in Contemporary Film–Making* (London: George Allen and Unwin).

Marks, L. 1994. 'A Deleuzian politics of hybrid cinema', *Screen*, 35, 3, 244–64.

Marks, L. 2000. *The Skin of the Film: Intercultural Cinema, Embodiment, and the Senses* (Durham: Duke University Press).

Martineau, B. 1984. 'Talking about our lives and experiences: some thoughts about feminism, documentary, and "talking heads"' in T. Waugh (ed.), *'Show Us Life': Toward a History and Aesthetics of the Committed Documentary* (Metuchen: Scarecrow).

Maynard, S. 1989. 'Black (and white) images: Aborigines and film' in A. Moran and T. O'Regan (eds), *The Australian Screen* (Ringwood: Penguin).

McArthur, C. 1980. *Television and History* (London: British Film Institute).

McNair, B. 1998. *The Sociology of Journalism* (London: Arnold).

McNair, B. 1999. *News and Journalism in the UK*, 3rd edn (London: Routledge).

McNair, B., M. Hibberd and P. Schlesinger. 2002. 'Public access broadcasting and democratic participation in the age of mediated politics', *Journalism Studies*, 3, 3, 407–22.

McQuail, D. 1987. *Mass Communication Theory: An Introduction*, 2nd edn (London: Sage).

Michaels, E. 1984. *Bad Aboriginal Art: Tradition, Media, and Technological Horizons* (Sydney: Allen and Unwin).

Michelson, A. (ed.) 1984. *Kino-Eye: The Writings of Dziga Vertov* (Berkeley: University of California Press).

Mitchell, W. J. 1992. *The Reconfigured Eye: Visual Truth in the Post-Photographic Era* (Cambridge, MA: MIT Press).

Molnar, H. 1990. 'The broadcasting for remote areas community scheme: small vs. big media', *Media Information Australia*, 58, 147–54.

Molnar, H. and M. Meadows. 2001. *Songlines to Satellites: Indigenous Communication in Australia, the South Pacific and Canada* (Sydney: Pluto Press).

Moore, C. and S. Muecke. 1984. 'Racism and the representation of Aborigines in film', *Australian Journal of Cultural Studies*, 2, 1, 36–53.

Moore, R. 1994. 'Marketing alterity' in L. Taylor (ed.), *Visualizing Theory: Selected Essays from V.A.R., 1990–1994* (New York: Routledge).

Moran, A. 1991. *Projecting Australia: Government Film Since 1945* (Sydney: Currency Press).

Moran, A. 1998. *Copycat Television: Globalisation, Program Formats and Cultural Identity* (Luton: University of Luton Press).

Morin, E. 1985. 'Chronicle of a film', *Studies in Visual Communication*, 11, 1, 4–29.

Morris, C. 2001. 'Multimedia dreaming', *New Internationalist*, 333, 21–2.

Morris, R. C. 1994. *New Worlds from Fragments: Film, Ethnography, and the Representation of Northwest Coast Cultures* (Boulder: Westview Press).

Muecke, S. 1992. *Textual Spaces: Aboriginality and Cultural Studies* (Sydney: University of New South Wales Press).

Muhammad, E. 1999. 'Black high-tech documents' in P. R. Klotman and J. C. Cutler (eds), *Struggles for Representation: African American Documentary Film and Video* (Bloomington: Indiana University Press).

Munro, D. 1994. 'Death of the documentary', *Stage, Screen and Radio* (July/August) 18–19.

Natter, W. 1994. 'The city as cinematic space: modernism and place in *Berlin, Symphony of a City*' in S. Aitken and L. Zonn (eds), *Place, Power, Situation, and Spectacle: A Geography of Film* (Lanham: Rowman and Littlefield).

Neale, S. 1980. *Genre* (London: British Film Institute).

Newton, J. 1988. 'History as usual? Feminism and the "new historicism"', *Cultural Critique*, 9, 87–121.

Nichols, B. 1976. 'Documentary theory and practice', *Screen*, 17, 4, 34–48.

Nichols, B. 1978. 'Fred Wiseman's documentaries: theory and structure', *Film Quarterly*, 31, 3, 15–28.

Nichols, B. 1980. *Newsreel: Documentary Filmmaking on the American Left* (New York: Arno).

Nichols, B. 1981. *Ideology and the Image: Social Representation in the Cinema and Other Media* (Bloomington: Indiana University Press).

Nichols, B. 1985. 'The voice of documentary' in B. Nichols (ed.), *Movies and Methods*, vol. 2 (Berkeley: University of California Press).

Nichols, B. 1991. *Representing Reality: Issues and Concepts in Documentary* (Bloomington: Indiana University Press).

Nichols, B. 1994. *Blurred Boundaries: Questions of Meaning in Contemporary Culture* (Bloomington: Indiana University Press).

Nichols, B. 2001. *Introduction to Documentary* (Bloomington: Indiana University Press).

Nimmo, D. and J. Combs. 1983. *Mediated Political Realities* (New York: Longman).

O'Connell, P. J. 1992. *Robert Drew and the Development of Cinema Verite in America* (University Park: Pennsylvania State University Press).

O'Donovan, M. 2001. 'AIDC [Australian International Documentary Conference] documents a growing industry', *Encore*, 19, 3, 12–13.

O'Pray, M. 1987. 'From dada to junk: Bruce Conner and the found-footage film', *Monthly Film Bulletin*, 645, 315–16.

O'Regan, T. 1996. *Australian National Cinema* (London: Routledge).

O'Regan, T. 2001. 'New stories for a digital age?' in B. Levy and F. Murphy (eds), *Story/Telling* (Brisbane: University of Queensland Press).

O'Rourke, D. 1997. 'Afterword' in C. Berry, A. Hamilton and L. Jayamanne (eds), *The Filmmaker and the Prostitute: Dennis O'Rourke's The Good Woman of Bangkok* (Sydney: Power Publications).

O'Shaughnessy, M. 1997. 'Producing *First Person*: an interview with Alan Carter, series producer *First Person*', *Continuum: The Australian Journal of Media and Culture*, 11, 1, 100–115.

O'Sullivan, T., J. Hartley, D. Saunders and J. Fiske. 1989. *Key Concepts in Communication* (London: Routledge).

Pack, S. 2000. 'Indigenous media then and now: situating the Navajo film project', *Quarterly Review of Film and Television*, 17, 3, 273–86.

Paget, D. 1998. *No Other Way to Tell It: Dramadoc/Docudrama on Television* (Manchester: Manchester University Press).

Palmer, G. 2002. '*Big Brother*: an experiment in governance', *Television and New Media*, 3, 3, 295–310.

Payne, R. 1997. 'Visions of silence', *Jump Cut*, 41, 61–76.

Peacock, T. 2002. 'Murdoch students learn how to talk back to TV', *The Australian* (6 November) 32.

Pennebaker, D. A. 1971. '*Don't Look Back* and *Monterey Pop*' in A. Rosenthal (ed.), *The New Documentary in Action: A Casebook in Film Making* (Berkeley: University of California Press).

Pennebaker, D. A. 1990. 'Looking back: D. A. Pennebaker interviewed by John Bauldie' in J. Bauldie (ed.), *Wanted Man: In Search of Bob Dylan* (London: Black Springs Press).

Peterson, J. 1986. 'Bruce Conner and the compilation narrative', *Wide Angle*, 8, 3–4, 53–62.

Petley, J. 1996. 'Fact plus fiction equals friction', *Media, Culture and Society*, 18, 1, 11–25.

Petrić, V. 1987. *Constructivism in Film: The Man with the Movie Camera* (Cambridge: Cambridge University Press).

Phillips, E. B. 1977. 'Approaches to objectivity' in P. Hirsch *et al.* (eds), *Strategies for Communication Research* (Beverly Hills: Sage).

Pilger, J. 1975. *The Last Day* (New York: Vintage).

Pilger, J. 1982. 'Stand up and be counted', *The Journalist* (January) 4–5.

Pilger, J. 1987. 'The Hawke-Pilger interview: manipulation of the media', *Australian Journalism Review*, 9, 1–2, 123–7.

Pilger, J. 1989. *Heroes*, rev. edn (London: Pan).

Pilger, J. and A. Barnett. 1982. *Aftermath: The Struggle for Cambodia and Vietnam* (London: New Statesman).

Plantinga, C. 1996. 'Moving pictures and the rhetoric of nonfiction: two approaches' in D. Bordwell and N. Carroll (eds), *Post-Theory: Reconstructing Film Studies* (Madison: University of Wisconsin Press).

Plantinga, C. 1997. *Rhetoric and Representation in Nonfiction Film* (Cambridge: Cambridge University Press).

Ponech, T. 1999. *What is Non-Fiction Cinema? On the Very Idea of Motion Picture Communication* (Boulder: Westview Press).

Preloran, J. 1987. 'Ethical and aesthetic concerns in ethnographic film', *Third World Affairs*, 464–79.

Prins, H. 1997. 'The paradox of primitivism: native rights and the problem of imagery in cultural survival films', *Visual Anthropology*, 9, 3, 243–66.

Protess, D. *et al.* 1991. *The Journalism of Outrage: Investigative Reporting and Agenda Building in America* (New York: Guilford Press).

Pudovkin, V. 1949. 'On film technique' in I. Montagu (trans.) *Film Technique and Film Acting: The Cinema Writings of V. I. Pudovkin* (New York: Bonanza Books).

Rabinger, M. 1998. *Directing the Documentary*, 2nd edn (Oxford: Focal Press).

Renov, M. 1989. 'The subject in history: the new autobiography in film and video', *Afterimage*, 4–7.

Renov, M. 1993a. 'Toward a poetics of documentary' in M. Renov (ed.), *Theorizing Documentary* (New York: Routledge).

Renov, M. 1993b. 'Introduction: the truth about non-fiction' in M. Renov (ed.), *Theorizing Documentary* (New York: Routledge).

Renov, M. (ed.) 1993c. *Theorizing Documentary* (New York: Routledge).

Renov, M. 1999a. 'Documentary horizons: an afterword' in J. Gaines and M. Renov (eds), *Collecting Visible Evidence* (Minneapolis: University of Minnesota Press).

Renov, M. 1999b. 'Domestic ethnography and the construction of the "other" self' in J. Gaines and M. Renov (eds), *Collecting Visible Evidence* (Minneapolis: University of Minnesota Press).

Renov, M. 1999c. 'New subjectivities: documentary and self-representation in the post-vérité age' in D. Waldman and J. Walker (eds), *Feminism and Documentary* (Minneapolis: University of Minnesota Press).

Riggins, S. (ed.). 1992. *Ethnic Minority Media: An International Perspective* (Newbury Park: Sage).

Romney, J. 1995. 'Access all areas: the real space of rock documentary' in J. Romney and A. Wootton (eds), *Celluloid Jukebox: Popular Music and the Movies Since the 1950s* (London: British Film Institute).

Rony, F. T. 1994. 'Victor Masayesva, jr., and the politics of "imagining Indians"', *Film Quarterly*, 48, 2, 20–34.

Rony, F. T. 1996. *The Third Eye: Race, Cinema, and Ethnographic Spectacle* (Durham: Duke University Press).

Roscoe, J. 2001. 'Real entertainment: new factual hybrid television', *Media International Australia*, 100, 9–20.

Roscoe, J. and C. Hight. 2001. *Faking It: Mock-Documentary and the Subversion of Factuality* (Manchester: Manchester University Press).

Rosenthal, A. 1980. '*In the Year of the Pig* and *Underground*: Emile de Antonio' in A. Rosenthal (ed.), *The Documentary Conscience* (Berkeley: University of California Press).

Rosenthal, A. 1988. '*The War Game*: an interview with Peter Watkins' in A. Rosenthal (ed.), *New Challenges for Documentary* (Berkeley: University of California Press).

Rosenthal, A. (ed.), 1999. 'Introduction', *Why Docudrama? Fact-Fiction on Film and TV* (Carbondale: Southern Illinois University Press).

Rotha, P. with B. Wright. 1980. 'Nanook of the North', *Studies in Visual Communication*, 6, 2, 33–60.

Rothman, W. 1997. *Documentary Film Classics* (New York: Cambridge University Press).

Rouch, J. 1985. 'The cinema of the future?', *Studies in Visual Communication*, 11, 1, 31–5.

Ruby, J. 1975. 'Is an ethnographic film a filmic ethnography?', *Studies in the Anthropology of Visual Communication*, 2, 2, 104–11.

Ruby, J. 1978. 'The celluloid self' in J. Katz (ed.), *Autobiography: Film/Video/Photography* (Toronto: Art Gallery of Ontario).

Ruby, J. 1991. 'Speaking for, speaking about, speaking with, or speaking alongside: an anthropological and documentary dilemma', *Visual Anthropology Review*, 7, 2, 50–67.

Ruby, J. 2000. *Picturing Culture: Explorations of Film and Anthropology* (Chicago: University of Chicago Press).

Ruoff, J. 2001. *An American Family: A Televised Life* (Minneapolis: University of Minnesota Press).

Russell, C. 1999. *Experimental Ethnography: The Work of Film in the Age of Video* (Durham: Duke University Press).

Sandusky, S. 1992. 'The archaeology of redemption: toward archival film', *Millennium Film Journal*, 26, 3–25.

Sarchett, B. 1994. '"Rockumentary": as metadocumentary: Martin Scorsese's *The Last Waltz*', *Literature Film Quarterly*, 22, 1, 28–34.

Saunders, W. 1994. 'The owning of images and the right to represent', *Filmnews* (May) 6–7.

Scannell, P. 2002. '*Big Brother* as a television event', *Television and New Media*, 3, 3, 272–82.

Schiller, D. 1981. *Objectivity and the News* (Philadelphia: University of Pennsylvania Press).

Schlesinger, P., G. Murdock and P. Elliot. 1983. *Televising Terrorism: Political Violence in Popular Culture* (London: Comedia).

Schwartz, D. 1986. 'First person singular: autobiography in film', *The Independent* (May) 12–15.

Scott, K. and A. White. 2003. 'Unnatural history? Deconstructing the *Walking with Dinosaurs* phenomenon', *Media, Culture and Society*, 25, 3, 315–32.

Seitz, M. 1982. 'Endgames', *The Progressive* (August) 52.

Senges, V. 2000. 'Interactive television: connect time is here', *Eurostar Magazine* (June) 14–18.

Shaw, C. 1999. *Deciding What We Watch: Taste, Decency, and Media Ethics in the UK and the USA* (Oxford: Clarendon Press).

Shohat, E. and R. Stam. 1994. *Unthinking Eurocentrism: Multiculturalism and the Media* (London: Routledge).

Singer, A. and S. Seidenberg, 1992. 'Television culture: the representation of anthropology in British broadcasting', *Visual Anthropology Review*, 8, 1, 122–25.

Singer, B. 2001. *Wiping the War Paint Off the Lens: Native American Film and Video* (Minneapolis: University of Minnesota Press).

Smith, B. 1999. 'Pilger and Bradbury', *IF: Independent Filmmakers*, 19, 26–8.

Smith, P. 1988. *Discerning the Subject* (Minneapolis: University of Minnesota Press).

Snyder, R. L. 1993. *Pare Lorentz and the Documentary Film* (Reno: University of Nevada Press).

Sobchack, T. and V. Sobchack. 1987. *An Introduction to Film*, 2nd edn (Boston: Little, Brown and Co.).

'Son of Big Brother'. 2002. *The Sydney Morning Herald* (10–11 August) 13.

Sounes, H. 2001. *Down the Highway: The Life of Bob Dylan* (New York: Grove Press).

Steemers, J. 1999. 'Broadcasting is dead. Long live digital choice' in H. Mackay and T. O'Sullivan (eds), *The Media Reader: Continuity and Transformation* (London: Sage).

Street, J. 2001. *Mass Media, Politics and Democracy* (Houndmills: Palgrave).

Stubbs, L. 2002. 'Albert Maysles: father of direct cinema' in L. Stubbs, *Documentary Filmmakers Speak* (New York: Allworth Press).

Stubbs, L. 2002. 'Ross McElwee: personal journeyman' in L. Stubbs, *Documentary Filmmakers Speak* (New York: Allworth Press).

Sussex, E. 1972. 'Grierson on documentary', *Film Quarterly*, 26, 1, 22–6.

Swann, P. 1989. *The British Documentary Film Movement, 1926–1946* (Cambridge: Cambridge University Press).

Taylor, R. and M. Glenny (eds). 1994. *S. M. Eisenstein: Towards a Theory of Montage: Selected Works*, vol. 2 (London: British Film Institute).

Thompson, K. and D. Bordwell. 1994. *Film History: An Introduction* (New York: McGraw-Hill).

Tierney, P. 2000. *Darkness in El Dorado: How Scientists and Journalists Devastated the Amazon* (New York: Norton).

Tincknell, E. and P. Raghuram. 2002. '*Big Brother*: reconfiguring the "active" audience of cultural studies?', *European Journal of Cultural Studies*, 5, 2, 199–215.

Torres, M. 1995. 'Creative control urged for indigenous projects', *AFC* [Australian Film Commission] *News*, 144, 2.

Tracey, M. 1982. 'Censored: *The War Game* Story' in C. Aubrey (ed.), *Nukespeak* (London: Comedia).

Tunstall, J. 1993. *Television Producers* (London: Routledge).

Turner, T. 1992. 'Defiant images: the Kayapo appropriation of video', *Anthropology Today*, 8, 6, 5–15.

Turton, D. 1992. 'Anthropological knowledge and the culture of broadcasting', *Visual Anthropological Review*, 8, 1, 113–17.

Urla, J. 1993. 'Breaking all the rules: an interview with Frances Peters', *Visual Anthropology Review*, 9, 2, 98–106.

Van Buren, C. 1997. '*Family Gathering*: release from emotional internment', *Jump Cut*, 37, 56–63.

Vaughan, D. 1976. *Television Documentary Usage* (London: British Film Institute).

Vaughan, D. 1999. 'The space between shots' in D. Vaughan, *For Documentary: Twelve Essays* (Berkeley: University of California Press).

Waugh, T. (ed.) 1984. '*Show Us Life*': *Toward a History and Aesthetics of the Committed Documentary* (Metuchen: The Scarecrow Press).

Waugh, T. 1985. 'Beyond *Vérité*: Emile de Antonio and the new documentary of the seventies' in B. Nichols (ed.), *Movies and Methods*, vol. 2 (Berkeley: University of California Press).

Wayne, M. 1997. *Theorising Video Practice* (London: Lawrence and Wishart).

Weiner, B. 1971. 'Radical scavenging: an interview with Emile de Antonio', *Film Quarterly*, 25, 3–15.

Wenders, W. 1986. 'Monterey Pop' in W. Wenders, *Emotion Pictures: Reflections on Cinema* (London: Faber and Faber).

Williams, C. (ed.). 1980. *Realism and Cinema: A Reader* (London: Routledge and Kegan Paul).

Williams, D. 2001. 'John Heyer (14/9/1916–19/06/2001)', *Metro Magazine*, 129–30, 248–53.

Williams, T. 2002. 'Blacks call for rules of engagement', *The Australian*, (26 February), 7.

Wilson, T. 1993. *Watching Television: Hermeneutics, Reception and Popular Culture* (Cambridge: Polity Press).

Winston, B. 1988a. 'Direct cinema: the third decade' in A. Rosenthal (ed.), *New Challenges for Documentary* (Berkeley: University of California Press).

Winston, B. 1988b. 'Documentary: I think we are in trouble' in A. Rosenthal (ed.), *New Challenges for Documentary* (Berkeley: University of California).

Winston, B. 1995. *Claiming the Real: The Documentary Film Revisited* (London: British Film Institute).

Winston, B. 1996. *Technologies of Seeing: Photography, Cinematography and Television* (London: British Film Institute).

Winston, B. 1999. ' "Honest, straightforward re-enactment": the staging of reality' in K. Bakker (ed.), *Joris Ivens and the Documentary Context* (Amsterdam: Amsterdam University Press).

Winston, B. 2000. *Lies, Damn Lies and Documentaries* (London: British Film Institute).

Woodhead, L. 1999. 'The guardian lecture: dramatized documentary' in A. Rosenthal (ed.), *Why Docudrama? Fact–Fiction on Film and TV* (Carbondale: Southern Illinois University Press).

Woodward, K. 1997. 'Concepts of identity and difference' in K. Woodward (ed.), *Identity and Difference* (London: Sage/The Open University).

Wootton, A. 1988. 'Looking back, dropping out, making sense: a history of the rock-concert movie', *Monthly Film Bulletin* (December) 355–6.

Wyver, J. (ed.). 1982. *Nothing but the Truth: Cinema Vérité and the Films of the Roger Graef Team* (London: Institute of Contemporary Arts and the British Film Institute).

Young, C. 1975. 'Observational cinema' in P. Hockings (ed.), *Principles of Visual Anthropology* (The Hague: Mouton).

Zimmermann, P. 1989. 'Revolutionary pleasures: wrecking the text in compilation documentary', *Afterimage*, 16, 8, 6–9.

Zimmermann, P. 1995. *Reel Families: A Social History of Amateur Film* (Bloomington: Indiana University Press).

Zimmermann, P. 2000. 'Pirates of the new world image orders' in P. Zimmermann, *States of Emergency: Documentaries, Wars, Democracies* (Minneapolis: University of Minnesota Press).

# Index